D0437748

GOSSIP FROM THE FOREST

GOSSIP FROM THE FOREST

The Tangled Roots of Our Forests and Fairytales

Sara Maitland

Photographs by Adam Lee

GRANTA

Granta Publications, 12 Addison Avenue, London W11 4QR
First published in Great Britain by Granta Books, 2012

A CIP catalogue record for this book
is available from the British Library.

1 3 5 7 9 10 8 6 4 2

ISBN 978 1 84708 429 3

Typeset by M Rules

Printed and bound by CPI Group (UK) Ltd, Croydon, CR0 4YY

For Mildred Lee Watson – the true princess.
(No green vegetables were hurt testing this hypothesis.)

Gossip: *sb.* God + Sib (akin, related.)
1. One who has contracted a spiritual relationship with another by acting as a sponsor at a baptism.
2. A familiar acquaintance or friend. Especially applied to a woman's female friends invited to be present at a birth.
3. Idle talk; trifling or groundless rumour; tittle-tattle.

Oxford English Dictionary

(This is one of my favourite examples of how the trivialising of women's concerns distorts language. The Gossip of my title is the encouraging, private, spiritual talk that we all want in times of trouble. Stories that are not idle; tales that are not trifling.)

CONTENTS

1

March

Airyolland Wood

It is dark, a soft, rustling night and not too cold. Adam, my son, and I are sitting on a moss-covered rock eating baked beans. He has pitched the small tent with the grace that goes with experience; I have heated the baked beans on the camping stove with the clumsiness that comes from lack of practice. It is dark now, and above us the branches of the trees are darker still, patterning themselves against the clouds. There is not much wind, but enough to make the branches a little restless. We can hear the burn and the branches and some other unidentifiable night noises, but it is quiet and calm. Airyolland Wood is a magical place for us and we are enjoying ourselves.

Airyolland is a tiny triangle of ancient oak wood that clings to the side of a steep valley in Galloway. It is a little fragment of what was once a far more extensive forest and we are lucky to have it still. A small stream, crystal clear and fast, rushes down towards the river in a series of sharp little falls; each sudden drop has a miniature deep pool at the bottom of it and the sides of the pool are rich with ferns, even this early in the year. The oak trees are old and tangled, many multi-trunked from long-ago coppicing, and they are festooned with epiphyte ferns, with moss, and with epicormic twigs sprouting whiskery from the rough bark. Their buds are fattening now, but there are no leaves, and the moon, slipping out from the filigreed clouds, occasionally breaks through the bare branches. The ground is both steeply sloped and complexly humped and carved; it is scattered apparently casually with erratic boulders – some as large as garden sheds and some much smaller – pushed here by a glacier and left when the ice retreated. Immediately to the south, abutting this wood, just across the stream, is a fairly typical patch of forestry plantation, huddling up against the little wood; above it is a well-greened field with a farmhouse just out of sight. The Southern Upland Way runs through here, and – totally incongruously – the single-track railway line from Glasgow to Stranraer cuts through the bottom edge of the wood. And still Airyolland is a magical place for both of us and we are enjoying ourselves.

As we came down from the high moor where I live earlier this afternoon, I could sense the spring pushing up the valley to meet us. There were daffodils out in the village and new lambs in the fields along the river. The hawthorn in the hedges is showing bright, pale green buttons of buds, and a wych elm on the edge of the wood is covered in tiny red-gold balls which will flower before the end of the month. In the grass on the slope as we enter the oak wood itself there are the first primroses, and underfoot the darker green shoots of what will be ransom – wild garlic – later on.

But the trees themselves show fewer conspicuous signs: oak leafs out later than most trees, except ash,[1] and the moss here is so thick and the rock so near the surface that there is surprisingly little undergrowth. The spring is coming nonetheless. Although it is still nearly ten days before we move the clocks forward, the evenings are getting longer and there are hard, pale little nubs down by the burn which will push up into fresh fern fronds over the coming month. Some of them are visibly beginning to do that exquisite fern thing: pushing up straight, sturdy stems and then uncoiling the tight spiral at the very top, so that briefly they look like Gothic bishops' crosiers. Earlier, while it was still light, there was a new twitter of birds, and there has been no frost for over two weeks.

We are here to catch the early sun tomorrow morning as it rises over the moor. The sun will spill light, colour and long shadows through the branches and across the green moss. That is what Adam wants to photograph. We are also here trying to learn how to work together as adults. So far so good, except that I demanded that we brought a cafetière with us, and he can hardly be expected to approve of such foppish ways, especially as he does almost all the portering.

'So,' I say, into the dark, 'which fairy stories do you know? Do you remember?'

'Goldilocks, Red Riding Hood, Cinderella, Snow-white. Jack and the Beanstalk.' There's a short pause, and then, 'The one with the swans and the shirts, Rumplestiltskin ... the princess with that long hair ...'

I am quite impressed. But it is somehow easier to remember these stories in this wood, as though the wood itself was reminding us.

'Where did you learn them? Who told them to you?' I ask.

'You,' he says. Then, 'School perhaps. I don't know really, I just know them.'

We expand our list of stories, dig for the details, re-run the plots and laugh a bit at some of them – for some reason, 'The Mouse, the Bird and the Sausage' pleases us immensely, and we chant together, giggling, a suddenly mutually recalled snippet:

The bird encountered a dog and learned that this dog had
considered the sausage free game and swallowed him down.
The bird was furious and accused the dog of highway robbery,
but it was of no use, for the dog maintained he had found
forged letters on the sausage and therefore the sausage had to
pay for this with his life.[2]

This is a totally absurd little tale from the Grimms' collection about some improbable housemates who fall out over the division of the domestic chores, and it has nothing to do with forests or magic. God knows what the psychoanalysts, or the universal folklorists, or the academic textual deconstructers, or anyone else for that matter, would make of it. It is important to remember how many of the fairy stories we do not remember; and it is worth thinking about which ones. A large number of them are funny and silly, but these do not tend to feature in the modern canon.

Later he says, 'OK. Tell me about the book.'

I say, 'Once upon a time it was all forest . . .'

It was all forest before the last Ice Age.

'Don't call it the Ice Age,' he says, *'call it . . .'*

It was all forest before the last *glaciations*, which is why we have coal mines – every coal seam is a dead forest, but we aren't going there now. We're going to begin about 10,000 years ago, when the ice began to retreat. For tens of thousands of years, in places up to 3,000 metres thick, it had pressed heavily on northern Europe and America; the sea level had dropped as more and more water was frozen up in the Arctic Circle and high in the mountain ranges; glaciers had pushed down from the mountains, carving new valleys with flat bottoms and steep sides. Now, gradually, it began to retreat, leaving behind a stripped land, ground down and naked.

As the ice retreated, living things moved in from the south, opportunist as always, and greedy for space. First lichens, those great pioneers that break up land, build soils, prepare the way; and then, gradually, mosses, fungi, ferns, and, last but not least, seed-bearing plants – low scrub, flowers, and eventually, trees. It takes thousands of years to make a good forest – but they did well in this wet northern land, and flourished and spread out. And so, once upon a time it was all forest. Forest enough to be lost in it for ever.

To be honest, this itself is a fairy story. It was never 'all forest'. Once upon a time, before people knew how much of it had been forest, the wide open down lands of southern England and the bare hills of Scotland and the wide flat fens and the rich green shires were all thought to be 'how it was' – natural, timeless and somehow pure. People tended to like it, rather in the way they liked the idea that the statuary of the classical world or the interiors of the great medieval cathedrals came in pure stone, pristine and restrained, and on the whole were rather sorry to learn that originally they had been gaudily painted. More recently we realised that these open spaces had once been forested, and we took that story on board instead. Our forests grew deeper and denser – fertilised by Arthurian romances and the Wild Wood in *The Wind in the Willows* and tales of Robin Hood – until we knew that once it had indeed been 'all forest'. And forest became the pure place of primal innocence, where children could escape from their adults, get away from the order and discipline of straight roads and good governance, and revert to their animal origins.

But it is more complicated than that really. There was more forest than there is now, but not as much as we like to think. Oliver Rackham, the leading academic of woodland history, believes that less than 7% of Scotland was ever ancient forest and that the great Caledonian Forest is as much a story as the Merlin who ran mad in it. More importantly perhaps, large swathes of this 'forest' were never the untrodden tanglewood of the imagination, but were inhabited, worked, used. Much of the so-called forest was what is more properly called 'wood pasture' – trees more widely spaced out, standing independently in grass, like savannah, cropped not just by deer and wild boar and aurochs, but later by cows and sheep and pigs. The wild animals followed the trees and grasses northwards from Europe easily enough, because Britain was still joined to the continent by a broad band of dry land until about 7000 BCE; and by the same route, Neolithic people followed the animals. There had in fact been people in Britain before the last glaciation, but they seem to have retreated southwards, fleeing the ice and the bitter cold. Now they returned, and almost as soon as they were established they started to manage and exploit the forest – for hunting, for grazing, for fuel, for food.

The same pattern was repeated across much of northern Europe, and indeed the people were much the same, too. The ice shrank back towards the polar regions, the forests chased it northwards as far as they could, and *homo sapiens* followed the forest. Right from the very beginning, the relationship between people and forest was not primarily antagonistic and competitive, but symbiotic. Until recently people could not survive without woodland, but perhaps more surprisingly, woodland flourishes under good human management –

coppicing, for example, increases the amount of light that reaches into the depths of the forest, and so encourages germination and new growth and increases biodiversity. This was not wild wood that had to be 'tamed', but an infinite resource, rich, generous and often mysterious. The forests were protective too. Of course you can get lost in the forest, but you can also hide in the forest, and for exactly the same reason: in forests you cannot get a long view. In his history of the Gallic Wars, Julius Caesar comments that the Gauls defended themselves in forts within 'impassable woods', although they were clearly not impassable to the Britons, whatever the Roman military made of them.[3]

Forests to these northern European peoples were dangerous and generous, domestic and wild, beautiful and terrible. And the forests were the terrain out of which fairy stories (or, as they are perhaps better called in German, the *Märchen)*, one of our earliest and most vital cultural forms, evolved. The mysterious secrets and silences, gifts and perils of the forest are both the background to and the source of these tales.

Modern scholarship has taken a number of approaches to this material, which presents a delightfully insubstantial and tricky body of work. Two approaches that I will mention here have been a Jungian psychoanalytic approach (arguing that the tales resonate for children, and adults too, because they deal in archetypes, in universal experiences, usually sexual ones), and a global ethnographic approach, which finds tropes from the tales in every culture everywhere; both these and other ways of looking at the stories are illuminating, but tend to lose the specificity of place. What is interesting to me is not the ways in which the tales of the Arabian Nights or of the Indian sub-continent or of the indigenous Americans of the Great Plains are the *same* as the stories collected and redacted by Jacob and Wilhelm Grimm and published initially in 1812, but the ways they are *different*.

The fairy stories from, for instance, the Arabian Nights do demonstrably have many of the same themes and narrative sequences as those in the Grimm brothers' collections, but they are not the same stories. One of the great services that the great Grimm expert Jack Zipes[4] has done is to show how 'site specific' fairy stories are. To put it at its most basic, in the Arabian Nights the heroes do not go out and get lost in the forest, or escape into the forest; this is because, very simply, there aren't any forests. But it goes deeper than this – they do not get lost at all; the heroes either set off freely seeking adventure – often by boat, like Sinbad the Sailor – or they are exiled, escape murder (rather than poverty), or are abducted. Children do not get lost in deserts; if they wander off, which they are unlikely to do because of the almost certain fatal consequences of being lost alone in deserts, they can be seen for as far as they can roam. Children get lost in cities and in forests. As I will discuss later, forests are places where a person can get lost and can also hide – losing and hiding, of things and people, are central to European fairy stories in ways that are not true of similar stories in different geographies.

Landscape informs the collective imagination as much as or more than it forms the individual psyche and its imagination, but this dimension is not something to which we always pay enough attention.

It cannot be by chance that the three great monotheist religions – the Abrahamic faiths – have their roots in the desert, in the vast empty spaces under those enormous stars, where life is always provisional, always at risk. Human beings are tiny and vulnerable and necessarily on the move: local gods of place, small titular deities, are not going to be adequate in the desert – you need a big god to fill the vast spaces and speak into the huge silence; you need a god who will travel with you.

It cannot be simply accidental that Tibetan Buddhism emerges from high places, where the everlasting silence of the snows invites a kind of concentration, a loss of ego in the enormity of the mountains.

It cannot be totally coincidental that the joyful, humanistic polytheism of the classical Mediterranean – where the gods behave like humans (which means badly), and humans may become gods, and heroes (god-human hybrids) link the two inextricably, and metamorphosis destabilises expectation – arose in a terrain where there was infinite variety, where you can move in a matter of hours from mountain to sea shore, where islands are scattered casually, and where one place is very precisely not like another.

Less certainly, but still suggestively, the gods of the Vikings, far north in the land of the midnight sun and its dreadful corollary, the six months night, are unique in being vulnerable. Most myths and legends look forward to a final triumphant consummation at the end of time; but Viking gods and heroes cannot offer much reassurance for all the noise they make, and they will march out to Ragnarok with only a slim chance of victory and a tragic certainty of loss.

I am not comparing the forms of religious myth, legend and folk tale (although sometimes, as in Ovid's *Metamorphosis* or some parts of Genesis, we can see all three merging together). I am just trying to give some better-known examples of how the land, the scenery and the climate shape and inform the imaginations of the people.

I believe that the great stretches of forest in northern Europe, with their constant seasonal changes, their restricted views, their astonishing biological diversity, their secret gifts and perils and the knowledge that you have to go through them to get to anywhere else, created the themes and ethics of the fairytales we know best. There are secrets, hidden identities, cunning disguises; there are rhythms of change like the changes of the seasons; there are characters, both human and animal, whose assistance can be earned or spurned; and there is – over and over again – the journey or quest, which leads first to knowledge and then to happiness. The forest is the place of trial in fairy stories, both dangerous and exciting. Coming to terms with the forest, surviving its terrors, utilising its gifts and gaining its help is the way to 'happy ever after'.

These themes informed the stories and still inform European sensibility, sometimes in unexpected ways. For example, concepts of freedom and rights, and particularly the idea of meritocracy – that everyone, regardless of their material circumstances, has an inner self which is truer than their social persona, and which deserves recognition – are profoundly embedded in the fairy story. You may be a beggar, but truly you are a princess; you may be seen to be a queen, but truly you are a wicked witch; you may have been born a younger son, but your real identity is as a king. Intellectually, these are modern radical ideas of the Enlightenment, but imaginatively they are already there at the core of the fairy stories. With them, growing out of the same root, I think, goes the ideal, so baffling to many other cultures, that romantic love, as opposed to parental good sense and a dowry system, is the best basis for marriage. Or at a less high-flown level, even up to the present day, stepmothers, despite so many people growing up with them, are still *always* wicked: culturally, to be a birth mother is good and to be a step-mother is at best highly problematic.

In Britain we often like to see ourselves as Sea People, island dwellers, buccaneers and Empire Builders; most British people like to emphasise their Celtic or Viking origins – and this self-image is probably enhanced by the new Britons who have more recently come across the oceans and settled. We tend to obscure the fact that, essentially, most of us are predominantly Germanic. This denial is made easier for us by the fact that until the modern period there was no Germany; but the waves of settlers who pushed the Celts westward were all Germanic – among them, the Angles and Saxons whose language is the basis of English. We share deep roots and cultural similarities with the people of northern Europe, as politi-cally we are beginning to acknowledge. To help with this, I tend to use the word 'Teutonic', a wider, less nationalised term than 'Germanic', to describe those cultural phenomena we draw from this tradition. This includes our fairy stories. At our deep Teutonic roots we are forest people, and our stories and social networks are forest born.

Now the forests themselves are at risk. About 5,000 years ago the process of deforestation began. With the discovery of iron working, the process speeded up because wood in its raw state does not burn hot enough to smelt; charcoal, however, does. To produce sufficient charcoal, as well as to meet the other human needs like grazing, hunting and timber production, forest management began. Overall, the earlier phases of such management reduced the area covered by the forests but extended their biodiversity. Over the following centuries the forests came under increasing pressure. The growing population and its needs required ever-increasing quantities of both arable land and fuel. The agricultural revolution of the eighteenth century increased the value of ploughed land, and through enclosure, agriculture encroached further on the forest and radically changed the psychological experience of space and view. The Industrial Revolution destroyed forests to create cities, transport systems, mines and factories – and the development of coal mining did not relieve this latter need because so much timber was needed for pit props and subsequently for railway tracks. In the UK, deforestation reached its limits immediately after the 1914-18 war. There is now very little ancient woodland still flourishing.

Nonetheless, the forests that remain are strange and wonderful places with a rich natural history, long narratives of complex relationships – between humans and the wild, and between various groups of human beings – and a sense of enchantment and magic, which is at the same time fraught with fear.

One problem about forests, especially ancient ones, is that they are chaotic from even a fairly short distance away. Their inhabitants knew intimately both the value and beauty of their woods, as well as the real dangers that lurked there. But from the point of view of an absentee landlord, ancient woodlands are non-economic; grubbing out patches of useless old trees and bringing the area under the plough was an obvious way of increasing rental income. The Industrial Revolution needed the wood but not the forests: well-managed plantation was an obvious way of increasing productivity. An unexpected development was the introduction of two opposing forms of 'fake' forest – the supposedly economically viable monoculture of mass forestry tracts on land that was never going to prove sufficiently profitable agriculturally; and the beauty of ornamental woodland – the parks, large gardens and arboreta of the rural upper classes. But forests, like fairy stories, need to be chaotic – beautiful and savage, useful and wasteful, dangerous and free.

Somewhere I picked up some of that horror about forests. When I was writing *A Book of Silence* I discovered that I was avoiding forests and their silences because I was frightened. Startled, I took myself off to Glen Affric – one of the remaining fragments of ancient pine forest in Scotland – to challenge and examine my fear. The forest was very beautiful, in a weird and ancient-feeling way. I discovered that, in reality, it was not 'fear' that I experienced, but something rather stranger. Glen Affric is famous for its lichens; they trailed from the birch and rowan trees like witches' tresses, long, tangled and grey. Perhaps initially it was that image which triggered an unexpected response: the forest gave me the same set of feelings and emotions that I get when I first encounter a true fairy story. For me, this is a visceral response and hard to articulate – a strange brew of excitement, recognition and peril, with more anticipation or even childlike glee than simple 'terror of the wild' because of the other sense that this is somewhere I know and have known all my life. The hairs on the back of my neck do not actually rise as the cliché would have it, but I know exactly what the phrase is trying to express.

I have always had a strong imaginative reaction to fairy stories. As an adult, I have read a lot of them and a lot about them. It was not hard to recognise the almost identical feeling that the Glen Affric forest gave me, but it was surprising. Naturally, then, I was intrigued by my so similar responses. I started to think about this, and have come to realise that these feelings do have a real connection, lying buried in the imagination and in our childhoods, as well as in the more regulated historical and biological accounts.

I grew up on fairy stories. Luckily for me, from early childhood my parents read to us widely and they also told us stories. Although, like all oral storytellers, they moulded and edited the stories to their own ends, they did not – as I remember it – make up new stories for us, but gave us a wide range of traditional ones – history stories,[5] Bible stories, and, particularly in my father's case, classical myths. But fairy stories have some big advantages for parents with six children because they are age appropriate for nearly everyone; they can be shifted and altered to match the moment's need; there is a fairly even balance of male and female characters; they are mercifully short; and they are memorable.

'Once upon a time,' the stories would begin … no particular time, fictional time, fairy-story time. This is a doorway; if you are lucky, you go through it as a child, aurally, before you can read, and if you are very lucky, you become a free citizen of an ancient republic and can come and go as you please.

These stories are deeply embedded in my imagination. As I grew up and became a writer, I found myself going back to them and using them, retelling them ever since, working partly on the principle that a tale which has been around for centuries is highly likely to be a better story than one I just made up yesterday; and partly on the deep sense that they can tell more truth, more economically, than slices of contemporary social realism. The stories are so tough and shrewd formally that I can use them for anything I want – feminist revisioning, psychological exploration, malicious humour, magical realism, nature writing. They are generous, true and enchanted.

My parents also gave us an unusual degree of physical freedom and space. We were allowed to go out into the big bad world and have adventures, both rural ones and – more surprisingly for middle-class children in the 1950s – London ones. I have not fully worked out the connection here, but it feels important to make a note of it.

I honestly do not remember when I became aware that there were mediators of these parental gifts – printed fixed versions of these stories. At some point I must have learned that they were different sorts of stories from Joseph's coat of many colours, from Helen's great beauty, and from Drake's game of bowls. By the time I reached that recognition I had also begun to separate out the different strands. Well into early adulthood I thought of the Classical Myths as being somehow superior to the fairy stories, more important and more dignified; more grown-up indeed, because adults around me read Greek mythology, admired and encouraged references to it, and thought the acquisition of Latin a necessary part of education, but to the best of my knowledge then, fairy stories were for the children. I suspect that this was both a learned response to my adults' preference for high over popular culture, but also, with the best will in the world, it is impossible to tell Greek mythological stories without at least hinting at sexual shenanigans of a pretty exotic kind, while this element can be much more efficiently repressed in fairy stories. Sex seemed highly grown-up and sophisticated to me then. It probably was not until 1979, when Angela Carter's *The Bloody Chamber* taught me a thing or two, that I realised just how sexy the bog-standard fairy story could really be.

And as I learned these distinctions about genre, I also learned to distinguish between different sorts of fairy stories and different ways of telling them. Quite early I discovered that I did not like Hans Andersen's stories. I knew they were fakes: they were too pious, too complicated and often too sad as well – all traditional fairy stories, I knew, have happy endings, it is one of the central codes of the genre. Oscar Wilde's got nearer to the real thing, but they only worked when they were read, not told; Tolkein was like that too, and also he wanted you to care about, rather than identify with, particular characters in longer sagas, and there was always an inexplicable sense that he was up to something else, even when he touched some deep roots.

Gradually I came to recognise that the best fairy stories are very ancient and originally oral and that you are allowed to retell them at whim and in your own way. Eventually, probably not until my teens, I became conscious that a large number of the most popular fairy stories had been recorded from verbal narrators by two German linguists, brothers called Jacob and Wilhelm Grimm: 'Rumplestiltskin', 'Snow White', 'Sleeping Beauty', 'Hansel and Gretel' and, of course, 'Cinderella'. They published a first collection of 86 tales, *Kinder- und Hausmärchen*, in 1812 and went on adding stories until the seventh and final edition, in 1857, contained 210 stories.

The Grimm brothers have come in for a good deal of criticism more recently, and much of it is justified. Specifically, while they inferred that these stories were collected verbatim from oral story tellers, simple local peasants, particularly old women, we know now that their sources were more often second hand, the stories gleaned from their middle-class social circle, although usually with a claim that they had first heard them from a servant or old nurse. Jacob and Wilhelm themselves, despite their linguistic and 'scientific' ethnographic intentions, edited the stories heavily, shifting their focus and making them more Christian, more family orientated, less explicitly sexual, more nationalistic and more sexist. One nice little example of this tendency is the fact that in the 1812 version of 'Rapunzel', the witch learns about the girl's princely visitor when Rapunzel wonders why she is growing fat, not having been taught about pregnancy. In the later editions, Rapunzel gives the game away by a slip of the tongue – she asks the witch why the witch is not as heavy as the prince to haul up on her long plait – thus becoming more innocent but more stupid to make the plot better suited to the nursery.[6]

Another criticism is of their 'nationalism'. They believed there was a distinct 'German' tradition, rather than a wider European one. They had a debate, for example, as to whether Sleeping Beauty was properly German, rather than 'too French' (the story had already been retold in a more literary form by Charles Perrault in 1697). Drawing on more ancient Germanic myths, they concluded that the trope was entirely Teutonic, and included the tale. Perhaps the reason why we imagine all those princesses being blonde (golden haired) is because their Teutonic character is so well embedded in the Grimm versions. Oddly enough, in the stories themselves blondness is very seldom mentioned – and many a princess (like Snow White) is explicitly dark haired. Certainly both brothers saw all the aspects of their work as a contribution to a common culture and shared historical understanding in the political cause of the unification of Germany; however they were deeply democratic and, indeed, lost jobs because of the radical tendency of their politics. We all know why individuals working at a similar period for the unification of Italy tend to be seen as heroes while their German equivalents are vilified, but we need to be careful with such a post-Nazi viewpoint.

The brothers also had various more personal agenda which surfaced in their editing: they emphasised the good but absent father (theirs died, and this changed their lives from idyllic to penurious overnight) and the cruel, malignant stepmother, who seemed, under the pressure of poverty and bereavement, to have banished the sweet, warm mother of their infancy. The editing work continued throughout the brothers' lifetimes, partly in response to direct requests from readers to eliminate material that was perceived as being inappropriate for children, and partly because Wilhelm, who became increasingly responsible for the work, wanted to add a wash of Christian piety to it.

I acknowledge the basic facts behind these criticisms, but, for me, these do not outweigh the extraordinary potency of the collection. The timing was good – I suspect that within decades it would have been impossible to have collected the stories even as indirectly as they did; the capacity for such easy telling was already diminishing. There is no British collection with this sort of authority. However much the supposedly pure stream of rural peasant culture was diverted and canalised, it was not allowed to get totally lost or desiccated. As Jack Zipes shows in his powerful contemporary translation and annotation of the *Complete Works* (Vintage, 1987 and 2002) (from which all the Grimm quotations in this book are drawn) they captured a language so unscholarly and vigorous, as well as an authentic narrative form, that the oral origins of the stories are made transparent without fuss. One of the major claims for an oral tradition, as opposed to a literary (printed) text, is that it is amenable to change, to an editing process that makes it accessible to new listeners, over and over again: told stories are impregnable against copyright law – no one can own or claim them. Every teller may, and does, change the story in reaction to individual understanding and a particular audience. Jacob and Wilhelm started their work on the *Märchen* as an academic and linguistic sideline to their serious study of German etymology, but their audience wanted something more domestic, and more child orientated – and they provided it, just as many doctoral students have edited their theses to make a publishable book. This reactive process has gone on freely ever since. Even when writers acknowledge the Grimm brothers as their source, they do not feel constrained by them. In the Grimm version, Cinderella's stepsisters were not 'ugly'; they were 'fair of face, but vile and black of heart' and there was no fairy godmother, but a little white bird in a hazel tree.

In relation to my book, the Grimm stories have a singular and important advantage: precisely because of their much-criticised nationalistic agenda, they stand a good distance away from the universalising global approach not only of modern scholarship, but of many important collections of fairy stories: Andrew Lang's 'colour' (Red, Blue, Lilac, etc) series is proudly drawn from any and all traditions, stirring up a rich brew of Arabic, Indian and European tales without distinction, a notable and proper project at the height of Empire, but one which nonetheless disguises and even edits out local specificity. Because the Grimm brothers were deliberately and determinedly seeking out a *Teutonic* folk culture, they emphasise Germanic aspects. And one of the central aspects of the northern European fairy story is that it takes place in the forest.

It is surprising how seldom this is noticed. When I have discussed my book with other people, even experts, they have expressed surprise at my claim that the forest is of primary importance in these tales. But in fact, over half the stories (116 out of 210) in the 1857 edition[7] explicitly mention forests as the location of some part of the story, and at least another 26 have very clear forest themes or images. For example, a story about a woodcutter or huntsman who, during the story, does not actually leave his house, or about a central animal (a wolf) or a tree (often a hazel), suggests to me that a forest is implicitly the location of the story. (The others are set in a wide variety of locations – often other agricultural settings, like farms, fields or mills; a few in towns; several in castles, palaces or other houses; some in clearly imaginary non-realistic places; and a couple in heaven. There is also a substantial number of usually shorter tales where there is no clue at all about the 'scenery'.)

Now fairy stories are at risk too, like the forests. Padraic Colum has suggested[8] that artificial lighting dealt them a mortal wound: when people could read and be productive after dark, something very fundamental changed, and there was no longer need or space for the ancient oral tradition. The stories were often confined to books, which makes the text static, and they were handed over to children. In this century, our projected tenderness or sentimentality towards children, as well as our somewhat literalistic addiction to scientific realism, has made us more and more unwilling to expose the young to the violence and irrationality of the forest and its stories. If we are honest, we know very well that children do not actually wish or need to be protected from this: at the physical level, one of the things that children like best is to be allowed to wander off, alone or with each other, into the woods and have adventures; and at the imaginative level, they are delighted when Hansel and Gretel push the witch into her own oven or the wicked stepmother is forced to dance in red hot iron slippers until she is dead. I suspect it is our own sense of refinement and culture, our pride (and our own self-protective fear because we do not want our children standing in judgement over or even laughing too much at us), that we are protecting, perhaps dishonestly.

The whole tradition of story-telling is endangered by modern technology. Although telling stories is a very fundamental human attribute, to the extent that psychiatry now often treats 'narrative loss' – the inability to construct a story of one's own life – as a loss of identity or 'personhood', it is not natural but an art form – you have to learn how to tell stories. The well-meaning mother is constantly frustrated by the inability of her child to answer questions like 'What did you do today?' (to which the answer is usually a muttered 'nothing' – but the 'nothing' is a cover for 'I don't know how to tell a good story about it, how to impose a story shape on the events'). To tell stories, you have to hear stories and you have to have an audience to hear the stories you tell. Story telling is economically unproductive – there is no marketable product; it is out with the laws of patents and copyright; it cannot easily be commodified; it is a skill without monetary value. And above all, it is an activity requiring leisure – the oral tradition stands squarely against a modern work ethic. One of the unexpected things we have learned from anthropology is the extraordinary quantity of 'down time' that hunter-gatherer societies enjoy – the hours and days they spend just sitting around and talking, singing, chilling out. Even in medieval Europe, the most humble worker laboured for shorter hours and on far fewer days of the year than we – despite all our 'labour-saving devices' and regulated maximum hours – can easily imagine. Traditional fairy stories, like all oral traditions, need that sort of time – the sort of time that *isn't* money. This is probably one reason at least why they were so readily handed over to children – socially, we can accept that children have 'free' time. Unfortunately, they do not have many of the other attributes that good story telling requires, like accurate memory, audience sensitivity, critical but affectionate listeners and good role models; the social separation of generations and age groups has added to this problem. (It is all in the telling: there is no event so thrilling that it can't be made dull by bad narrative, and no event so trivial, senseless or petty that cannot rivet attention when narrated by a good teller.)[9]

The deep connection between the forests and the core stories has been lost; fairy stories and forests have been moved into different categories and, isolated, both are at risk of disappearing, misunderstood and culturally undervalued, 'useless' in the sense of 'financially unprofitable'.

So that is what this book is about: it is an attempt to bring them back together, so that they can illuminate and draw renewed strength from each other.

'Hang on,' said Adam, after hearing an edited version of all this. 'You talk about British woods, British history and being specific and all that. But the Grimms were German, not British, and these are all German stories. How are you going to plonk them down in British woods?'

This was pretty smart of him and I was not unimpressed, but I argued stoutly, 'No, they are not German stories; they are Germanic stories. The British are Germanic people from the northern

European forests, and I believe we had the same stories. Well, not just the same stories, because we also have Celtic fairy stories and some Viking fairy stories, but they are really different.'

'You're just guessing.'

I admitted that I was a bit. And I told him that it will always be hard to tell with oral stories, because they are always changing and shifting and we just cannot know. But there is some evidence. The oldest printed fairytale we have in English is 'Tom Thumb', from 1621. It is nearly identical to the Grimms' version – not simply the same type of story (there are midget hero stories in all sorts of cultures), many of the episodes and details are the same too. It must have been widely known because Phineas Taylor Barnum (1810–1891), the American circus impresario, gave Charles Stratton, his famous performing dwarf, the stage name of 'General Tom Thumb' in the early 1840s – only twenty years after the Grimms' stories were first translated. There are lots of little clues like that. And the Grimms' stories became popular in English very quickly. Even during the Second World War, W. H. Auden praised the collection as 'as one of the founding works of *Western* culture'. But I told Adam he was right in a way – I *am* guessing. It is a deep guess though, from how the stories fit into our forests and how our forests fit into the stories. It is a guess that works.

By this point in our conversation, Adam and I had long finished with the baked beans and had crawled into our sleeping bags in the tent. I last slept in a tent forty years ago, and Adam slept in this one a few months ago high up above the snow line of the southern Andes. It was cosy but a little strange to be snuggled up so close together, although the dog thought it was heaven and wriggled around our feet ecstatically. Occasionally she jumped up, rigid, attentive, aware of something outside in the wood even though we could not hear it, and then turned round and round, stirring herself into the sleeping bags as her ancestors must have stirred themselves into grassy nests in long-vanished forests.

'So, how do we go about it?' he asked.

'We walk in some woods,' I said.

We would walk and talk about fairy stories and forests. We would talk to contemporary forest people – people who still live or work in the forest. I want the forests in the book to be real – real walks, real people, and real 'nature'. I want the book to be specific, not general. And then I want to match up what is in the forests with fairy stories, see how the themes of the fairy stories grow out of the reality of the forest, and the other way round too – show how people see the forests in a particular way because of the fairy stories. So then I hope I can retell some of the Grimms' stories so that the connection gets made again and maybe both fairy stories and ancient woodland get protected, valued, seen for what they are: our roots, our origins. And it will be fun.

It felt adventurous. I snuggled down with some satisfaction. Then he said, 'Mum, do you know about mycorrhiza?'

'What?'

'Well, trees need their own fungi. They've only worked this out quite recently; but it turns out that trees – well, most plants actually – have a sort of double or twin life. They are partnered with fungi called mycorrhiza, and they cannot live without them – or even germinate. I don't mean aggressive, parasite fungi; I mean they make a team, you can't have one without the other.'

(The next day, back at home, I looked up *mycorrhiza*:

> Most land plants are dual organisms. Attached to their roots is a
> fungus whose hyphae are thinner and more richly branched
> than the root itself; they invade more soil than is directly
> accessible to the roots. The host plant supplies the fungus with
> the carbon needed to make its hyphae. The fungus does much
> of the job that schoolchildren used to be taught was done by
> the root hairs. It supplies the plant with nitrogen, phosphorus
> and other nutrients, and sometimes water too; it can even
> defend its host against competition from non-mycorrhizal
> neighbours. Neither functions well without the other; seedlings
> use their seed reserves to make contact with the fungus, and die
> if they fail to find a partner.)[10]

'So maybe that's what the book is: forests and fairy stories are like trees and their mycorrhiza.' After a pause, he added, 'Well, I suppose the forests don't need the fairy stories.'

But I love this image and wanted to run with it. 'Yes they do,' I said firmly.

The fairy stories teach us how to see the forests, and how to love them too. They are spooky but special in our imaginations. Woods are part of our fantasy of childhood because of the fairy stories. That love protects our woodlands. An astonishing number of people who had voted Conservative and seemed happy to cut benefits for the disabled, make students pay for their degrees, risk massive unemployment, and all the other cuts, were suddenly up in arms about a perceived threat to the forests – and that was only a consultation document. Our almost hidden and often bizarrely ignorant love for wildwood comes from the fairy stories and keeps the forests safe. If you have got a decent chunk of ancient woodland near you, you will be safe from development or wind farms or whatever. People do not love fen or moor or arable farmland or even mountains in that way; the people who live in them may love them, but the protest about making the forests more commercially viable came from a far wider constituency. I believe the relationship between forests and fairytales is mutual, symbiotic.

In this book I want to see forests and fairy stories like this – partners necessary to one another and at risk if *either* fails or cannot find and connect with the other. The relationship is specific; there are different mycorrhiza for different species of plant, so the forests of this book are not generalised. In each chapter I will go and seek out a different and particular forest. Luckily, there are lots of different kinds of forest in Britain – very distinct both as to the species that flourish there and as to the history that has led to their survival (or in some cases introduction). Between them, I sense that they can give access and depth to the central themes of the northern European fairy stories. Simultaneously, the stories can make us see and know the forests afresh.

I turned over, almost ready to sleep, pleased with things so far.

Then Adam said, 'OK, then. Tell me a story.'

'I don't tell them, I write them. I'm a *writer*. Telling-aloud story-telling is something special; I don't have those skills. I fake them.'

'Well, give it a go now to get me in the mood and then you can write it up properly later.'

I searched for a story that would make all these points, and could not find one. Then I looked for a story that is about mothers and sons. Oddly, there are not that many of these – mostly the fairy stories are about fathers-and-sons or mothers-and-daughters. (Not that this should matter too much: when he was eight and I read him *The Lord of the Rings*, Adam was – to this feminist mother's great pride – so offended by the masculinity of all the characters in the Fellowship that I had to read the whole text re-grammaring one of the hobbits – we chose Merry because it seemed the easiest name to do it with – as female throughout.) Then I thought about being frightened of imaginary forests and snug in this real one.

'OK,' I said into the dark.

Thumbling

Once upon a time there was a woman who wanted a baby.

She had a husband – a decent man, if a little dull. He was hard working and kind, which is a good start, and although he did not much like to chat, and never about the things she wanted to talk about, they lived together with a steady affection in their little cottage in a village on the edge of the forest.

They were well regarded in their community – he was quiet and well tempered and she kept their home clean and bright. Her butter churned into milk; her dough rose into bread, and whenever she went out and about her fingers were busy with her spindle and her tongue with the concerns of her community. And certainly they did with sufficient frequency and pleasure those things which should lead to the making of babies. But no baby came.

The woman wanted a baby. Sometimes her wanting soured her and she was not always as tender and gentle as she should have been. Her man wanted a baby too, and perhaps his wanting made him less playful and open than he should have been. Too many evenings they sat by the fire in a dull silence, which was gloomy rather than harsh. Eventually her boredom would make her say something, and his expression would deepen from dullness to irritation.

One evening, her hands still busy with her spindle, she broke one more sombre pause.

'Other people's houses are livelier than this,' she said. 'I do wish we had a child.'

'Yes,' he said, 'so do I.' His surprising effort to respond, as his parish priest had urged him, made him sound cross and accusatory.

She was stung.

'Even if it was as small as your thumb,' she said.

He flushed suddenly, his hands moving down to cover his crotch, his legs crossing themselves awkwardly. They both knew what she had said.

'Well, there you go,' he said gruffly. To be honest, there was not much else he could say.

And there it went. As so often happens when people who are not communicating too well with each other make wishes, they got what she asked for. Nine months later she had a baby, and it was as small as his thumb.

Her midwife had an easy time of it. She sat cracking jokes and relaying local news, until she reached down and cupped the tiny baby in one hand. Although startled, she could see at once that the boy was not deformed in any way, and opened his mouth to yell lustily. She sensibly abandoned the string she had had prepared and instead pulled a fine thread from the spool below the spindle to tie the pulsing cord. Her gossip was less certain. The midwife handed her the baby and she looked at him in amazement. It seemed too improbable a thing to live and too fragile a thing to rush down the street to the priest's house. But it was definitely healthy and breathing well. She was only meant to baptise the babies who might be dead before the priest could come.

'Oh, do it,' said the other two women laughing now.

So she dipped her finger in the bowl of water and said, 'What shall I call him?'

'Thumbling,' said his mother, giggling. Whatever this was, it was not dull.

So he was christened Thumbling, wrapped in a tiny scrap of lamb's wool and, after a few ingenious experiments, fed on his mother's milk expressed onto the eye of a fat needle. And later, when her husband came in and was shown the tiny baby, he was moved to both tenderness and merriment; he stroked the little head with one finger, beamed with pride, and quite spontaneously kissed his wife and told her she was wonderful. They were both very, very happy.

He never got any bigger, but in every other way Thumbling grew quite normally. He learned as quickly as anyone else's baby to control his head, to crawl across the tabletop, to yell when he was hungry and to sleep when he was tired. The only difficulties he had were practical, and his parents had creative amusement and great joy in finding practical solutions. As he began to toddle, it turned out that even his father's smallest finger was too large for the little one to cling on to, so the man whittled and smoothed a tiny stick to help his baby. Later he made a game of football they could play on the table, his breath against his son's little feet. The woman learned to spin wool finer than had ever been done before and to knit his little garments on pins. This fairylike work was much admired and she began to get commissions, even from the Lord of the Manor, to make up cloth as fine as spiders' webs to adorn full-sized human beings. Everyone in the village loved Thumbling. He was enchanting, magical, charming. He grew nimble in brain and body, full of tricks and funny little ways. The villagers were proud of him and felt he was a credit to them. They came to visit his mother to see him, and filled her house with chatter and laughter. She had no time to be bored and no need to nag her man for conversation any more; and it is easier to talk about your feelings when you are overflowing with joyful pride than when you know that you do not make your beloved happy and feel guilty about it. The couple were too contented and too loving to exploit Thumbling. His father resisted all pleas to bring him to the inn to dance and caper for drunks; his mother quietly declined invitations to show her women friends what he looked like naked. And they loved him too much even to feel tempted by the generous cash offers that passing salesmen made them – to take him away and show him in the big cities.

They adored their son both despite and because of his oddity, and all the more as it became clear that she was not going to conceive again even though there was now both more frequency and more pleasure for them both in doing those things which should lead to the making of babies. They spoiled him of course, but it was hard to see why that might matter in the long run.

As Thumbling got older his mother got ever happier. As her friends' and neighbours' boys grew, they grew away from their mothers. They went off on their own to explore, or they went off with their fathers to work, or they got in fights and annoyed the neighbours – but Thumbling was always too small to do any of this. He stayed with his mother. When he wanted to go off into the forest to play his own games and have his own adventures, she could throw a fine net over her potato patch and it was a forest for him. He could explore all day and build himself nests and dens and climb high, high into his potato trees and fight with fierce beetles, but her net held him safe and he could not get away.

As her friends' and neighbours' boys grew, they made friends of their own and encouraged each other in obstinacy and sullenness and dumb insolence. They had secrets. Their very glances hurt their mothers' feelings. They had gangs and girls they thought more beautiful than their mothers and things to do they did not wish to talk about. But Thumbling did not have friends like that; he would never leave her for a pretty little sweetheart, or a heartless trollop unworthy of his blithe beauty and his quick wit. She was lucky; her son would always be at home as coddled as a baby and as safe as an old man. He would always love his mother best. He would always sit on the rim of her mixing bowl and chat as she stirred in the raisins for the pudding; he would always and forever curl up in peace in the hollow of her clavicle, warm against her neck, drowsy with the rhythm of her spindle. And her man would always come home from field or wood, weary from a long day's work, but light in the pleasure of his home, and they would all three sit at, or on, the table and talk together and laugh because Thumbling was so funny and sweet and innocent and he was theirs for ever.

Then one night she woke suddenly and from the warmth of her man's arms she could hear her son weeping. And she knew at once that he was weeping for the friends he would never have, for the work he would never do, for the woman he would never kiss and for the child he would never father. He was weeping for the great dark forest through which he would never walk; for the long slope of the road between the great green trees that he would never come down to the new places where his fortune might be waiting. He was weeping for his freedom.

Love and happiness had made her courageous, with a far nobler bravery than the bored endurance which she had imagined was fortitude in the time before he came to her. Courage made her generous. She wept too. And then she started planning.

A week or so later, during their comfortable evening meal, her husband was gently bemoaning the inconvenience of a task he had to do. He was planning some coppicing deep in the forest. But if he took the wagon with him in the morning, what could he do with the horse all day? If he had to come home to get the wagon, he would waste half a day's work. He could not think of anyone with the time to help him. There were lots of solutions really, and she knew he would think of one of them. She was about to offer to drive the cart up herself in the afternoon when Thumbling piped up:

'I'll drive the cart up, Father.'

His father laughed. 'Oh yes, little one, and how would you go about that? You could not manage the reins to start with, and you might get lost.'

'You could tell me the way. And . . .' She could see he was thinking fast. '. . . and if Mother put me in the horse's ear I could tell it which way to go.'

Before her husband could laugh again, she said, almost breathless in her haste, 'That's a brilliant idea.'

Both father and son looked at her, amazed. Their surprise made her feel ashamed.

So the next day, in the afternoon, she lifted her tiny son up and tucked him into the ear of their faithful horse. It was dark and velvety inside, warm and safe as her own lap, and she heard the high joy in his voice as he called out, 'Giddy-up and through the gate.'

She watched the wagon, with no visible driver, cross the bridge and turn neatly up the track into the forest. It disappeared into the trees and she went back into her silent, empty house and cried a little.

It was a desolate four hours before she heard the clip-clop of hooves and she ran out into the yard. Her husband was driving up from the bridge and she could see from his posture that something was wrong. She waited while he turned the wagon into the yard, but not until he climbed down.

'Where is he? Where's Thumbling? What's happened?' She could hear the shrillness in her own voice.'

'It's all right,' he said slowly. He climbed down and led the horse into the barn while she stood there. Soon he came out again, carrying a heavy bag in one hand. He put his arm round her shoulder and led her into the warm kitchen.

He dumped the bag on the table and she heard the clink of gold coins.

He looked at her, questioning something, obviously thinking as he looked.

'I sold him,' he said.

She could not speak; she could not even think. Loss. Rage. Shock. All of them at once. They struck her dumb.

'He asked me to. Some idiots saw the horse driving itself and heard his instructions. They followed the wagon and saw me take him out of the horse's ear. They were fascinated. You know what's he's like – he was showing off, full of himself; he made them laugh, dancing on my shoulder. They offered me a small fortune for him. They wanted to take him to the city and exhibit him. Of course I said no. So they offered me a large fortune for him. I was about to say no again, when he whispered in my ear that I should accept the offer and he'd go with them and then escape and come home and we could all be rich. So I said I would.'

She wanted to hit him; she wanted to howl. She managed to say, 'But what if . . .?'

'I know,' he said, 'I do know. But he has been weeping in the night for his freedom.'

She stared at him. After a sombre pause, he said heavily, 'I had to let him try.'

'Yes,' she said, almost in a whisper, 'yes, you did.'

He took her into his arms then and she wept and he comforted her as best he could.

It took a terrible three days for Thumbling to get home. She was desperate.

On the third night she could not sleep. Nor could he. They lay rigid beside each other in the bed, not daring to speak. Then they heard some extraordinary noises coming from the scullery. They shot out of bed, pressed through to the back of the cottage and peered through a slit in the door. There was a bloated wolf, struggling to fit back into the drain through which he had obviously entered. They felt giddy from sleeplessness and anxiety, and could make little sense of what they could clearly see.

Then they heard a well-known, piercing little voice, somewhat muffled inevitably, but calling, 'Get me out of here. Now.'

The father whacked the wolf with an axe and the mother ran for the big meat knife and slit open the dead beast carefully. Inside its maw, somewhat bloody and in need of a good wash, was their son. He was laughing.

He was full of himself too. He told them of his adventures.

He had escaped from the impresarios easily enough by hiding in a mouse hole. He had fallen in with a gang of thieves and got them all arrested. He had been swallowed by a cow, but shouted so loudly that the village priest thought the animal was demonically possessed and had had it killed. Still inside the cow's third stomach, he had been gobbled down by the wolf. He had tricked the wolf into the scullery and then let it eat so much that it could not get out again. He obviously thought he had been pretty damned clever for a small chap. And actually he had.

She cleaned him down by the kitchen fire, trying to be angry with both her men, but laughing and laughing at his ridiculous adventures and her own immense relief and joy.

'Bedtime,' she said firmly when he was all clean and sweet

smelling and warm. She carried him to his tiny bed and popped him in. He calmed down suddenly and she tucked him up.

'Can I have a wolf skin counterpane?' he asked. But before she could answer, his eyes closed. Just before she straightened up, longing for her own bed, he murmured, 'Actually, Mother, it was quite scary, some of it. But I coped and I made us a fortune.' There was a short pause, and then he added slyly, 'Better than a fancy princess, anyway. I think I'll stay home from now on.'

So he did and they all lived happily ever after.

2

April

Saltridge Wood

There is a freshness of green in beech woods in the late spring. Beech leaves open quite slowly; they break out of their pointed scaled buds and seem to dance, an extraordinary pellucid shade of green. Although the trunks and branches of beech trees look especially solid, the twigs that carry the leaves are delicate, feathery almost, and spread out, by and large, in horizontal fan shapes. It takes a beech tree quite a while to fill in its canopy solidly, and so in the spring and even in the early summer the sunlight breaks through, dappling the ground underneath them. It seems impossible to describe the green of early beech woods in sunshine: it is somehow a pure essence of green, to which other lesser greens can be compared to their detriment. In fact the first green of larch trees is very similar, and underappreciated, but larch needles do not move and bounce the light in delicate breezes the way beech leaves do. There is something in the dancing of beech leaves that adds to this greenness. Of course, beech green cannot be the 'best' green – that would be nonsense – but it still feels true, somehow, and lifts the spirits.

It is not just the green that makes spring beech woods so pleasing. The trunks of beech trees are grey and smooth. It is into beech bark that lovers most satisfactorily carve their hearts and initials: the

graffiti stand out clearly on the smooth surface, and the messages
grow with the tree. The more gnarly trunks of oak, the long ridges
of elm, or the scales of pine not only make for a less emphatic visual
statement, they tend to grow back over any carving and obliterate it.
Etymologists think that the word 'book' may be derived from the
word 'beech' (*boc* is an old variant for both), and that in northern
Europe the earliest books were perhaps written on thin slices of
beech wood.

These almost severe-looking trunks create a rich contrast to the
delicate green leaves. Beeches tend to grow straight and then branch
out horizontally higher up and carry their foliage above the
branches; from the ground, looking up into the leaves, these dark
spread-fingers of smooth wood resemble ribs, creating what has
been often described as a cathedral effect; or perhaps, rather, the
beeches inspired the cathedrals' fan vaulting. A secondary consequence of this arrangement is that when beech trees get old and less
robust these heavy branches tend to peel off, leaving long rips like
wounds. Oak trees, by contrast, tend to die from the tops, leaving
dead wood like stags' antlers protruding above their living leaves,
somehow more grotesque than tragic. Since, relative to their height,
beech trees have comparatively shallow roots, they tend to respond
to high winds by being uprooted rather than broken off: the whole
root plate is lifted out of the ground, leaving a hole, again like a
wound. These various natural formations combine to give old beech
woods a very moving atmosphere of religious awe and painful
sorrow. It is compelling in its loveliness.

There is an additional pleasure in walking in beech woods: very
little undergrowth flourishes there, so the ground is clean and firm.
In autumn, beech leaves turn a very uniform golden-brown-red
colour and, since there is little growing through to break up the
carpet of fallen leaves, it lies there right through the year, so that
beneath the bright green ceiling is a smooth red floor. Beech roots
spread out on the surface around the base of the tree like mossy but-
tresses, but away from the immediate vicinity of the trunk there is
little to disturb either one's feet or one's view through the forest. The

exceptions to this tend to be spring flowers like bluebells and ransoms flowering before the dense canopy fills in. (Sanicle, a white,
summer-flowering umbellifer, is a famous exception to this – it
grows happily under beech trees on chalky soil.) Fallen beech leaves,
however, are rich in potash, and because they decompose readily,
they enrich the soil, so outside the immediate shaded circles of the
beech trees themselves – for example, along the sides of tracks
through beech woods – there is often a rich botanic array. Since new
beech trees germinate in the shade of their parent tree – though not
much else does – beeches tend to be strongly gregarious; where
there is one beech tree, there will be more.[1] And because beech is
shade bearing, there are often thickets of saplings waiting for the
death of the trees above them in order to grow into the space they
have left. Stands of beech trees and nothing else are quite common.

In late April,[2] I went with two old friends – and Solly, their
enchanting miniature wire-haired dachshund puppy – to walk in
Saltridge Wood, a typical beech wood just north of Stroud in the
Cotswolds. The Cotswolds, 'the most English and the least spoiled
of all our countrysides',[3] are made up of a long lift of limestone hills
and constitute the largest Area of Outstanding Natural Beauty in
England (790 square miles). The whole area is famous for its gentle
green hillsides, called wolds; its rich farmland with deep valleys,
old hedgerows and water meadows; its historic market towns and
villages; the beauty of its natural stone – pale gold in the north
and creamier south towards Bath; its atmosphere of gentle, old-
fashioned prosperity;[4] and its ancient beech woods. The Cotswolds
have come to represent a sort of apogee of rural 'Englishness'.

Because beech trees hate to be waterlogged they are often found
growing higher along steep-sided valleys; Saltridge Wood is perched
on a long ridge between the picturesque villages of Cranham and
Sheepscombe. It was a gratuitously pretty day, the weather designed
for the walk – warm for late April and brightly sunny, with some
charming little cumulus clouds overhead and sweetly golden green
in the wood. Saltridge belongs to the National Trust, so the tracks
are well made up and waymarked and access is straightforward. We

climbed up from Cranham's ancient grassy common, where I saw my first house martins of the year swooping and floating on the sunny air, across small green fields enclosed in sturdy hedgerows just coming into full leaf. From the track through the wood we looked down over wide views of arable land dotted with lambs and cows, cottages, farms and larger houses with orderly gardens and mown lawns; there were sheets of cowslips in the fields, with ponies apparently grazing them. Inside the wood there were bluebells and the ransoms had set their buds, white wet swellings above the dark green leaves, although it was too early for their damp, sharp, oniony scent to have permeated the air. There were primroses under the forest wall and patches of sweet woodruff showing their refined chalk-white flowers above the elegant little six-leaved 'ruffs' or whorls that decorate their stems, and probably give them their name. Woodruff does not take on its rich hay-and-almonds scent, which made it such a popular domestic deodorant in the Tudor period, until it is cut and dried, but, standing in the shade along the path-side, it offered a visual promise of its future olfactory refinement. And the wood was radiant with birdsong; at the end of March and beginning of April the woodland birds that have wintered south of the Mediterranean arrive back to mate and raise their broods; they join the winter resident species, and the range of songs, calls and chatter continues throughout the summer in a remarkably rich chorus.

Perhaps partly because they grow so finely here in what is seen as the iconic English landscape, beech trees in Britain are held in very high regard. In particular they are seen as somehow a quintessential female tree, in elegant but delicate contrast to the sturdy, manly oaks. Fine ancient beeches are called 'queens' (while similarly ancient Scots pines are called 'grannies'). Based on no real evidence beyond anecdote, I believe that the beech is the species that people are most likely to be able to identify on sight, and the one which is most often named as their 'favourite' tree. Even more than the oak tree nowadays, the beech is valued, even loved, as having a kind of national status.

Thinking about beech woods, I realised we have several layers of complicated history: the actual history of our woodlands and the actual history of our fairy stories, neither of which we fully understand. But more to the point, at the level of our emotions and imagination these two histories have both fostered each other, and at the same time confused us all. We end up believing that because we love forests we also we know everything about them – that beech trees are peculiarly British, for instance, and that 'once upon a time' the forest was continuous and dense across the whole country. (There are other examples that will emerge elsewhere in this book.) We act as though the forests of fairy story, of the imagination, are entirely real, and anyone who challenges our slightly sentimental account of the woods is behaving like a wicked witch, out to destroy small children. Oliver Rackham, with justified irritation, has drawn attention to our collective fantasy about woodland. No matter how much biologists and historians research and write about what is actually happening, we prefer our own fairy stories and legends. Rackham writes:

> The anthropology of woodland has come to be a fascinating
> subject in itself. Why does the public believe a complete pseudo-
> history that is at variance with the real history? Why is there ...
> 'a hunger for false information'? Why does pseudo-history grow
> to accommodate new events that ought to explode it?[5]

I suggest that it is not a 'pseudo-history' in the sense he experiences it, but a profound confusion between two histories that do not know themselves or each other. Our deep but unconscious desires have created stories about forests and fairy stories that make walking in the spring sunshine in Saltridge Forest feel so rooted in fairy-tales that we cannot see the trees for the wood.

This is quite odd. There is nothing particularly British about beech trees. In fact, beech spreads all across western, central and southern Europe – from the south-east of England and the north of Spain to the western shores of the Black Sea, and from southern

Norway to Sicily. Across mainland Europe it is the principal tree of broadleaf woodland in upland areas, which means it was the dominant large tree in central and southern German forests where the Grimm brothers collected their stories. In France it is used extensively in commercial forestry, as it never is in Britain. England is at the very northern limit of its natural range – the geographical areas where it will germinate and mature spontaneously. Ancient beech wood is fairly restricted in Britain, confined to Epping Forest, the Chilterns, the Cotswolds, north Norfolk, the lower end of the Severn valley, the New Forest, and sporadically along the south coast as far west as Dorset.[6]

Even within its natural range in the south, the beech is a bit of a Johnny-come-lately. Indeed, until well into the twentieth century there was an ongoing debate as to whether it was a native species at all. 'Native' trees are deemed to be those that were growing in Britain before it was cut off from mainland Europe. Any species that arrived later must almost certainly have been imported and deliberately planted. Sweet chestnut, for example, is not native; it was introduced by the Romans, along with rabbits, nettles and ground elder.

About 10,000 years ago, when trees began to crawl north following the retreating ice cap, the first pioneers were birch and then pine. These were followed by hazel – although, mysteriously, this seems to have spread *southwards* from north-west Scotland. Oak, alder and lime (at one point the dominant tree over much of England) came next, then elm and ash. Finally, holly, maple, hornbeam and, it is now generally agreed, beech made it into southern Britain in about 7,000 BCE, just before the land link between Britain and the rest of the European continent was flooded by the rising sea levels.

The history of trees and woodland is tortuous, and parts of it still contested. Many people know we can tell the age of individual trees by counting their 'rings', the dark circles on a cleanly cut trunk, as a new ring is laid down for each year of growth. However, not all trees make clear rings – holly, for example, does not – and until recently this technique could obviously only be used by cutting down the tree, although it is now possible to take a 'core' out of a living tree without destroying it. With living trees, size and general health are not very reliable as trees mature at different rates depending on very local (and even individual) conditions – although where the tree has been coppiced regularly, the size of its bole is helpful in determining its age.

Establishing the age of a wood, rather than a tree, is even trickier, because in a healthy wood the age of any particular tree is not relevant: the wood might have grown up around an older freestanding tree, or the wood might be a great deal older than any of the trees in it. The term 'ancient woodland' (or, more technically, 'ancient semi-natural woodland') describes woods that are known to have existed before 1600 in England and Wales, and before 1750 in Scotland.[7]

Landscape historians have developed various methods for deciding where ancient woodland was and what trees were growing in it. Direct documentary references (in the Domesday Book, for instance) are reasonably conclusive, and place names provide strong clues. Unfortunately, in the case of beech this is not reliable because the word itself gets too easily confused with 'beach', 'book' and 'buck'.

A more favoured approach has been to look for what are known as 'indicator species' – these are not trees, but ground plants that, for one reason or another, are found only (or predominantly) in ancient woodland. They are often plants that either need shade to flourish or have inefficient methods of dispersing their seed, so they do not readily spread to new habitats. The more of these indicators (appropriate to soil and climate) that are present, the more firmly the dendrologists can assert that a particular wood is ancient. But this is not straightforward: the lists vary according to the region, and if you take all the lists together, a grass – *Melica uniflora* – turns out to be the only 'universal' indicator, although the sweet woodruff (*Galium odorata*), flowering so elegantly in Saltridge this April, appears on every list except the one for Cornwall. Nor

is there full agreement about which species should be on any particular list.

Modern scientific methods have demonstrated the presence of
beech from before the cut-off date of around 7000 BCE. In particular, pollen analysis has enabled us to know what trees were around
and when. Since beech pollen is not well dispersed by wind and is
therefore unlikely to have blown in across the Channel, its presence
in sites dated to 9,000 years old proves that beech is in fact a native
tree.

Nonetheless, the high status of beech in Britain is fairly recent. In
Sylva, his 1664 book about woodlands, John Evelyn is dismissive of
beech, claiming that it is 'good only for shade and fire'. The main
function of the beech woods of the Chilterns was to provide fuel for
London, until in the later eighteenth century improved transport
made coal a more attractive option. Even in strong beech areas,
beech wood was never used for timber-framed houses – oak was
always preferred. Beech had few traditional uses, except that the
beech mast was used as pig fodder – and its botanical name, *fagus*,
derives from the Greek verb *fagein* (= to eat) because of this. Later,
it was sometimes roasted as a coffee substitute.

Appreciation of the beech's charms grew in the nineteenth century – partly because it was pleasing to painters, as they moved out
of their studios and began to paint *en plein air*. Individual beech trees
are distinctive, but the round groves of beech trees on the tops of
hills proved even more attractive to the landscape artist; they make
a useful focal point in wide views of grassy downs. Paul Nash
(1889-1946), who painted the Wittenham Clumps in Oxfordshire
repeatedly, said of them, 'It was the look of them that told most.
They were the Pyramids of my small world.'[8] Now everything about
beech trees is honoured: the pinkish-white colour and compact
grain of the wood has become popular with contemporary joiners
and wood turners.

Today, the ascendency of beech trees and beech woods is firmly
established. In Saltridge, in the sunshine, I could entirely understand
this – there was a joyful magnificence in the huge trees and the clear

ground beneath them. But I still find myself oddly resenting beech woods. I know some of the reasons why. Part of this comes from the deeply embedded irritation that most northerners, and Scots especially, feel about heavy cultural and national value being attached to any phenomenon which only occurs south of the Humber. But in the case of beech trees there is a socio-political edge to this annoyance. Although its natural range stops in East Anglia, beech will in fact flourish throughout most of Britain if it is planted. It will grow well as far north as most other trees. Perhaps because having beech trees required positive action and so demonstrated ownership and power, in the eighteenth and nineteenth century beech became the ornamental species of choice. The aristocracy and 'gentry' planted it in avenues and parks and inserted it into their home woods and plantations even as they enclosed the old commons and common woodland. Tommy Donnelly, the ancient tree specialist for the south-west area of Scottish Natural Heritage said to me that whenever I saw old beech trees in Galloway, I should 'look for the mansion'. They would prove to be someone's idea of poshing up their landscape, and they speak to me not only of southern dominance, but of Landlordism, of Enclosure and Clearance. (This political reading of the beech's social standing is probably reinforced by an often-repeated little slogan of my father's: 'Tyranny is like a beech tree; it looks very fine but nothing grows under it.' He certainly did not mean this to be taken as a comment on the tree rather than on his own strong democratic beliefs, but it has stuck in my mind.)

The coupling of oak and beech as king and queen of the forest, male and female, is another cause of irritation; it is an unusually silly anthropomorphism. At the same time, I also resent the fact that the beech has usurped the throne of the birch tree, which, in earlier times, was seen as the 'queen' of the forest – 'the majestic sceptre of the wood', according to the fourteenth-century Welsh poet Gruffydd ap Dafydd.[9] And as late as the early nineteenth century, the poet Coleridge described the birch tree as 'The Lady of the Woods'.[10]

Birch trees have as delicate and graceful, as 'feminine', an appearance as beech, and are far less grandiose. They were the first trees to return to Britain after the last glaciers retreated, and they flourish higher up and further north than other trees dare; their natural range covers the whole of Britain. 'Birch', often in the form of 'Birk' or similar, is the commonest place-name prefix in the country. They are still pioneers, the first trees to move into clear-felled forestry land or to push their way into heathland or neglected fields. Beech is shade bearing, but birches love the sunshine and open spaces. Birch pollen is produced in abundance and carries widely on the wind, so birch can appear anywhere – and does. Despite their fragile appearance and relatively short life span (seldom more than 80 years), individual birch trees are immensely tough – Rackham reports specimens that have fallen over collapsing cliff edges, tumbled to the bottom and then simply re-rooted and carried on growing. They are highly resistant to frost, capable of flourishing on the poorest soils and serve to consolidate loose earth on bare slopes, preparing it for other species. Recently, birch has been earning the respect of commercial foresters for this reason: it will plant itself, saving time and energy; is just as profitable for pulp as the more laborious conifers; and improves the ground rather than acidifying it as spruce and even larch do. While the spread of beech may well be, at least in part, responsible for the reduction of other species, particularly the lovely lost limes which were once the most common tree of our ancient woodlands, birch creates new territories for trees. Birches begin their season with long catkins, and their looser crowns and more waving fingers mean that the sun-dappling effect, 'more golden than under any other native tree',[11] lasts much deeper into the summer. In autumn their leaves turn a bright yellow. Their trunks, too, are smooth and peel into thin sheets, and are a radiant white colour (the adjective 'silver' in relation to birch seems to have been coined by Tennyson in the late nineteenth century). Though less imposing than beech trees, birches have their own particular charms.

There are two further cultural reasons for restoring the birch to her ancient throne. Birch, unlike beech, good only for 'shade and fuel', is a remarkably useful tree. It has been utilised throughout the United Kingdom, and especially in the Highlands of Scotland. John Loudon (1783–1843), the botanist and landscape architect, extolled the usefulness of birch wood:

> [Highlanders] build their houses, make their beds and chairs, tables, dishes and spoons; construct their mills; make their carts, ploughs, harrows gates and fences, and even manufacture ropes of [birch]. The branches are employed as fuel ... the spray is used for smoking hams and herrings. The bark is used for tanning leather and sometimes, when dried and twisted into a rope, instead of candles.[12]

In addition, birch is used for wickerwork, for specialised articles like helms, wheels and parts of barrels; for dyes and medicines. Birch oozes a natural oil called betulin, which gives birch bark its silver colour and is also the principal ingredient of 'wintergreen', the old-fashioned cream for aches and pains (the botanical name for 'birch' is *betula*); birch is also used in the making of gunpowder and, bizarrely, contemporary omelette whisks.[13] Above all, its fermented sap was the original Gaelic *uisge beatha*, the 'water of life', a popular and potent drink before grain whisky stole the honour and the title.

Curiously, beech trees are almost entirely absent from folklore. They have little place in legend, and virtually nothing in the way of associated customs or proverbs. Birches, on the other hand, are magical trees: Druids claimed them as the sister tree to the oak; witches' broom sticks were traditionally made out of birch, and so, in some parts of the country, were maypoles. Birch trees, together with fish, are among the very few items from the natural world that cross over, with their positive magical attributes intact, between the fairy stories of the Celtic and the Teutonic traditions.

In fairy stories, individual trees are always strongly positive forces, but there are no beech trees; there are birches, oaks, limes (linden), ash, willows, pines, larches, junipers and above all hazels, but no beeches. Given that the beech is so well established in Germany, this cannot simply be a translation issue.[14]

So although I walked happily that day in the dancing spring sunshine along the limestone ridge in Gloucestershire and enjoyed myself and admired the beech woods, I recognised an underlying resentment. The beech trees were imperious and very beautiful . . . but so were wicked stepmothers. Being 'the most lovely of all'[15] may not make you good, may not make you the heroine or the natural princess. Perhaps that is more precisely the difference I am struggling to express: the beech may be the queen, the symbol of English woodland, but the birch is the princess, the heroine of our woodland fairy stories.

Much of this, of course, is of necessity imaginative speculation, because the dissemination of fairy stories is at least as complicated as the dissemination of tree species. Oliver Rackham says that we cannot even imagine how the wildwood (the wood before any human interventions) may have looked, and we cannot reproduce or recreate it. I believe the same is true of the fairy stories. By the very nature of an oral 'text' you can only know how it was *this* time, the time you heard it. Field anthropologists have become sensitive to the fact that asking someone in an oral culture to tell you a traditional story will distort the story; the teller will mould the story to the listener's expectations – at least as far as such expectations are understood. This is not deliberate deceit or secrecy; it is the job of a story teller to do so.

A written text is fixed from the moment of its inscription. Because it is a physical object, we can usually date it with some accuracy, both by the language and often, too, by its physical manifestations – its graphology and the actual materials it is made of (for example, is it carved in stone, pressed into clay, written on parchment or paper?). Because it was written into an immediately fixed form, we can also often know who wrote it and, in some cases, learn about the text through what we know about the author, and vice versa. None of these ways of de-coding the history of a written text works for an oral story, which is just a murmur of air, invisible and flexible. And since the art of oral story telling has, to a very large degree, been lost, we cannot even reconstruct such stories out of our own collective experience of telling and hearing them. Many historians believe that memory itself has changed with the shift to literacy – that we learn and remember things in a different way today from how we did in the past.

This is made more difficult still by a deep disagreement about the origins of fairy stories. As I discussed in the previous chapter, broadly similar themes and tropes emerge in stories from a number of highly disparate cultures, but the stories themselves are, so to speak, site specific. There are, basically, two schools of thought to account for the similarities: the first suggests that the stories deal with such fundamental human dilemmas, issues and problems that they arise spontaneously and independently in any given human culture. The other theory is that each of the stories is disseminated through telling, handed on from traveller to traveller, and that each new audience becomes a teller – a sort of anthropological 'six degrees of separation'. To be honest, I don't think either version really quite adds up, though I have no better theory to offer.

In fact, there is a good deal of disagreement about the emergence of any of the forms of expressing the imagination. Currently, anthropologists and social geographers suggest that all art began with ritual and arises initially out of a religious rather than an aesthetic response: the cave paintings of southern France or Central Eastern Africa (or anywhere else) were more fundamentally about hunting rituals than about interior decor. The idea, put too simply, is that first there was ritual, repeated ceremonies to placate, please or manipulate the gods. The life-and-death importance of these ceremonies made it crucial that they were practised correctly each time, and to make this simpler, rhythm developed – eventually supported by percussion instruments (usually some sort of drum) which punctuated the rituals and assisted their correct repetition. Rhythm developed into music. Both visual and narrative images came later – first, solid objects (sculpture), then representation (two-dimensional metaphors for three-dimensional realities); first, songs, then poetry, then stories.

As far as we can tell, oral tradition stories fell into three categories: myths, which dealt with religious matters; legends – heroic
tales with some claim to historical truth; and fiction – stories that
were not meant to be believed, at least at a surface or literal level,
whether or not they revealed profound metaphorical truths of one
kind or another. However, it is surprisingly hard to distinguish
between the three.

It is, for example, impossible to know exactly how and in what
way people understood the truth of some very ancient stories. Did
the Hebrew people believe in Adam and Eve and the snake in the
way that contemporary fundamentalists seem to? It seems unlikely:
after the second chapter of Genesis, the name Adam occurs only
twice in the whole Hebrew Scriptures, on both occasions in poetry,
and both times meaning 'humanity', without any explicit moral
message and no reference to the story itself. Eve is never mentioned
at all, even in the laws and instructions enjoining obedience and
submission on women.[16] Similarly, it is clear that many sophisticated
Greeks and Romans did not believe in the myths or in the deities
described by the myths, but still believed the stories were worth
retelling, enjoying and referring to in a broader cultural way – as
Ovid does in the *Metamorphosis*.

Because hagiography emerges in a similar cultural context and
contains some surprisingly similar tropes to fairy stories, it is worth
wondering exactly how medieval Christians understood these stories
about saints. Some of the saints were clearly historical figures, and
a good deal was known about them biographically. But others dis-
tinctly lacked plausibility. Margaret of Antioch was one of the most
popular saints in northern Europe (judging by the number of
Church dedications to her); did her devotees really believe that she
was swallowed by a dragon, but that her purity disgusted the mon-
ster so much that he opened his mouth and let her walk out through
his throat – thus making her an appropriate patron of women in
childbirth? Did the women who certainly did seek the prayers of St
Uncumber believe, in our contemporary sense, that this Spanish
princess of no known historical period got out of her marriage by

growing a miraculous beard overnight – and that she would, in exchange for a handful of oats, get rid of other women's unsatisfactory husbands too? Certainly European hagiography shares an extraordinary number of themes and scenes with fairy stories. Are these legends, or fictions, or something in between that we lost a sense of with the rationalism of the Enlightenment?

A great deal of work has been put in over the last two centuries trying to work out exactly what we have got with the body of fairy stories; but the results are surprisingly meagre and unsatisfactory. Folklorists and anthropologists have come up with various ways of taxonomising fairy stories and their parallels in other cultures. The two most popular analyses at present are the Aarne-Thompson system, which tries to organise fairy stories according to specific motifs in their plots, and Vladimir Propp's morphological approach, which analyses the stories by the function that various character types and actions perform. Both systems are extremely complex (the Aarne-Thompson system ends up with 2,399 different types of fairy story, which hardly seems terribly useful, although, to be fair, this does include a range of stories that might not immediately meet some criteria of a 'fairy story') and, more problematically for me, they inevitably look for what is common to the diverse, worldwide stories, as opposed to what is specific to any particular story. In fact, neither system has even come up with a working definition of a fairy story.

One problem, which brings our fairy stories at least back within the shades of the woods, is that we have no 'virgin stories', or true fairy wildwood. Once a story has been recorded in any form at all, it moves out of the oral space in which it originally evolved. Throughout the historical era fairy stories have always existed in two forms – the oral stories, and the literary versions of them. What is unclear is how much the literary versions affected the oral versions, as well as, more obviously, the reverse. Just as beech trees and, for totally different reasons, Norwegian spruce were inserted into already existing woods, so literary retellings of fairy stories may well have fed back into the existing tales, altering them in ways we do not fully understand. In her wonderful book *The Forest of Mediaeval*

Romance,[17] Corinne Saunders examines the magical forests of high literary culture that shares so many elements with the fairy story, but is completely different. And not just different in tone and style – in the romances there are virtually no children (never mind children as protagonists); in the fairy stories, there are virtually no sword fights or battles. The heroes of romance have names and 'back story'; in fairy stories, even the principal characters seldom have names, and when they do, they are often simply descriptive (Snow White, Little Red Riding Hood) or generic (John, Gretel, etc.). In the Grimms' stories, practically no one goes mad; in the romances from Merlin to *Orlando Furioso*, madness is a regular occurrence. In fairy stories there is, ultimately, no such thing as unrequited love and remarkably little infidelity; in the romances, both of these are almost a necessity. Nonetheless, it is obvious that the two forms have affected each other. By the time the demotic fairy stories were being collected they had incorporated elements drawn from literary romance – sometimes satirically.[18]

Before Jacob and Wilhelm Grimm began their project, writers did retell fairy stories, but they did so in a literary and conscious manner; they did not try to replicate the rhythms, forms or morals of the oral tradition. Charles Perrault (1628–1703) is often treated as one of the earliest 'collectors' of fairytales, but he did not see his own work in that light. He was throughout his life a committed 'modernist', arguing the superiority of French contemporary literature over the classics ('Even Homer nods' was a catch phrase of his). He saw himself as laying the foundations for a new literary genre, French rather than Greek. Although his fairy stories were drawn from pre-existing oral tales, he developed them for sophisticated court-based readers in a highly literary manner. The great innovation that the Grimm brothers introduced was the attempt to replicate the form and language and rhythm (rather than the narrative content) of oral fairy stories. This is why it is slightly odd that they are so criticised now for editing and altering the stories to make them accessible to a new group of readers – bourgeois children whose reading materials were strictly mediated by adults. This is what, to the best of our knowledge, the tellers of stories within the oral tradition have always done.

I am suggesting that we walk in all the forests with a double map: a rich, carefully researched but still incomplete map of the history (economic, social and natural) of woodland that spans not just centuries but millennia; and a second map which relocates the forest in our imaginations and was drawn up when we were children from fairy stories and other tales. To make everything even more difficult, the first map is a palimpsest: the older history has been scraped off by biological scientists over and over again and rewritten in the light of new discoveries – with details like 'beech trees were . . . were not . . . were indigenous'. The second map is a magic map, which shifts and changes every time you try to use it to find out where you are, where you came from and where you might be going.

And to add to the already heady mixture, it is so very pretty in Saltridge beech wood in the springtime. The light shifts and dances; although it is too early in the year for real butterflies, the pairs of freshly emerged beech leaves look like butterfly wings, and quiver on the wind like green butterflies. There is so much to look at, so much to learn, and yet at the same time it is all supposedly 'natural' and easy and our home and heritage. It feels hardly surprising that Hansel and Gretel got lost.

Suddenly, as we walked, chatting comfortably, a very bad thing happened, just like in a fairy story: a vicious dog, not very large, but necessarily a great deal larger than Solly, hurled itself down the track, growling, and for no reason whatsoever attacked the poor puppy. In the ensuing melee, including a reckless but heroic rescue in the finest traditions of medieval romance by my friend, there was a good deal of human and dog blood shed, a great deal of noise, and a real sense of shock. The attacking dog was no wolf, and no doubt his owners were not witches – although we felt they were wickedly casual about the whole episode – but the abrupt ferocity and the unexpected change of mood from golden to wild and threatening added to the confusion that the walk was making me feel.

Soon, though, the aggressor and his useless owners disappeared

into the wood. We calmed ourselves and continued. We came out of
the wood and dropped down from the ridge, past the cricket field
which Laurie Lee, the author of *Cider with Rosie*,[19] donated to the village. Even apart from its donor, this cricket pitch has to be one of
the most romantic community amenities in the country – poised
high above the white stone village and overlooking the green valley:
the 'myth' of English rural life happens in this case to be entirely
true. Victorious over the evil force that had threatened our passage
through the forest, we ate lunch in the garden of the village pub,
half bemused by loveliness and the sense of being in a fairy story.

It was a stiff climb up the scarp afterwards, and halfway up, just
below the edge of the wood, we sat out among the flowers on the
common and dozed a little in the warm sunshine before plunging
back among the trees and continuing the walk. The path wound up
and down, often running along the edge, between trees and fields;
and there were huge old beech trees and slim straight younger ones
and it all felt idyllic, a dream of green springtime. The wood felt
enchanted and generous; it was like a fairy story, but I knew it was
all more complicated than it felt.

The White Snake

Once upon a time there was a young man with clear eyes, a quiet mind and a gentle heart.

Not surprisingly, since these rare and precious virtues seldom lead to worldly success, he was a servant. The King, his master, treated him with benign contempt despite his dependency on the man's goodness and good sense, but nonetheless the man continued to serve him loyally and rose gradually to a privileged position as steward and secretary, managing the household and keeping his master's confidential papers.

One day the Queen lost a valuable ring and, since the man had access even to the monarch's privy chambers, the King decided that he must have stolen it. Despite the man's protestations of innocence, the King announced that if the ring were not returned by the following morning the man would be executed. Since he had not stolen the ring and indeed had no idea where it might be, the man was, not surprisingly, distressed by this announcement. He spent the rest of the morning putting his affairs in order and paying such small debts as were outstanding so as not to inconvenience people afterwards and then, in the afternoon, he went out for a last walk in the woods which he loved. And there, in a sunny glade strewn with fritillaries, purple spotted and delicate, he encountered a white snake, with bright gold eyes and a green forked tongue.

Conversing with snakes is dangerous, for they are subtle and in league with the Devil himself; but a man with clear eyes, a quiet mind and a gentle heart can do with impunity what others should not risk. Instead of seizing a stick and beating its brains out, the man approached the snake quietly and gently, and smiled at it. The snake stared back unblinking for a few moments and then, with a side-slip wriggle, it smiled, then turned and vanished into the long grass.

'Strange,' the man thought to himself, but within moments he realised that it was stranger still, because a nightingale began to sing somewhere just out of sight and suddenly he could understand its song and the depths of its passion and joy. Walking home in the gloaming, he realised that the snake had given him the capacity to understand the language of all the living things in the wood. And when he was back in the great courtyard of the castle, he could hear the giggly little gossip of the sparrows, which told him that a fat duck had swallowed the Queen's ring when she had stupidly let it fall out of her window. Boldly, he arrested the duck and forced it to regurgitate the jewel, and after breakfast the next morning, he was able to return it to the King and avoid the death penalty.

The King was grateful and perhaps felt a little guilty, so he offered the man any post of honour that he chose. But, not entirely surprisingly, the man had lost confidence in royal generosity and declined. Instead, he asked for a horse and a little money so that he could leave this unreliable employment and seek a more independent future of his own. Eventually the King accepted this request and before the day was over the man had packed his few goods into a saddle bag and ridden off – as the heroes of stories must always ride – down the long track through the forest to seek his fortune.

When night fell he climbed into a tall tree for safety's sake and curled up to sleep in a high fork of two branches and listened to the wisdom of bats, the adventures of owls, the endless sexual problems of nightjars and the tiny homely gossip of the four hundred different invertebrates who had made their homes where he now nested.

He travelled on. Late in the morning he noticed the trees turning from limes and oaks to alders and willows, and before long he came down to the side of a small lake; the track ran beside it and he enjoyed the happy sight. However, he soon noticed a splashing commotion in the reeds along the bank and, leaving his horse, made his way down to the water. There were three salmon smolts, bright silver, with their soft scales flaking from their panicked thrashings, for they had half stranded themselves in the thick reeds and could not fight their way back into the current that would carry them down to the sea. They were panting, exhausted, and bewailing their fate. He felt an instant gentle sympathy so he picked them up one by one and chucked them out over the reed beds and into the deeper water. They regrouped joyfully and stuck their heads out of the water, laughing and shouting, 'Thank you, thank you. We salmon can remember the river our mothers swam in and the very gravel we were spawned on, and we will not forget your bright eyes, your gentle heart and your kindly mind. One day we will repay you.'

He travelled on. One afternoon he noticed that the road ran uphill and passed through scrub woods of pine and rowan, where the ground was dry and sandy. He heard a shrill, cross voice complaining that his horse was trampling a whole city to death and, looking down, he saw an ant hill, a great mound with the laborious workers and soldiers coming in and out, unresting and unhasting. On the pinnacle sat the Queen, regal and lovely with her tiny waist and elegant elbowed antennae. She was so small and yet so determined to protest and protect her people that his gentle heart was touched and he turned his horse aside, tethered it, and spent a couple of hours diverting the track so that future travellers would not harm the colony. The Queen drew up her army in formal array and they saluted him, chanting their great ant-warrior songs, and the Queen called out boldly, 'Thank you, thank you. We ants remember; we solve complex problems by ingenuity and teamwork, and we will not forget your bright eyes, your courteous heart and your kindly mind. One day we will repay you.'

He travelled on. The track climbed higher and he noticed that the trees changed to silvery birches and scrubby juniper, and there were harsh crags of rock above the wood and fungi and moss around his horse's feet. And from a rock cliff towering above him, he saw three black shapes come hurtling down, squawking and grumbling. It was three raven fledglings, not yet able to fly, but hurled from the nest by their intemperate parents. They flopped and flapped on the ground, and moaned and lamented. 'We are helpless children,' they croaked, 'Our parents are an unkindness. We can't hunt and so we'll have to starve. Woe! Woe! Woe, ever-more!' The unnatural unfaithfulness of the parents reminded the man so much of his late employer that he was moved to sympathy. He jumped down from his horse and, with a single blow, hacked off its head and left it as carrion for the young ravens to feed on. They hopped onto the dead equine and started glutting themselves on its eyes. The man watched them, amused, and when they had eaten their fill they called out together, 'Thank you, thank you. We ravens remember, we apply intelligence and strength and travel huge dis-tances, and we will not forget your bright eyes, your generous mind and your warm heart. One day we will repay you.'

He travelled on, using his own two legs now, but with no regrets. And soon the track ran down into a wide green valley, through woods of oak and holly, through orchards of apples and cherries, and through pastures where the cows stood belly deep in grass under the shade of elms and ash trees. Eventually he came to a big city where there was such chaos and noise and hubbub that he could barely hear himself think, let alone the small voices of the wild.

And there in that city he fell in love with the Princess. You'd think he would have steered clear of royalty after his past experi-ence, but no, in his generous heart and quiet mind he rejected all stereotypes and saw only her loveliness and her loneliness. He believed her hard shell was to protect her inner self from the flat-tery of the crowd and the over-indulgence of her father. He saw dignity in her haughtiness and good sense in her snobbery. Why should she give herself to a man who was unworthy, untried, unproven? So he went a-courting in the green springtime and declared himself a suitor, although many princes had died in that same cause, for she set her would-be lovers impossible tasks and demanded their lives when they failed.

First she led him to the seashore and tossed in a gold ring. He had to fetch it out from the depths and keep on trying until he either found it or drowned. He stood on the beach well aware there was nothing he could do and so just standing and looking and listening and enjoying the warm sunshine and the laughing waves. Then, suddenly, three salmon came leaping towards him, their long silver-and-red-flecked sides breaching the surface with power and delight. They had grown now in size and strength and had metamorphosed so that they could live in the salt of the ocean. Bravely, they let a wave cast them up at his feet, where they deposited a single oyster shell before the next wave pulled them back into the deep. The young man opened the shell and there was the ring. He laughed and took it to the palace.

But the princess had her pride and she did not want to marry a servant. She demanded a second task, another proof. She took ten sacks of millet seed and strewed them about her orchard. He had to gather them all, every last grain, back into the sacks by morning, or die. He stood under an apple tree, well aware there was nothing he could do and so just standing and looking and listening and enjoying the warm sunshine and the dancing froth of blossom. Then, suddenly, he heard a tiny rustling, a whisper nearly as silent as the growing of grass, a restless movement across the whole orchard; and there were thousands upon thousands of ants, a great army, orderly and well-disciplined, marching to the command of their queen and gathering every single seed back into the sacks. And the young man laughed and showed them to the princess.

But the princess had her pride and she did not want to marry a servant. She demanded a third task, another proof. She told him he had to bring her a golden apple from the Tree of Life. He did not know where the Tree of Life might be, and he was well aware that there was nothing he could do, so he put his small affairs in order, calculated that he had no debts to pay and went out for a last walk in the woods which he loved. He sat under a green linden tree and listened to the pied flycatchers chat about King Solomon's mines and the hot, damp, insect-filled air far away in Africa where they had passed a pleasant winter. Then, suddenly, there were black shadows moving overhead and he looked up and there were three ravens playfully performing the aerobatic routine that ravens normally keep for their own lovers: rolling on their backs, falling through space, flipping over before they hit the ground, and croaking with amusement. And as he looked, one of them dropped a golden apple from the Tree of Life directly into his waiting hand. And the young man laughed and ran back to the city.

He divided the apple in two and gave one half to her, and together they ate it and her heart filled with love for him because of his clear eyes, his quiet mind and his gentle heart. They lived happily ever after.

Things are not always what they seem. This story began with a snake and ended with an apple, but paradise was not lost, it was found. They say that ants form destructive armies and march out against people; they say that fish are slippery and cold blooded; they say that ravens are messengers of doom and death. They say that gentle hearts win no fair ladies. None of these things is necessarily true.

Never underestimate the joy that a man can gain if he has clear eyes, a quiet mind and a gentle heart.

3

May

The New Forest

May is the magic month in the greenwood. Gradually, through its bright four weeks, the roof of the forest thickens into summer density, the fan-vaulting of winter branches filling in and blurring with leaf dance. There is a mysterious brightness, a golden quality to the May green which will soon deepen into the heavier dark richness of full summer:

> Nature's first green is Gold,
> Her hardest hue to hold.
> Then leaf descends to leaf,
> So Eden sank to grief,
> So dawn goes down to day
> Nothing gold can stay.[1]

In early May I went to the New Forest and discovered that, by glorious chance, it was the peak of the bluebell extravaganza. The drift of bluebells in the early summer, seen through and under trees just greening – blue water, blue mist, blue dreams – is always almost a fairy story itself; not rare, not unexpected, and occurring throughout Europe, from the north of Scotland[2] southwards through Belgium, France and the Netherlands to Spain and Portugal, and, through introductions, into Germany and Italy as well – domestic, but still fabulous. Botanically, bluebells are called *hyacynthoides non scripta*; 'non scripta' is the Latin for 'not written on', and the name distinguishes them from the classical (and mythical) hyacinth whose every petal was inscribed by Apollo with the letters AIAI – 'alas' – to express his mourning for his beautiful beloved. The bluebells in British woodlands are not mythic, are not touched by the gods. They are common, annual, ordinary, and their magic is small, unimportant and straightforward. They are the flowers of fairytales. A drift of bluebells in the late-spring sunshine, the warming air giddy with their sweet scent, is heart stopping.

In fact, bluebells are not confined to woodland; what they really need is damp, cool ground, and they are frequently found in ditches and along shadowed walls and hedgerows well outside the wood-land margins; in Cornwall they grow on rocks right down to the shoreline where no trees have ever grown. But it is in the forest that they are most pronouncedly themselves. I think this is perhaps because in woodland you can never see exactly where the carpet ends; the sun dappling of the ground through the trees above and within the lakes of blue makes them seem to vanish rather than stop; there are always catches of colour receding further and deeper into the wood. Bluebells are particularly lovely under beech trees, because they flower just as those delicate, vivid leaves come out and the light within the wood is mediated between fragile bright green and the strange smoky shimmer of the flowers. The clear red-gold ground under beech trees adds a particular depth of tone in those patches the bluebells have left empty.

It is impossible to describe – and, oddly, nearly as difficult to paint or photograph. The whole effect is so over the top that most attempts to record it come out schmaltzy or chocolate-boxy, do what you will. Nor is it quite clear exactly how the bluebells pull off this annual stunt act: close up, it is not that spectacular a flower; the three or four small blossoms on their slightly floppy stems all look humbly downwards and face in a single direction. Taken one by one, the plants seem quite unimposing, the dark green strap-like leaves apparently outdoing the more modest flowers in volume and strength of colour. If you pick them,[3] their stalks are long and flaccid, dripping a limp dampness onto your hands from white silky stalk bases. They fade fast into nothing. And yet ... in full bloom, in their wide pools of blueness, they create an ineffable atmosphere of everything that is loveliest about our ancient forests. Before there were so many cars, the railways ran Bluebell Excursion trips so that people could be nourished by seeing them, even through a window in passing.

Driving through the New Forest in May sunshine, I saw them as they spread away from the unfenced roads, back into the sunny distance of spring woodlands. I kept having to stop my car and look, convinced that this misty swathe, this sweet, grounded cloud, had to be the apotheosis of springtime and of woodland magic. The New Forest has a good mixture of trees, from modern plantation through to old heathy scrub, and includes both oak and beech stands. But the bluebells do not much discriminate. They tend to leave the thinnest, least fertile soils to bracken and they do not like the acid subsoil under plantation conifers, although they will return slowly once the trees have been cleared; beyond that, they are ubiquitous – they need only time, damp and space to perform their spring ritual.

Yet there is nothing particularly special about the bluebells of the New Forest; lots of woodland boasts 'better', or at least more famous, bluebells. I had not come in search of them deliberately. They were just an added bonus.

I parked the car at Lover at the northern end of the forest, almost solely because I liked the name,[4] and walked in the woods there in clean May sunshine. It was a special walk, and not solely for the springtime and the bluebells, but because I saw a snake in the forest. Although still early in the year, the warmth must have called it from hibernation. It was a small adder lying out in the sun on a long ride, a grassy track between trees, so called because they were originally created to ride down, especially when hunting. Here, the grass had been walked flat in places, and it was on a patch of bare sandy earth that the snake was warming itself. I cannot see a snake without a sudden inhalation of fear. I am not alone in this; many people have a deep horror of snakes, which is hard to explain unless the Genesis story has sunk in deeper than we like to think; neither the Freudian tale of penises and paternal rape fantasies, nor the evolutionary one of ancient remembered dangers quite work – men are as terror-struck by snakes as women are and venomous serpents were never a primary threat in either jungles or savannahs. We do not experience quite this horror in the presence of the big cats and still less of hippopotami, although both are far more serious threats. But even though I know that the snake is most unlikely to bite me, that if it does it will not do me an enormous amount of harm, that in the worst possible case there are effective anti-venoms readily available, and that a bee sting is more dangerous and many plants are more toxic, still snakes are mysteriously scary.

Snakes do not appear often in the fairy stories, but they are always faintly sinister when they do. In 'The Three Snake Leaves', a little-known and dark tale, for example, a poor young man makes his fortune as a soldier and marries the King's daughter, who is 'very beautiful but very strange'. One of her peculiarities is that she binds any would-be husband to a vow that, should she die first, he will be buried with her. The young man is so infatuated, however, that he agrees; she dies; he is locked in the crypt with her. As he waits his slow fate a snake crawls into the tomb and, not wanting it to eat his wife's corpse, he kills the creature and cuts it into three pieces. However, a second snake appears and, using three leaves it has brought with it, reunites the sections and resurrects the first snake. The young man copies the snake's actions and restores his wife; he has the sense, however, to keep the leaves safe. Having said in the last chapter that there was very little adultery in the fairy stories, I immediately find myself recounting one of those few stories in which it does occur (might this explain the snake?): after a while, the princess falls in love with a ship's captain, kills her husband, and throws his body into the sea. However, he is rescued by a faithful servant and revived in his turn by the carefully kept leaves. The princess's father wreaks stern vengeance on her, and the young man inherits the kingdom. Interestingly, the snake shows no personal involvement or interest; it reanimates its own partner and then slithers away out of the story. The snake does not speak to or *give* the leaves to the hero, but just goes away, leaving them behind. Elsewhere, animals engage actively with the heroes and heroines; even wicked animals, like the wolf in 'Little Red Riding Hood', show some interest in and involvement with the humans they encounter, and talk to them; but snakes just go coldly about their own dark business.

All three of the British snakes (the adder, the non-venomous grass snake and the much rarer but harmless smooth snake [*Coronella austriaca*]) live in the New Forest, but I knew this particular one was an adder by its extraordinary beauty – its elegant proportions, strong zigzag pattern and large, dark eyes. Adders are not uncommon in Britain, although, because of their timidity and habits of retreat, I have not seen many – it remains for me a nervy thrill. I've never seen a pair mating; they 'flow' sinuously along each other's sides, licking backs and flicking tails. A male adder, interrupted by a peer during this ritual, engages at once with the second male. Together, they perform the 'adder dance', raising themselves up vertically and pushing at each other as though arm wrestling. They say that the male who has already flowed with the female always wins these encounters, strengthened by arousal, perhaps. I would so like to see this.

One specific feature of adders is that they need an unusually complex habitat to accommodate their diverse behaviours – sprawling in the sun to gain energy, hunting, hibernating and hiding. This is why they flourish in the New Forest. The New Forest is the largest area of unploughed, unsown lowland in Britain, and in consequence it has extensive areas of diverse habitats which have disappeared from elsewhere: 36,000 acres of old deciduous woodland; 29,000 acres of heath and grassland; and another precious 8,200 acres of wet heathland and bog. These are all broken into small patches like mosaic tessera. There are also over 20,000 acres of plantation trees, some from the eighteenth and nineteenth centuries, but mainly planted since the 1920s. There is, in addition, a 26-mile coastal strip looking out over the Solent towards the Isle of Wight.

This splendid variety has led to the survival of a rich diversity of life forms, too: plants, birds, insects, reptiles and mammals, some found nowhere else in southern England, hang on in the new Forest. For complicated historical reasons, it has been continuously used for common grazing – by cows and pigs, and particularly the ponies, which are now a notable tourist feature and more than earn their daily hay. As I have already suggested, woodland does best when it is properly used by humans – coppicing and pollarding extend the life of individual trees, and also expand biodiversity by breaking up the canopy and creating sunlit spaces within the trees. Well-managed stock-grazing has a similar positive effect – the open, diverse terrain of the New Forest has been enhanced and developed by the free ranging of domestic animals, as well as by the presence of its own native fauna.

The New Forest combines all these natural advantages with being easily accessible from other areas of the country, criss-crossed by roads and dotted with villages. Although one of the elements that preserved the New Forest was its low fertility, making its land less valuable, this has changed and Hampshire has high property prices, a rich population and therefore fewer pressures to develop high-density housing or industrial areas. The New Forest is highly protected – a large part of it is designated as a National Park, and there are various Sites of Special Scientific Interest (SSSIs) and conservation zones. The consequences, of course, are car parks, bicycle routes, well-constructed walkways and an inordinate number of 'tourist attractions' and their accompanying signage: the price of preserving the wild places can be managing the wild places so heavily that they cease to be wild at all.

Oddly enough, this has been part of the history of the New Forest. It has been a 'made' forest, an amenity forest, for nearly a thousand years. Indeed, the whole area is *more* wooded now than it was at the end of the first millennium.

Most places have several histories. For example, they have a 'natural history' in their geology, climate, flora and fauna and so on, and they also have a 'political history', which tells us about who owns them and to what end and how that came to be the case. These are never totally separate histories; they are usually closely related to each other. Like all histories, they are human histories, and they affect and entangle with each other and cannot be divided tidily.

Out of the relationship between these (and other) histories emerges a different sort of history: an imaginative history, a complex cultural narrative about how a place or particular type of landscape is perceived and pictured. The word 'landscape' itself shows how this history is both part of and different from the first two histories. Originally the word 'landscape' was an art history word – it meant a picture, a painting of a terrain, and thence a view of a terrain, and finally the terrain itself – as though we called human beings 'portraits' because a portrait is a picture of a human being. This history, too, weaves itself inextricably into the others and affects them; for example, there is now a planning concept called 'landscape amenity', which means that terrains socially (and politically) deemed to be beautiful are exempted from certain forms of further development. Some of the criteria for this are drawn more directly from 'natural history' (ancient woodland, high mountainous land, especially if it is rocky and fierce, and waterfalls are currently more likely to be 'protected', along with places occupied by a particular, culturally derived range of flora and fauna), and others are drawn from 'political history' (Bronze Age standing stones, medieval ecclesial buildings and eighteenth-century parkland, for example). This selection of landscapes affects the designated terrain directly and therefore inevitably affects other places, since if you do not put your factory, motorway or wind farm here, then you will put it *there*.

But even if it is impossible to draw clear lines between these histories, it is still worth trying to do so. If the northward retreat of the ice marked a crucially important moment in the natural history of northern European forests, the period around the turn of the first millennium – a thousand years ago – proved equally significant for their political history, and particularly in England. At that time a general European-wide cultural shift occurred which changed the understanding of leadership. The perception of what a king was shifted from a 'first among equals' status, reflected in various types of election or appointment, to someone with a unique form of empowerment, whereby royalty was embodied in the person of the monarch not by merit but by right, and the honours of the function became personal attributes, and later divine grace itself. In England, which did not make the move in the slow, steady way that seems to have happened elsewhere in northern Europe, this change was abrupt and difficult. In 1066, William of Normandy arrived from northern France with the new view of his own rights as King firmly in place, and after the battle of Hastings, he set about imposing these concepts on his newly conquered people. The change was sudden and imposed. There was a further complication: because of the country's small size, and despite the still-flexible northern border – the clear limits of the country – all the land surface belonged to someone. This was not the case in much of the rest of northern Europe, where forest, stretching over much more huge expanses of land, was simply 'free'; it often had no official owner.

One of the symbols of these newly conceived royal rights was the claim that the monarch owned all wild animals – they belonged to the Crown regardless of whose land they happened to be on at any given moment, and therefore a king had a unique right to hunt them. (When the Normans arrived, this principally meant deer and wild boar, but it could include hare and other species.) Moreover, if the King had a particular right to hunt, he therefore had a right to places to keep 'his' deer and to protect them from being hunted by other people. William set about 'afforesting' – declaring by procla-mation that the monarch, to the exclusion of everyone else, had the sole right to hunt over any piece of ground he fancied. Any Royal Forest so declared was no longer administered under the common law or the traditional local administration, but fell under Forest Law. Prior to the Norman Conquest, woodland – particularly wood pas-ture – in England was extensively used for grazing stock, for fuel, for building materials, and for extending arable land by grubbing out trees and shrubs and putting the land to the plough. Declaring a piece of land to be Royal Forest did not mean that it was *owned* by the Crown, but that its management fell under the Forest Law designed primarily to protect the game. These laws overrode various older rights under common law, for example, the rather splendidly named rights of purpresture (fencing off of any part of the forest for grazing or building on it), assarting (clearing forest land and felling trees for agriculture), pannage (letting pigs forage), agisment (pasturing other stock), estover (taking firewood) and turbary (cutting peat or other turfs). The Forest Law also included limitations on harvesting other forest products, on carrying weapons and on keeping dogs. If you lived within the New Forest, for example, you were allowed to keep a mastiff as a guard dog, but had to have its claws removed, so that it could not hunt deer. In actual fact, most of the old rights continued to be exercised, but their management was removed from local control and vested in the King's Foresters.

(Just to confuse things further, land could become Royal Forest without being a forest in the common sense of the word. In this new legal sense, 'forest' meant a place where there was something to hunt, rather than a place where there were lots of trees. Hare, for example, are not forest animals, but they are beasts of the chase, and for the purpose of coursing them, tracks of open grass land could be afforested. The noble sport of falconry or hawking requires open land too – so the King could afforest appropriate areas for that as well; in 1066, large areas of what became the New Forest were not wooded at all.)

All the Plantagenet kings used their rights not just to hunt but to confer privileges and gifts of meat and wood on their faithful retainers and to furnish indecently large banquets. William the Conqueror loved hunting. He afforested *ubicumque eam habere vouit*, 'everywhere he felt like it', and he, and his immediate heirs, felt like it eventually in about a third of southern England. The list of Royal Forests goes on and on – from Allerdale in Cumbria to Exmoor, from Shropshire to Kent, but especially in the central shires (though, curiously, not in the

North-East beyond York), the Plantagenets afforested over eighty
tracts of land, some of them very large. It is important to remember
just how much of the pathetic acreage of ancient woodland that
remains – especially in England – was protected from being grubbed
out (having the trees cut down and their roots extracted, which was
necessary prior to ploughing) because it had been afforested by the
Crown. Most of the forests we know by name were Royal Forests:
Sherwood and Epping and Bolsover and Dean and Woodstock and
Hatfield and Windsor and, of course, the New Forest.

This enthusiasm for hunting had rich symbolic meaning for the
new status of the King, but it also seems to have been a personal
passion of William the Conqueror, not merely an assertion of his
power. William had fallow deer introduced into England (before
this, there were only the native red deer and roe deer), and probably also pheasants. And after his death in 1087, his zeal was
recorded bitterly in the *Peterborough Chronicle*:

> He loved greediness very much;
> He set up many deer preserves and also enacted laws
> That whoever killed a hart or hind
> Should be blinded . . .

Oliver Rackham argues that blinding as described here – and
castrating, another punishment for infringing the Forest Law – were
actually never applied; and, moreover, only the nobles were ever
charged with such offences and were punished with fines, which was
more useful to the English Crown, which was relatively impoverished in comparison with its European peers. But from the point
of view of the narrative imagination and the evolution of popular
culture, the belief that such punishments existed where they had not
existed before the arrival of the Normans was to prove significant.

The Norman Conquest heralded a massive social change in
England, at the expense of the old Anglo-Saxon population. This
can still be seen in contemporary English language: the words for
domestic animals while alive remain Anglo-Saxon in derivation –

cow, pig, sheep; but when meat arrives on the table it becomes French – beef (*boeuf*), pork (*porc*), mutton (*mouton*). It is not hard to work out who was eating meat, a strong indicator of prosperity in Europe even now, and who was doing the agricultural labour, then – and still – one of the steadiest indicators of low pay. As a corollary, it is interesting to see that the live animal remains the insult word – stupid cow, greedy pig and silly sheep.

Forest Law was imposed from above. It was also new, replacing older customs, and it emanated directly from the foreign conqueror; it was different from the old well-known and well-understood laws which, however severe, had the comfortable force of tradition behind them. Not surprisingly, then, afforestation caused bitter anger, at all levels of society. A limitation on the right to afforest was one of the causes addressed by the noblemen who drew up Magna Carta in 1215, devoting four clauses of the document to the matter, including demands that 'All forests that have been created in our reign shall at once be disafforested. River-banks that have been enclosed in our reign shall be treated similarly'; and 'All evil customs relating to forests ... are to be abolished completely and irrevocably.'

The New Forest, which William the Conqueror afforested in 1079, was created out of a wide swathe of what is now Hampshire – then, as it still is, a rich mixture of ancient woodland, open heath and coast. In order to establish good hunting grounds, the residents were evicted and communities destroyed, although the 36 parishes of tradition must be an exaggeration – the soil was always poor and infertile here, so the land can never have supported such a thriving agricultural population.

There was deep resentment. As is common with folklore, this sense of grievance grew until, in the seventeenth century, Richard Blome recorded:

William the Conqueror (for the making of the said Forest a harbour for Wild-beasts for his Game) caused 36 Parish Churches, with all the Houses thereto belonging, to be pulled down, and the poor Inhabitants left succourless of house or home. But this wicked act did not long go unpunished, for his Sons felt the smart thereof; Richard being blasted with a pestilent Air; Rufus shot through with an Arrow; and Henry his Grand-child, by Robert his eldest son, as he pursued his Game, was hanged among the boughs, and so dyed.

William Rufus's death remains mysterious – an unsolved assassination or an unfortunate accident. It is the sort of event that feels as though it belonged more to a fairy story or legend than to history.

Throughout Europe this centralising power of the monarchy cut deep into rural life. The response of the 'old' pre-conquest landed class, if they did not join the new order and reap its rewards, was armed resistance. In England, Hereward the Wake is perhaps the most famous rebel. In alliance with some highly dubious Viking invaders, he sacked Peterborough Abbey and then hid out in the Fens, waging a kind of guerrilla warfare until he was defeated on the Isle of Ely in 1071. The North-East proved particularly hard to subdue (as usual), the landed classes there having a long history of independence and of claiming special freedoms, particularly from taxation, for themselves, as 'the patrimony of St Cuthbert'. The huge, stern cathedral in Durham, one of the great works of Norman architecture and designed to house the shrine of the saint, was founded in 1093 to 'buy off' the recalcitrant northern earls.

These were conservative rebellions – they were against 'new' laws and the new style of monarchy. They were not 'revolutions', or radical struggles for rights and privileges for those who had never had them, they were insurrections against change. They were the resistance of those who had been doing well out of the old system and wished it to continue.

From this perspective, Forest Law did something else, something inverted and strange. As well as preserving wildwood and forest from the onslaught of agriculture, Forest Law created a uniquely useable space where the illegal could become the heroic. Resisting Forest Law was a crime not against one's neighbours but against an invisible centralised government; not against the common traditions that, however unwelcome, bound communities together, but against a distant authority, and one whose legitimacy could be questioned under the rules of the old dispensation. The forest was thus not only one of the things that these malcontents were contesting, it also became the place into which they could escape in order to contest it at all.

Efficient slave cultures need open land: it has to be difficult to run away. Egypt, for example, is perfect for this purpose – the chances of disappearing off into the desert are slim: escapees can be spotted from miles away, and if the owners do not catch them, the desert will probably kill them. Forests are precisely the opposite – they are very good places to hide. Slip away between the trees, lurk in the greenwood, vanish into the thickets of wild wood: step outside the laws that bind you to the present and you become the Out Law – the free hero of romance and folk tale.

The most famous of these outlaws is Robin Hood, who probably never existed at all – legend, anecdote and fantasy create composite characters who come to represent a whole idea. But such characters, the heroes of folk legend, are usually based on some sort of reality, and there is no reason to think that Robin Hood is an exception. In this sense, these legends are very different from fairy stories and more related to literary romance. The developed story of Robin Hood epitomises all the arguments here.[5] He was a landholder, a minor nobleman, Robin of Locksley Hall, and in some accounts even the Earl of Huntingdon. He was treated unjustly by 'bad' King John and his wicked place-man the Sherriff of Nottingham while the 'good' king, Richard the Lionheart, was off fighting the crusade, so he fled into the forest and became an outlaw, but an outlaw seeking personal restitution, not social change. Meanwhile, he lived free, he 'robbed from the rich to give to the poor', he supported the oppressed and was true to the 'real' king. It was not the law, but the abuse of the law that he resisted. From early on, accounts of Robin Hood present him as 'merry' and courteous – with a particular respect for women – and as an excellent archer, but also as a 'natural leader' (officer class) who inspired to-die-for (often literally) loyalty from his men, who were all his social inferiors; these accounts also present a romantic and sunny forest, where Maid Marion can be treated like a princess and where excellent dinner parties can be thrown for friendly visitors.

This sense of the forest as both the place of oppression and the place to avoid or punish oppression goes very deep and still remains strangely resonant. Running away, camping out and living off the land have all kept their romantic heroism, even as children are more 'cabin'd, cribbed and confined'[6] than they have ever been before.

The admiration for the noble and somehow free outlaw has left a strange shadow on our consciousness: poaching is treated as different from other forms of theft. At a cultural level, one great and continuing myth is that 'natural products' are free and should be freely available to everyone with the energy and wit to go and find them:[7] 'scrumping' apples may be 'naughty', but it isn't bad, while stealing fruit from a shop is criminal. This extends to poaching game as well. The contradiction is made explicit in *Tom Brown's School Days*, of all unexpected places. Our hero and his friends have spent a day in the woods, climbing trees and collecting birds' eggs (this shows they are good, healthy, 'manly' types). On the way home they fall foul of a farmer who accuses them of stealing his hens – although they are in fact innocent on this occasion. A helpful prefect, Holmes, 'who was one of the best boys in the school', arrives by chance on the scene and, in an extremely high-handed manner, liberates them from rustic arrest. However, once away from the menial farmer's impertinent attempts to protect his own property, Homes goes on to lecture them:

> Knocking over other people's chickens and running off with them is stealing. It's a nasty word but that's the plain English of it. If the chickens were dead and lying in a shop you wouldn't take them, I know that, any more than you would apples out of Griffith's basket; but there's no real difference between chickens running about and apples on a tree, and the same articles in a shop. I wish our morals were sounder in such matters.[8]

But it does no good – Tom and his companions are briefly chastened, but go back to poaching and bird theft, apparently with the amused tolerance of their usually highly moralistic creator. Regardless of the law, in a different, imagined parallel world the outlaw-in-the-forest has imbued the poacher with a romantic freedom, even a sort of virtue.[9] Sneaking off into the forest and living by your wits permeates literature. In *John McNab*,[10] John Buchan has members of the Cabinet poaching, to the ultimate amusement and admiration of the land owners (and also, therefore, in the twentieth century, the deer and salmon owners) themselves. It is one of the mainstays of children's adventure stories: from *Children of the New Forest* to Enid's Blyton's *Famous Five*, poaching is presented as a noble sport and a mark of desirable independence. BB in *Brendon Chase* and Roald Dahl in *Danny, the Champion of the World* make poaching an heroic or at least an endearing act, in a way that 'stealing' never is. The young Charles Stewart (the future Charles II), hiding up an oak tree with a price on his head, suddenly stops being a pampered tyrant and becomes a loveable hero: he has escaped into the forest and become an outlaw. The strange wave of popular support that the thuggish Raoul Moat attracted in 2010, despite being a murderer (and blinding policemen), feels to me as though it was related to the fact that he ran off and hid from the law in the woods.

Outlawry is an expression of a fundamental freedom which is to be found in the forest. But it is a conservative and regressive romantic freedom; it is based on some idea of 'natural rights', and it ends either with the restitution of the older established order, or in tragic exile and death. The Forest Outlaw is always privileged – and is allowed, even applauded for, activities that in the poor would be regarded as criminal. This too is embedded in language – a 'villain' is now a bad guy, a criminal, and particularly one with malevolent intent, but originally the word meant nothing more – or less – than someone at the bottom of the tidy feudal pack – a landless agricultural labourer, a 'low born rustic'. The poor become the crooks, but the rich become adventurers.

The high-handed and noble option of the Out Law was not

easily available to the poor displaced by the development of Forest Law, although it certainly impacted on them bitterly. Their resistance took the form, as it so often does, of a dark humour, even impertinence, expressed in jokes and stories.

Kings do badly in fairy stories.

This probably feels odd, even wrong, at first reading. *Everyone knows* that fairy stories are about Princes and Princesses. But they aren't. Jack Zipes has counted. In the Grimms' collection, there are 29 stories (out of 256) in which one of the principal characters is either a prince or princess,[11] though it is rare for both of the eventual partners to be royal. There is only one story in which a king is the protagonist. And these 30 royals are outnumbered by tailors (11), soldiers (10), servants (8), and 29 other skilled tradesmen or their children. There are 78 stories in which the protagonist is a farmer, a peasant or a 'poor person', or the child of one. Moreover, it is easy to forget that that the Grimms' collection includes about a dozen stories – similar in theme and structure to the more expected fairy stories – which feature saints, most often Mary, not in biblical tales, but as hagiography. If you see Joseph as a skilled tradesman and Mary as the daughter of poor parents (although, like a fairy-tale heroine, eventually becoming the Queen of Heaven itself) – which is how they were perceived for much of the Middle Ages – then this makes another half dozen stories to add to this list.

In a great many of the stories the young and the poor set about outwitting the kings. Young princes and princesses are often complicit in their father's downfall or in subverting his plans. In story after story the King sends the lower-class hero off on impossible quests, hoping to get rid of him and keep his daughter for more profitable marriage; in story after story young women, both princesses and commoners, outwit the King to marry his son. Kings tend to be snobbish, cruel, incompetent and – in the end – outflanked.

These are stories about 'just deserts', not about inherited privilege; cunning as well as industry and courage are to be admired.

Proud princesses get their comeuppance and the poor get rich by trickery more often than by virtue. In no stories, however, even in the pietistic editorial hands of Jacob Grimm, does anyone find happiness by becoming reconciled to their poverty – happiness means being rich and powerful as well as beloved. These are radical, not conservative, tales; stories about overcoming distressing poverty and alienation, subverting the normal social order and achieving a new life of comfort and security.

In fact, it is not just kings who come off badly in classic fairy stories – fathers do too. Fathers are closely linked to kings – as God is to the world (both Father and King), so a king is to his country and a father to his household. They have immense power and control. Following the lines from the *Peterborough Chronicle* I quoted above, the poet concludes:

He loved the stags as much
as if he were their father.

There seems to be a strong element of satire here: a king is meant to be a father to his people, not to some deer, and his fatherhood is complicated because he is caring for the deer *in order to* kill them.

Fathers tend not to get very sympathetic treatment in fairy stories in general – good mothers die and stepmothers are evilly intended, but fathers are simply useless. Unlike mothers, fathers do not die (there are very few fatherless children), they are merely negligent or absent: what on earth was Cinderella's father doing while his new wife enslaved his own child? Or worse, in 'Beauty and the Beast', as in many similar tales, the father sacrifices his daughter to protect himself: the Beast will only spare his life if he promises to send his daughter along as a substitute, and even though he believes that the Beast is going to kill her, he agrees. The king-father in 'The Seven Ravens' weakly marries a witch he does not love and then fails to protect his children from her; he tries to hide the boys in the forest but completely mismanages this endeavour, mainly through his own stupidity.

Above all fathers, like kings, even when they are not weak or self-ish, lack wisdom and discernment. They fail to notice that the youngest of the three sons is actually the hero; or that the humblest of their daughter's suitors is actually the bravest and the best. They favour the status quo at the expense of their own real interests.

The winners in these stories are not the powerful and prosper-ous, but the poor – the apparently stupid, the apparently uncouth, the apparently idle. Feminist criticism has interpreted fairy stories as inher-ently sexist. Between the 1812 and the 1856 editions of the Grimms' tales, the female characters do become more passive, but even the earliest versions of the stories advocate rather different moral strate-gies for men and women, so there is some real truth in this charge, but it has led us to overlook perhaps how profoundly anti-patriarchal they are. Kings and fathers are incompetent and often risible; they are defeated, outwitted and trapped into marriage or forced to give away half their kingdom (and presumably the other half when they die) and their lovely daughters to those whose claims rest not in their strength or power but in their cunning, their kindness and, very often, their simple good luck.

Who are these soldiers and tailors who come up the long path through the forest and create havoc in the town or castle? In their specific forms they are social characters from the eighteenth and early nineteenth centuries, when the tales were being recorded. Zipes argues that the high number of soldier heroes in the Grimms' collection is 'most likely a direct result of the Napoleonic Wars and the vast increase of soldiering as a profession in the European pop-ulation'.[12] In the army of this period there was an enormous divide between officers and common soldiers, who were badly paid, ill treated and commonly despised; they were regularly punished by flogging for minor breaches of discipline and attempts to desert, and sometimes even less serious failures of obedience were met with capital punishment. Their lives were miserable, and if they were wounded or recalcitrant they were dismissed without any further support or even severance pay. In eight of the ten soldier tales the protagonists are explicit about their hatred for the army, for the king whom they 'served', and about their desire for revenge. Another tale is about three soldiers who have deserted, which comes to much the same thing. They are desperate, dangerous and determined. Having little or nothing to lose, no investment in living a peaceful social life and no obvious future, they are fearless, cunning and inventive. They are also outsiders – in a broadly agricultural society, soldiers were displaced in the literal sense of the word: they are tramps and vagabonds, they have spent much of their life on the road, and they arrive at the scene of action by chance and travel.

The tailors, too, are transient, rootless and dissatisfied. Although there were rich master tailors in the old cities of Germany, these are not the tailors of the fairy stories. By the time the Grimm brothers were collecting their tales, the old guild and apprentice system was breaking up. Too many tailors spent much of their life as journey-men, always looking for a better, more stable position, often forced into shoddy workmanship and cost-cutting exercises, and because they were travelling on they had little to gain by establishing repu-tations for high-quality work. In addition, tailoring was an attractive option for young men who were neither rich nor strong, because it needed very little capital investment to set up as a tailor and the job was not physically demanding in the way that most other skilled work was. Tailors had a reputation for being cunning, dishonest, quick witted and puny.

What the two professions have in common is that they produce deeply disgruntled characters with little to gain from social norms, landless and displaced, driven by a sense of injustice, forced to travel and live by their wits, and all because of poverty itself. Tailors and ex-soldiers are the specific late-eighteenth-century version of some-thing more universal – the dispossessed and angry poor. They do not look like hero material in any expected sense of the word to a lit-erate society brought up on a more romantic heroism, but in fairy stories they (as part of a larger, looser group of itinerant workmen – amongst them a shoemaker, a musician, a journeyman, and a sur-geon) easily outnumber the princes and the rich merchants. And they are triumphant.

They come out of the forests seeking their fortunes; they go back into the forests to find their true identity. They trick the kings and marry their daughters. They are not the 'lumpen proletariat'; they are skilled workers on the cusp of industrialisation. In the century following the publication of the *Märchen* they will become Chartists,[13] trade unionists, communists.[14] The last armed insurrection in Britain, the Battle of Bossenden, took place in the ancient sweet chestnut forest of the Blean in 1838, when the agricultural workers of Kent took up arms against the royal militia. Oddly enough, their leader, the self-titled Sir William Courtenay, believed he had the magical power of immortality. They were defeated of course: the tropes of fairy stories are inspirational or consolatory, not prophetic.

It was inspirationally beautiful in the woods that May day with the bluebells and the adder and some tiny baby rabbits and my own high-minded thoughts. In a perfectly organised world I would have heard a cuckoo as I walked. This is not a wild fantasy; May is the month when you are mostly likely to hear that familiar disyllabic call echoing through the woods, and it would have fitted very neatly into my thoughts, since the bird arrives from a long journey and sneaks into the nests of other birds, tricking them into raising its young often at the expense of their own brood. It would have made a splendid analogy. But I did not hear a cuckoo that day. I was quite glad because, although my heart always lifts a bit for the very first cuckoo of the year, which really does shout out the spring, I find the incessant repetition of that strangely penetrating call rather annoying. Once a cuckoo starts, it seems able to keep it up all day. Even without a cuckoo, though, the forest was full of bird music, celebratory, joyful, exuberant. Then, when I was nearly back to my car, I heard a sound I had never heard before, a brand new bird song – an accelerating run of crisp metallic notes, ending up with a tremolo trill. (I have read it described as the 'sound of a spinning coin on a marble slab'.) I had to listen to an audio tape later to identify it: a wood warbler, a summer visitor from tropical Africa to deciduous woods throughout Europe where the forest floor is reasonably clear of undergrowth. And when I listened to the tape, I learned something else: the wood warbler has an alternative, completely different song that it inserts, as it were, between the verses of its main one. I had heard that too in the forest, a fast sequence of intense, soft, somehow sad notes, but had not realised it was one and the same bird singing both songs in the afternoon sunshine of the bluebell woods, the King's hunting forest.

Histories of the imagination are hard to trace and impossible to prove, but it is surely at least provocative that in Scotland, where the Crown was always much weaker and slower to move towards the new European concept of the King, there was much less afforestation – and a different sort of fairy story. The magic of the Celtic tales is deeper and grander; the heroes come with long pedigrees and noble education and they never laugh at themselves, nor at the social systems they emerge from. Merlin may roam mad in the Great Caledonian forest, but he serves the King first and foremost; despite a less-than-grandiose childhood, Arthur always was the true king by inheritance, by blood – he was no indigent soldier, no sneaky little tailor, and certainly not the 'child of a poor man', a servant or

agricultural labourer. Merlin's magic is a high magic, far more powerful than the little domestic magic of the old women, the witches,
and the woods themselves in the classic fairy stories; but it won't save
him or Camelot or the Kingdom. The little tailor, the sly and boastful servant girl and the surly, discontented soldier, however, will
become rich, sexually satisfied and in power. The Crown's attempts
to exclude them from the forest, deprive them of their traditions
and keep them in their places will fail. They will sneak back into the
woods, where they will learn a thing or two and emerge to claim
their rights, achieve power and live happily ever after.

Rumpelstiltskin

Once upon a time there was a funny little man and he was dancing in the forest.

He, at least, called it dancing, though to you it might have looked more like gambolling and frolicking, tumbling and prancing, because he was not graceful. He danced in the hazel coppice and he looked like those trees – short and bristly with skinny misshapen branches. But, like those trees, he promised sweetness and ripeness and generous joy. Later, in the moonlight, high up the mountainside, he danced with trembling aspens and the bristly junipers and he looked like them too – solitary, clinging to the poor soil, spindly and grotesque. He was leaping and somersaulting and singing for joy:

> *Today I'll brew, tomorrow I'll bake*
> *And soon I'll have the Queen's namesake;*
> *Oh how hard it is to play my game*
> *For Rumplestiltskin is my name.*
> *He is me. I am him.*

And he ought to be the hero of this story, but they have made him into the villain.

Once upon a time there was a greedy king and a boastful, ambitious – though admittedly rather lovely – miller's daughter.

He wanted to be rich and she wanted to be queen. They were as selfish and worldly and mean-hearted as each other, and they lied and tricked and exploited their inferiors to get what they wanted.

They ought to be the villains of this story, but they have made themselves into the heroes.

It is not fair.

The funny little man was dancing in the forest because there no one could see him dance, or so he thought. In the forest he was hidden. In the forest there were no sneers, no averted glances, no stifled giggles or covert disgust. In the forest there were no mirrors. In the forest he could be who he chose and how he wished. He was full of joy that night. He danced because, come morning, he was planning a good deed, and in his folly he imagined that a king and queen would be grateful, would smile at him and would let him play with their darling baby. Poor fool.

He was me. I was him.

It is not fair. So I am going to tell the story again – it is my story and I have the right.

Once upon a time there was a self-important miller; he had worked his way up from not much and wanted all the world to know it. He scrooged his workers, bullied his wife and spoiled his children, as such men do. His favourite child was his oldest daughter, who was very like him only prettier, and on her his ambition was set. Nothing was too good for that little madam. She grew up wonderfully self-centred and with a total lack of useful skills; she believed the world owed her not simply a living but adulation and chocolates and jewels and furs. Her father, who inevitably called her 'my princess', believed that she ought to be a queen, and by the time she was seventeen she entirely agreed with him.

The miller was a man who could not help boasting. Swagger was like sweat for him, it oozed out of his flesh and smelled slightly rank, although he never noticed, any more than he noticed that his childhood friends laughed at him and that his new acquaintances despised him. His voice was loud and his purse was full – what more could a man need? he thought complacently.

One day the miller met a king – a venal, greedy young man with sharp eyes, a weak chin and a rather unimportant kingdom, but a real and proper crowned king nonetheless. In an expansive mood brought on by brandy and arrogance, the miller told the king that his daughter could spin straw into gold.

Well, the king was not stupid, or at least not very stupid, and he was both eager for gold and somewhat dubious, as anyone might be. He did what kings have tendency to do when something they want a lot looms up on their horizons – he sent some soldiers round to arrest her and drag her off to his castle. This was not, of course, quite what the miller had intended, but he was convinced that the mere sight of his daughter would melt the King's heart, and any form of introduction to royalty tends to rot the good sense of men like him. So he managed to fool both himself and her that this was not an arrest exactly, but more of an invitation to visit the castle. He gave her a good deal of advice, which would have been shrewd if he had not failed to understand that the King was more driven by avarice than by lust. A surprising number of men are, when push comes to shove, but this is often hidden by the fact that avarice can easily enough take the form of greed for power and power can most easily, and pleasurably, be expressed by sexual conquest. So the miller accompanied his daughter to town and, more in a spirit of investment than of generosity, bought her some rather exotic lingerie and some very expensive jewellery.

Yes, these are nasty people and my take on them is without good humour or kindness. Or even much forgiveness. But I am just a funny little man who dances on his own in the high forest and dreams that one day someone will love him. I have cause for bitterness, as you will see.

So, the young woman arrived at the palace with an eager anticipation. Her father had, of course, failed to inform her fully of his folly, so she was little startled to be led not to a lavish bedchamber where some appropriate minion would help her decorate herself for the festivities, but to a small, cramped attic filled with straw, in which there stood a spinning wheel. The King accompanied her and announced:

'Now get to work; and if all this straw isn't gold by morning, I'll have you executed.'

A humbler, more sensible and more merry-hearted girl would have laughed at the King, admitted she had not the least idea how to set about such a task and told him that indeed she could hardly spin flax or wool into thread, let alone straw into gold, and that her father was a boastful fool and the King an idiot for believing him. But after the haughty looks she had cast at her sisters and the contemptuous flounce with which she had crossed the village square, accompanied by a guard of uniformed soldiers, she could not face the shame. She smiled archly at the King, hoping to deflect him, and was still smiling flirtatiously when he left the room and slammed the door. When she heard the key turn in the lock her smile collapsed, and before many minutes had passed she was weeping.

When she looked up there was a funny little man looking at her sympathetically. He enquired politely as to her difficulties.

He is me. I am him.

At this point I did not know she was a nasty piece of work. Passing about my business in the corridor, I had heard someone crying and popped my head round the door to see if I could help. No magic about that – the King had left the key in the keyhole. There was this pretty little thing, her face all swollen with tears, and anyone would have offered to help if he could.

Now, most people have forgotten this, but spinning straw into gold is not that hard: there is a knack to it and it takes practice, but anyone with the will can learn. It is easier with straw than with many things because it is the right colour to start with. You sit at the spinning wheel and you think of all the golden things in the forest: of lichens in flat, round disks on granite; of wild narcissus under the first fresh leaves in springtime; of the patterns on the back of *Carterocephalus palaemon*, the Chequered Skipper butterfly; of globe flowers seen through hazel branches, bright as sunshine; of the stripes of a bumblebee sipping on clover; of the iridescence on the undersides of dung beetles; of the flash of goldfinch in a hawthorn hedge; of chanterelles on shaded moss; of owl eyes blinking in the deep wood; of tormentil and asphodel and agrimony and broom; of horse chestnut leaves in autumn and of ripening crab apples; of grass seed heads catching the low sun in winter. If memory fails, even buttercups and dandelions will do, though the work is slower with such common joys. You gather all these together in heart and head and eye and then – and this is the tricky bit – you need to spin the spinning wheel very, very fast and without breaking the rhythm. *Whizz, whizz, whizz. Whirr, whirr, whirr.* And that is it really, though of course a loving heart helps, as always.

After the straw was all spun into gold, the miller's daughter asked the funny little man, 'What must I pay you?' He wanted to ask for a kiss, but he was courteous and gentle, so he asked for her necklace and she gave it to him.

The King, of course, was too greedy to let it go at that. A whole room filled with gold thread was not enough for him, so he dragged her off to another larger attic and all three of them went through the same process *Whizz, whizz, whizz. Whirr, whirr, whirr.* This time the funny little man wanted to ask for a hug, but he was gentle and courteous, so he asked for her ring and she gave it to him.

She was so pretty and grateful that the funny little man was glad to have been of service to her.

But the third night was different. The King had been thinking, and although he despised her for being a miller's daughter, his enthusiasm for the gold overrode his snobbery. He said that if she would spin one more roomfull he would marry her. And far from refusing point blank, she agreed. Her snobbery overrode her good sense. She was happy to marry a king who would make her a queen, even though he had proved himself venal, greedy and cruel.

Not just folly, wicked folly. The funny little man was shocked. He thought he would teach her a lesson. So he slipped into the room and spun the straw to gold. *Whizz, whizz, whizz. Whirr, whirr, whirr.* And when she enquired what she would have to pay him this time, he asked for her first child. He thought that would give her pause, but after a bit of pouting and grumbling she agreed. She promised.

He never imagined she would consent; he never meant to take the child.

He wanted to make her think and he wanted to do a gracious thing. He wanted someone to be grateful to him – not laughing or sneering but grateful, admiring even, and appreciating. That is not a big ask, surely.

I do know. *He is me. I am him.*

So they made a deal and a year later he learned that the Queen was safely delivered of a child and he came back. He thought he would pretend to take the child, though he never would do so really. He had earned it, but he would not claim it – and she would be grateful and would smile at him and would let him play with the baby. He had it all planned.

She reneged on the contract. She promised, she promised and she did not come through. She was a liar and a coward and a suspicious, selfish woman.

He gave her one more chance: he offered to play a game with her. She had to guess his name. She cheated, flourishing the riches that she had stolen from her own husband and sending spies to catch the little man dancing in the forest.

He did not want her baby. Unlike her, he was kind and gracious and generous. He only wanted a chance for the world to see those things in him and be glad and grateful. He knew that babies need their mummies and do not need to be stolen away by funny little men who everyone laughs and sneers at.

There are rules; there are rules in fairy stories:

- The true queen is gentle and kind and good as well as beautiful.
- Hard work is rewarded – magical hard work by those who live in the forest is especially rewarded.
- The old, the ugly and the weak should be respected, treated tenderly and not mocked.
- Promises must be kept.

So why is the funny little man the villain, and the greedy king and the spoiled queen the heroes?

It is not fair.

I should know. *I am he. He is me.*

4

June

Epping Forest

Late in June, and despite getting lost in the strange mixed countryside of tiny sunken lanes, motorways and approaches to Stansted Airport, I rather surprisingly managed to arrive in time at Bishop's Stortford railway station, where I met Robert Macfarlanc, the writer of *Mountains of the Mind*, *Wild Places* and *The Old Ways*, off a train from Cambridge so that we could go and walk in Epping Forest.

We drove south from Bishop's Stortford and crossed under the M25 to approach the forest from the north. There is something pleasing about the idea that one of the largest areas of ancient forest in England is *inside* the M25, and therefore effectively part of London. In fact, the city and the forest have an intimate, mutually beneficial relationship: the city grew because there were forests (providing fuel) around it, and Epping Forest survived because of the city.

In the 1130s most of what is now Essex, including Epping Forest, was declared Royal Forest by Henry I and was indeed used by the monarchs for hunting.[1] As in other Royal Forests, the interests of the Crown, landowners and local inhabitants were managed under the Forest Law, and over the next couple of centuries the commoners (those who held common rights in the forest) established the usual

arrangement of rights to wood cutting and, in this case most sig-
nificantly, to 'intercommonage' – the right to graze stock throughout
the whole forest, not merely within the manor where they lived. By
the eighteenth century there was a considerable tradition of hostil-
ity between the landowners and the commoners. For example, here
the rule was that landlords owned the maiden, or timber, trees, but
that the commoners could cut wood from pollards for fuel. There
are frequent accounts of landlords bringing complaints to the forest
courts that maidens had been lopped and thus turned into pollards.
Equally, the commoners were actively resistant to all attempts to
limit free grazing, even those legally sanctioned by the Verderers
(the local officers of the Forest Law); they tore down all new fences
and attacked the workmen constructing them.

By the end of the eighteenth century the Crown, having no more
interest in either hunting or raising venison in Essex, became not
merely willing but eager to sell its rights to the forest back to the
actual owners from whom it had freely taken them seven hundred
years before; many of these owners still retained their medieval
rights as Lords of the Manor. Here as elsewhere, they made energetic moves to buy back the forest rights and then enclose the land –
thus preventing the commoners from exercising their customary
free grazing and wood gathering. These tensions were replicated
throughout the country – and not just in forests. The long tradition
of common rights and open grazing was in effect very nearly abolished
between 1790 and 1880 because of the rising value of agricultural
land and because of the high capital investment for the major land
improvements of the Agricultural Revolution.

Enclosure was a greater assault on the rights of the agricultural
communities than royal afforestation had ever been and needs to be
seen in a larger context than simply in terms of how it affected the
status of forests. Enclosure was a key factor in a wider, profoundly
radical cultural shift (in the sense that Thatcherism was radical),
conceptually and structurally. It was a vital part of industrialisation
and the move towards active modern capitalism: ideas of private
ownership, profit and 'usefulness' (that what makes something

'valuable' is its ability to generate monetary value – so that sub-fertile moorland, wild forest and mountain regions come to be seen as being 'without value') overtook older ideas of community and responsibility and duty. From the Highland Clearances in the North to the substantial urbanisation of the British labouring classes, the social consequences of the changes were enormous, and of course complicated and not all negative. The depth of the change can, as always, be seen in the way it is moralised. Landowners' profits, at the expense of traditional agricultural life, quickly acquired a high ethical imperative: common rights were morally bad for the poor, as this free-range grazing and 'easy' acquisition of fuel encouraged idleness and allowed individuals to avoid decent wage labour and settled work. During the long-running nineteenth-century battle for the right to enclose Epping, the forest was described as the 'nursery and resort of the most idle and profligate of men'.[2]

But enclosure was a hard-won victory. It was bitterly contested, both by legal recourse and by straightforward physical opposition throughout the country. Not all Highlanders went as passively as the narrative of doom requires; the troops were called out to sup-press anti-enclosure uprisings in many parts of the country, from Kent to Galloway. The commoners of Epping proved particularly recalcitrant, and gained the support of some local landowners, who brought their plight to the attention of both Parliament and the Corporation of the City of London. Here, Epping's proximity to the capital became significant because it transpired that the Mayor and Corporation were in fact commoners – that is, they held common rights – as tenants in some of the parishes of Epping Forest. Unusually, therefore, the commoners of Epping had among their own number an enormously rich, influential and powerful member.

In 1851, Hainault Forest, immediately adjacent to Epping, was legally disafforested. Within weeks, the vast majority of its trees had been grubbed up and the land converted to enclosed and ploughed fields. Encouraged, the landowners of Epping who desired enclo-sure began to fence 'their' parts of the forest, without waiting on the

legal niceties. Between 1850 and 1870 more than half of Epping
Forest (over 3,000 acres) was fenced – although not grubbed out.
However, the forest communities were also inspired, in the opposite
direction, and started to use the law more directly to protect their
ancient rights. In 1866, Thomas Willingdale filed a suit in Chancery
claiming that his lopping rights to trees in Loughton Manor had
been infringed by the ring fence the owner had illegally erected.
Like many other Victorian Chancery cases, this one dragged on and
on, and Willingdale died while it was still being argued. However
the Corporation of the City of London, increasingly aware both of
the dangers to the forest and of the deeply unsettled mood of the
community, took up the issue by bringing proceedings against all
enclosures. Unlike individual commoners, it could afford to do this,
and so this became a rare occasion when the whole concept of
enclosure was challenged (rather than specific incidences of it). In
the end it came down to one particular legal question – intercommonage. This ancient practice in Epping made the landlords' ability
to buy back the rights impracticable. The judges ruled, rather pleasingly, that the rights of intercommonage were so ancient and
complicated that it would be impossible for the landowners ever to
demonstrate that every single entitled commoner had given consent
and been compensated, and that since the right was individual
rather than collective, each and every commoner had the right to
veto a change. Therefore, any enclosure in Epping Forest was illegal.

But the Corporation of London had its own agenda, which did
not have much to do with traditional forest community life. Above
all it wanted to secure the forest for 'the health and recreation' of its
own constituency – the citizens of London. So it proceeded to buy
up, from the disgruntled landowners, the 'waste' ground of all nineteen manors in the forest. By 1878 it had acquired 3,500 acres and
induced Parliament to pass the Epping Forest Act, which made the
Corporation itself the Conservator of the Forest, with the primary
obligation 'at all times to keep Epping Forest unenclosed and
unbuilt on as an open space for the recreation and enjoyment of the
public'.

This was a brand-new development – a forest, or indeed any other large space, whose primary function was to provide recreational space for people *who did not live in it*. Today this seems entirely natural – Epping was a direct forerunner of the national parks and of the amenity role which the Forestry Commission has now adopted as a major management aim. But in 1882, when Queen Victoria opened Epping Forest to its new existence, there were no precedents. For example, no one had much idea about how to balance the needs of the public with the preservation of the ancient woodland itself; as the Epping Forest guidebook puts it, 'early management was rather experimental'. One mistake that we now know they made was to buy up the lopping rights (this is not the same as enclosure) as it was felt that pollarding and coppicing were 'bad for' trees; since then, it has become clear that these activities actually extend the life of individual trees and enrich the biodiversity of an area of woodland. Pollarding in Epping has now been re-introduced, although much of the old skill and tree lore has been lost and must be re-learned or re-created. At another level, though, it was extraordinarily successful – Epping Forest became a 'Cockney Paradise'.[3] Urban dwellers made it abundantly clear how much they liked getting out of town – on one bank holiday in 1920, 102,000 visitors poured through Chingford Station heading for the forest. The open spaces of Chingford Plain and High Beech offered the visitors donkey rides, coconut shies and similar entertainment; twice a year, there were big travelling fairs. Huge tea rooms, named 'Forest Retreats', catering for up to 2,000 people at a time, were opened and drinking water fountains made available. Beyond these facilities, the forest was open and, released from both the gross overcrowding of the expanding city and the repressive ownership of most open land, with its onerous trespass laws and lack of access, it was extensively used by Londoners for walking, for early bicycle clubs and for a more general sense of freedom and play. This role has continued: Epping Forest is now designed and managed primarily for leisure – waymarked and amenity pathed and car parked and caféd and toileted. Interpretation boards tell you what you are looking at and footbridges stop you getting your feet wet. There are picnic tables and viewing points. There are sixty football pitches and three cricket grounds. The Corporation also owns a public golf course, licenses angling, hires out boats, makes provision for horse and bicycle riding, and offers natural history and local archaeological courses.

Meanwhile, in terms of maintaining the natural forest – another duty the Epping Forest Act laid down – the new managers did not do at all badly. Epping Forest was the first public 'nature reserve' in the country. It has maintained an impressive diversity of habitats, and therefore of plants and animals. This diversity is partly based on the remarkable variety of soil types within the forest, but is partly due to some very forward-looking policies: at a time when birds of prey and terrestrial predators were being energetically exterminated elsewhere, usually in support of exclusive game and hunting activities, the Corporation extended protection beyond the requirements of the act and brought owls, hawks and stoats under its protective mantle. Today, areas covering two-thirds of the forest have been designated as Sites of Special Scientific Interest (SSSIs), and English Nature has assessed the forest's bio-diversity as 'outstanding' for its variety of invertebrates, dragonflies, amphibia, breeding birds, mosses, liverworts and fungi. There are over 50 species of tree (although this includes introductions and garden escapees); 200 species of bird – including 60 breeding varieties; 650 flowering species; all three types of British newt; over 4,000 different insects, including 1,337 beetles, and 525 different moths and butterflies. Given that nowhere in the forest is out of walking range of a London tube station, this is remarkable. Moreover, because Epping was taken over by the Corporation, it was no longer part of the Crown Estate when the Forestry Commission was set up after the First World War, so it never came under the pressure to be 'productive' as the other Royal Forests did, and consequently there has been no mass conifer plantation or clear-felling.

We parked in a car park full of motor bikes and a mobile café. We went into the forest.

It was June. The sun was shining. After we had walked a little way, Macfarlane took his shoes off. He did not urge me to do so too, but after a small self-conscious moment I did and he said that only barefoot can you truly feel a forest. It was strange; in my hippyish youth I was a notorious barefoot wanderer – even along Oxford pavements; but it was, I suddenly realised, a very long time since I had felt the extraordinary intimacy of the ground against naked toes, naked soles. It also made me look where I was walking with a new concentration – aware not just of brambles or old sharp refuse, but of the texture of beech mast, wet grass, moss, fallen leaf mould, bare wood. And suddenly it reminded me not of my student days, but of my childhood. My mother was a great believer in the positive health effects for the young of going barefoot in the countryside. I had forgotten. Manley Hopkins is right: 'nor can foot feel now, being shod'.[4] It was as though my body itself had its own sweet memories of freedom and innocence.

We wandered: it was a walk of extraordinary variety, of both habitat and mood.

In places the forest felt deep and ancient; the trees are mainly oak, beech, and particularly hornbeam, which flourishes only in the south-eastern corner of Britain (and, perhaps because it is rather slow growing, it has not been transported north as an ornamental or hedging the way beech trees have). Hornbeams make exceptionally fine pollards with their sinuous silver grey bark and the flutes and gnarls of long survival (there are hornbeam pollards in Epping known to be over 300 years old). We followed paths that seemed to have no purpose except to be followed. They led to glades and clearings, places of meeting, but there was no one to meet. We may have seen a dark feline creep off. Macfarlane wondered if it might be the infamous Beast of Ongar, but I preferred a witch's familiar, vanishing to warn her of our possible approach. We came out of the thick trees and onto pasture where there were grazing cattle and open ponds, with dragonflies and late tadpoles; Macfarlane, who plunges into every bit of cold water he encounters in *The Wild Places*, did *not* swim here, although I suspect he was tempted, and if he had done, I would have been too.

Then elsewhere, without warning, the atmosphere seemed to change abruptly and the wood felt grubby with picnic refuse and evidence that we were walking where too many people had recently trodden, certainly with their shoes on. One strange thing about this walk was the constant awareness of how near 'civilisation' we were all the time. We were never really beyond the reach of engine noises from the roads which cut through the forest – not lanes or tracks, but major trunk roads. One moment we were in old woodland with all its silent muttering and the harsh musky smell of ransoms – wild garlic, which follows hard on the heels of the bluebells – and then suddenly we were crossing a busy road or hearing a blare of engine revs. It was oddly unsettling and unresolved.

This sense of the public aspect of the forest, as opposed to my more usual experience of silence and hiddenness, never quite disappeared. We walked through cathedrals of beech trees, their leaves still delicately green, but now much denser than in April and May. But the clearings they stood in felt open for gatherings, and the graffiti carved deep into the smooth trunks provided constant reminders of people coming into the woods for their own reasons, although apparently always reasons of love. Macfarlane expounded his 'tentative theory' that people do not, cannot even, carve anything vile or obscene into living bark; I had never thought about this before, but all the trees we encountered seemed to prove his point.

Somehow it felt as though we were always somehow on the periphery. Macfarlane later described this slightly distanced feeling: it was, he said, as though 'we were really wandering in a memory or wish-fulfilment of the ancient forest, which we wanted to be far wider and deeper than the actual forest was'.[5] Gradually it dawned on me that this is exactly what Epping Forest is: it is a dream or memory of ancient woodland. A feeling of barefoot childlike enchantment is an entirely appropriate response to Epping Forest. This is a forest which is the way it is and where it is in order to replicate the pleasures and playfulness of lost forests, lost childhood.

Then we found the swing.

In one of the more isolated parts of our walk, we came into an open glade, the ground smooth and red-gold under a massive beech tree. The wide canopy roofed the whole space so that we were sheltered within a green tent. And there someone had managed to tie a rope to a branch at least thirty feet above the clearing, although it was one of the lowest solid branches of the tree; the rope hung down straight into the middle of the green chamber. This was impressive, and it was hard to work out how it had been accomplished. The tree trunk was too smooth to climb and too fat to swarm.[6] I like to think that whoever created the swing did it by shooting an arrow from a home-made bow, with a light lead cord attached, and then used that to haul up and secure the thicker rope, but I am guessing. The seat of the swing was a stout piece of straight dead wood, attached to the bottom of the rope. In any event, it was a skilled, complex task obviously requiring planning, knowledge and creative imagination. The swing was sturdy; we both swung on it and it supported our adult weight through long arcs of freedom. But nonetheless, there was an innocent, amateurish feel to it; it came from another world than the Health-and-Safety-controlled playgrounds or even the 'adventure' jungle swings offered to visitors in well-regulated 'family friendly' parks.

For me there was a great joy in finding the swing. Apart from the pure physical delight of swinging on such a long rope, it felt like a sign that there are still children in the forests. The makers of this particular swing must have been fairly big children – constructing it was clearly a task beyond a pre-teenager. But there must have been young people who came to this secret space with the equipment and skills to complete a difficult engineering task with great competence. They must have had practice and training in using serious tools and been allowed to take them out of some careful workshop and into the woods: this is something very different from strewn beer cans and used condoms – although both of these would themselves represent very traditional uses of the hidden places in the woods.

I worry that not many more generations of children will be allowed this kind or level of independent personal success – this genuine achievement of combined creative imagination, thoughtful problem solving and physical skill. Wandering off into the woods and being alone and unsupervised anywhere is discouraged now and frequently treated as dangerous.

We are doing something very alarming to our children – and, making it worse perhaps, we have fooled ourselves that we are doing it for their sake, for their safety. The amount of unsupervised time outside the home that young people get to enjoy is being reduced year on year (the average child has lost a whole hour a day already this century). It starts at birth – babies are no longer put out in prams to enjoy fresh air, clouds overhead, people passing, and, if they are lucky enough, green leaves and dappled shadows, and, above all, to enjoy themselves, their freedom and self-sufficiency. We all know there is something wrong with this, because the well-intentioned parent then buys them mobiles and electronic moving objects which hang over their cots as an artificial substitute. And as they get older the situation gets worse. In the face of both consistent anecdote and good research which tell us that mooching about, alone or with your peers, wandering around, especially in natural environments, and being allowed to choose for yourself how you will spend some of your time is good for physical health, educational achievement and imagination, self-awareness and a sense of security, we wantonly deprive children of this space. We say it is for their safety, but this is nonsense. The number of children murdered by strangers per year has not increased since the Second World War (with the exception of 1996 – the year of the Dunblane shooting, where the children died not because they were alone in the woods but, rather, precisely because they were not: they were well supervised and 'safe'). Far more children are abused in the home or by adults they know than by strangers. Serious accidents in the home are more common than those on the roads. Obesity, unarguably related to lack of exercise, is more likely to shorten our children's lives than anything that may happen to them out on the street or in the countryside.

We adults are selfishly letting our fairly imaginary fears deprive our children of opportunities to enjoy something that adults continually report as one of the most pleasurable memories of our youth – times of being outside, alone or with our siblings or friends. The fact that these small-scale wilderness experiences are closely linked to creativity, good mental health and enhanced well being is secondary – the primary gain is delight and freedom. In his intriguing book *Last Child in the Woods*,[7] Richard Louv argues passionately that we must allow our children, for their own sake, more space and opportunity to go alone into what he insists on calling 'nature'. He then boasts that he gives his teenagers this permission *so long as they take a mobile phone with them*. This is simply long-distance supervision; they are *not* allowed to be alone, they are not trusted to look after themselves, they are, in effect, not judged competent.

We have compounded the problem by replacing 'nature studies' – a hands-on knowledge of what is actually happening that until recently began in primary school with 'the nature table' – with 'ecology', which too often is something that happens in books and on TV, far away on polar ice-caps and in equatorial jungles. Too often this approach presents nature as something fragile, threatened and best left alone. Children can end up thinking they 'love' wild animals – but never any wild animals they have actually encountered: pandas, not rats; tarantulas, not bees.

Love without knowledge is a dangerous thing. In an article in the *Daily Mail* in February 2011, during the furore about the Cameron government's consultation paper on the Forestry Commission Estate, Max Hastings wrote an article in which he said of commercial forestry:

Although many of its dreary plantations are indeed the much-discussed 'havens for wildlife', they are the wrong sort. Vermin and predators prosper in their dark depths, and take a heavy toll on songbirds and small mammals.

The concept of a 'wrong sort' of wildlife shows dangerous love coupled with ignorance.[8] What form of wildlife is not 'predatory'? What is the right sort? Many songbirds are 'predatory' in as much as they eat insects; badgers are predatory – in Spain, their principal food is rabbits, and in Britain they devour Hastings' 'small mammals' as well as earth worms, frogs and other reptiles. Are weasels 'right' small mammals or 'wrong' predators? (The derivation of the word 'weasel' is probably from the Anglo-Saxon *weatsop*, meaning 'a vicious bloodthirsty animal'.) Spiders are predatory. And obviously birds of prey are predatory. Meanwhile, 'vermin', according to the OED, is an entirely *social* category, properly applied to species that take preserved game, or that are believed to do so. The idea of a 'wrong sort' of wild life is patently ridiculous and a symptom of a very 'wrong sort' of androcentric sentimentality, which is good neither for 'nature' nor for the individual who feels it.[9]

In consequence of both child-raising and educational approaches, I seriously fear that we are failing to nourish the beautiful and precious quality of resilience in our children. I mean the simple honest awareness that horrible and dangerous things do happen, but that you can cope; with a modest application of good sense you can not only survive, you can gain from the experience.[10]

I see both forests and fairy stories as a specific antidote to this. Forests because, oddly enough, they are relatively safe terrains for exploration. This is partly because there are no lethal animals lurking in them. No one has died of an adder bite in Britain since 1974. There are few cliffs to fall off and small chance of drowning. They present challenges but not, on the whole, serious danger. But it is also because in fact you do not have to go very far into woodland to feel that excitement of aloneness and secrecy, as Robert Macfarlane and I discovered. You can hide in a wood within earshot of your grown-ups, in a way that you cannot usually on a mountainside or beach. Moreover, forests offer an extraordinary range of free things to do – adventurous things and contemplative things. Forests offer infinite possibilities for creative play – especially, I think, because they often provide a choice of physical levels; climbing up a tree is different from hiding inside one. A long view through or over woodland is radically other from hiding behind or within a thicket. And, where the stories are still told, everyone knows that forests are magical.

The fairy stories themselves are also training grounds for resilience. Terrible, terrible dangers threaten the children in fairy stories – from cruel and abusive parents to giants, wolves and witches. But in every single case, not through special skills or miraculous interventions, but through the application of good sense (and, interestingly, good manners), the children do not merely survive, they return home wiser, richer and happier.

In the Grimms' collection there are, in fact, surprisingly few stories that are about children, rather than adolescents or young adults. It can be a little hard to work this out – Snow White, for example, is called 'Little' in the original title itself, and the story says explicitly that she becomes 'more beautiful than the Queen herself' when she is only seven. However, after she eats the apple and falls into her coma we are told that although she lay 'a long, long time in the glass coffin', 'she did not change but looked as though she were asleep'. Nonetheless, when she recovers she is old enough to get married more or less instantly. The Little Goosegirl, despite the soubriquet, is clearly an adult, or very nearly so, because the story begins with her setting out to her own wedding; and the apparently very young princess who plays with a ball in the garden, is lectured by her father, and throws the poor frog across her bedroom in a tantrum in 'The Frog Prince' is also old enough to marry him when he is restored to his human form. The line between adult and child is more blurred in the stories.

Nonetheless, there are actual children in these tales. Red Riding Hood is described as 'a dear little girl', and is perceived and treated as a child who has to learn a lesson about caution and obedience.[11]

Hansel and Gretel are definitely quite small children, as are the less well-known pair in 'Brother and Sister' and Marlinchen and her

stepbrother in 'The Juniper Tree'.[12] Above all, there are the various
Thumbling (Tom Thumb) stories in which the hero is not just a
child but a very tiny one.

Curiously, the stories about actual children are very often much
darker and less playful than the ones about adults. Truly horrendous
things happen to these children. They are the victims of abusive
households.[13] They (sensibly) run away[14] or are deliberately abandoned in the forest. Here appalling things occur – surprisingly often
the danger is about being eaten. The Wolf eats Little Red Riding
Hood; the witch in her gingerbread house plans to eat Hansel; in
'The Juniper Tree' the father is tricked by the wicked stepmother
into eating his own son, served up as a tasty stew; in 'Brother and
Sister' the boy is enchanted into the form of a fawn and hunted
within an inch of his life; Thumbling is swallowed by a cow. This is
rather strange because it is not a very probable danger, compared
with, say, the dangers of fire, eating something toxic or drowning.
Within the historic period there have been very few animals in
northern Europe likely to eat anyone; it feels to me a symbolic peril,
perhaps arising more out of a real fear of hunger: 'be careful
because the hungry are dangerous'.[15]

But – and this is the point – every single fairy story ends happily.
The children demonstrate excellent coping strategies. They are
highly competent and are rewarded for this. In as much as these stories have a pedagogical or ethical thrust, it is not, 'Don't go into the
forest', or, 'Stay at home and be safe.' It is, 'Go into the forest, but
go cannily.' Some strangers are dangerous; some, however, are very
helpful – you cannot tell which by appearances (beautiful, young or
smooth-spoken are not reliable indicators of virtue; but ugliness, age
and strange appearance are not evidence of malevolence), so learn
to discriminate. Be polite, caring of your environment, and hard
working. Above all, keep your wits about you.

Hansel and Gretel are imperilled. They are taken into the forest
to be abandoned. Hansel thwarts their parents' first attempt by
laying a trail of pebbles which allows them to find their way home:
this is sensible. The second time, however, he tries to lay a trail of

breadcrumbs: this is a wrong move and they get lost in the forest. Eventually they find the gingerbread house – but they are greedy and try and eat the house, so they are captured by the witch. In a series of cunning ways – Hansel sticks a chicken bone through the bars of his cage so the witch thinks he is too skinny to eat; Gretel lures the witch into her own oven – they outwit their enemy. They become very rich and go home in triumph.

Little Sister and Little Brother are abused at home. They run away into the forest. Despite his sister's explicit warnings, the boy is self-indulgent – first drinking from an enchanted stream, so that he is turned into a deer, and then wanting to go out even though there is a hunt going on. The sister, however, keeps her head, makes careful plans, correctly nurses his wounds and eventually negotiates a successful settlement with a king which leaves her as queen and her brother freed from the spell. (There is a sub-theme in those stories that are about actual children: 'Trust your big sister. Girls are more likely to be intelligent and self controlled than boys.' This theme is entirely absent from stories about adolescents and adults. It makes me wonder who was telling these particular tales, given how frequently the care of smaller children fell to the oldest girl in any rural family.)

Marlinchen and her stepbrother, in 'The Juniper Tree', are also abused. In fact, her mother murders the boy and tries to cast the blame on her own daughter. She feeds the dead child to her husband (who finds him delicious). But Marlinchen keeps her cool and gathers up the bones, listens to advice from the birds, and brings about her brother's full recovery.

Thumbling is so small that in one tale he is carried away on the steam from the cooking pot. But he faces a series of extreme dangers, both from the natural world and from 'bad' people. What is fascinating here, as he hides in mouse holes, wriggles into buildings, outwits robbers and cows and fish, makes a substantial fortune and returns home safely in the end, is that he does this precisely by exploiting his apparent disadvantage – all his triumphs occur because, with great ingenuity and cunning, he uses his tiny stature to his own profitable ends. He is resilient, and resilience leads not just to survival but to triumph.

At the moment, there is an odd sense culturally that we do not *want* children to feel competent and able in the world; we do not want them to roam freely and make swings for themselves – we prefer, rather, to keep them in the house, to choose and organise their activities for them (and to pay for this with our money and our time, which keeps them further under our control), never to let them be alone or 'mooching around' doing 'nothing'.

We do not just keep young people away from the woods – and, of course, from other wild places. We bowdlerise the fairy stories, saying – even believing – that they are 'too cruel'. It is interesting that most of the cruelty comes in the form of punishment of bad parents by their children – are we sub-consciously afraid of something? Nowadays, wicked stepmothers even in these non-realistic stories are never made to dance in red-hot iron shoes, shoved in spiked barrels to be drowned or burned at stakes. Children are allowed no comeback. But what is lost along with the savagery in this more self-regarding approach is the chance for children to learn that they can cope, they can survive, they can overcome fear and horror.

Interestingly, we have also abandoned another genre of literature, one which encouraged children to see themselves as capable on their own in the wild. There is a sort of novel for younger readers that was immensely popular up until the last quarter of the twentieth century and that has now well-nigh disappeared: stories of adventures in which children are on their own and deal with problems under a veneer of realism; novels like *Swallows and Amazons* or *The Famous Five* or, to take a forest example, *Brendon Chase* by BB (the naturalist and artist D. J. Watkins-Pitchford, who was also his own illustrator).[16] In *Brendan Chase* three children run away and live for a year in the wood, camping in the base of a hollow oak tree and 'living off the land'; they have to evade adults, but also find supportive friends. What is interesting is that they do this not to escape a terrible home life, nor from terror about their boarding schools, but more or less for the fun of it, acting with a healthy but callous indifference to their adults' anxiety.

Another change is that when they are finally caught, their perfectly loving parents respond with punitive sternness. No contemporary children's story would end 'I will not describe the just punishments and penances which they had to undergo before they had fully expiated their sins.' But nor would any modern story allow children the fun, freedom and self-sufficiency that the three boys have in the forest. Robin, John and Harold have little need for grown-ups, but an intimate knowledge of and joy in the woods and the seasons.

In his foreword to the Jane Nissen Books 2000 edition of *Brendon Chase*, Philip Pullman wrote:

> This is the sort of book that will never be written again … the slaughter is endless. Not only do they kill; they steal wild birds' eggs and catch butterflies. To a modern sensibility this is worse than advocating the compulsory use of hard drugs. Why should anyone want to read it? Firstly to learn some valuable lessons about nature … *Brendon Chase* shows how it's possible to take pleasure in shooting and killing and simultaneously to love natural things with a passion that approaches ecstasy. And out of that love comes knowledge.

We have kept the magical element of fairy stories in modern books for young people; fantasy worlds are now the location of adventures and moral combat. But we have abandoned the immensely reassuring realist element of these old tales: the forests are dangerous but you can survive; use your own intelligence and courage and you will come back safely.

We do not only keep children physically out of the forests – just as seriously, we are depriving them of the language of the woods. It is nearly impossible to understand, or even to see, things you do not have a name for. In 2008, a new edition of the *Oxford Junior Dictionary* – designed for children aged between 7 and 9 – decided that the modern English primary school child had no use for a remarkable range of fairly basic 'nature words', including:

- catkin;
- brook;
- acorn;
- buttercup;
- blackberry;
- conker;
- holly;
- ivy;
- mistletoe.

Conker! Blackberry! And where I live, the former now lie on the road until the cars squash them, and the latter rot in the hedges until the frost takes them; presumably even rural children do not know what either are, let alone what to do with them.

Of course, the words that have replaced them – like database, export, curriculum, vandalism, negotiate, committee, compulsory, bullet point, voicemail, citizenship, dyslexic and celebrity – are useful words to have, but I was walking in Epping Forest with Robert Macfarlane, a master of enchantment, who sums it up in his wonderful essay, 'A Counter-Desecration Phrasebook':

> A basic language-literacy of nature is falling from us. And what is being lost along with this literacy is something perhaps even more valuable: a kind of language magic, the power that certain words possess to enchant our imaginative relations with nature and landscape.[17]

The editors of the *Oxford Junior Dictionary* defend these omissions by arguing that their selection of words reflects the fact that Britain is now a multicultural modern country; but I cannot understand how it makes something more multicultural to eliminate a whole culture. The child of the *Oxford Junior Dictionary* is an urban, deracinated technocrat, not so much multicultural as de-cultured: a child deprived of magic.

It is obvious that playing in a forest for which you have no responsibility, in which you never have to labour, in which you have no investment, and to which you have been mechanically conveyed by an adult is not the same thing as playing in the forest which is both your home and your workplace and whose well-being is your well-being. Our robust and lovely fairy stories come out of that older forest, they reunite us with our cultural roots there, and children should have access to them particularly as it gets harder to access the real thing; these stories teach them both that the forest is magical and generous and also that it is dark and terrible. The stories could remind children about something they are being taught to forget: that intelligence and knowledge and love allow a person to overcome the worst disasters and be better off for it.

It seems sad that the paternalistic nineteenth-century Corporation of the City of London was prepared to make an investment for its subordinates more generous in spirit than we are willing to make for our children. They need the freedom of the forests and their stories.

Hansel and Gretel

Once upon a time there were two little children, gaunt with hunger, glazed with grief, lost in the forest. They walked hand in hand through tanglewood and terror until they came to a house made of gingerbread. A wicked witch lived there.

This was a long time ago. Now they are grown up; grounded and prosperous. They have never forgotten what they had learned in the woods. They used the witch's treasure trove wisely, investing first in healthy food and then in education. They continue to love and cherish each other. They always treat the world with respect and the world repays them with safety and joy.

Now Hansel is head forester to the King. He goes daily and with authority into the greenwood, walking under the trees and along small paths with knowledge and pleasure. He looks after the trees, coppice, pollard and maiden alike. He decides what can be cut and what should be cut. He interprets the Forest Laws as generously as possible, always seeking a balance between the needs of the villagers and the well-being of the trees. Some people think he lets the grazing swine back into the cut thickets a little too early, but others find his interpretation of dead wood somewhat too restrictive. He takes on young men and trains them carefully. He is well respected by his seniors and unusually popular within his community. He married a good-hearted woman, the daughter of a miller, and they have five children, and now, since this Lammastide, a first grandchild – a little girl whom they have called Gretel after his sister. He has built his house of stone, not sweet-meats; it has glass windows and stands solid again the wind and rain. It is a welcoming house of hospitality and laughter, although it is often rather untidy because he is an indulgent father. When people call him a 'warm man' it is sometimes unclear whether they mean 'rich' or 'kindly'. He is both.

With Gretel it is different. She lives alone in the forest. She is quiet, almost silent, solitary by choice. If you pass her way you will often find her in her garden. Plants – vegetables and herbs and flowers – grow well for her. Her garden is a place of colour and sweetness. She usually stands up, easing her back with her hands, and calls out a low but cheerful greeting. Once, when she was younger, she set off along the road through the forest to join the Holy Sisters in the convent at Waltham. But after a few years she came quietly home again. 'I couldn't live with enclosure,' she says calmly, if asked. Her house is built of wood with a thatched roof, but it too is sturdy and cosy. It looks rather more like a gingerbread house than Hansel's does, because it is painted in bright pale colours, and because under the eaves and around the windows are filigree strips of carved wood, which most people think are pretty but frivolous, and beside her little twisty iron gate at the bottom of her garden path there is always a bowl of sugar plums which local children know are put out for them.

The sturdy stone house and the pretty wooden house, which are neither of them like the other houses of the village, stand about two miles apart – an awkward distance: too long for a stroll, but not far enough for an expedition – so that Hansel and Gretel do not in fact meet very frequently. Sometimes if he is returning from work at Gretel's end of the forest Hansel will take a slightly longer path and pass along the hedge that runs across the bottom of her garden; and sometimes he will go in through the back gate and stand chatting while she weeds her flower beds, or go through her doorway and sit at her kitchen table and share a drink with her in the early evening. Or if there is a heavy fall of snow or a wild storm, Hansel will deliberately walk over to check that no harm has come to Gretel. Sometimes, though not often, some business of her own will bring Gretel to the village, and before going back under the trees she will stop by Hansel's house; he is usually out at work on these visits, but she passes neighbourly time with her sister-in-law and they like each other.

And just occasionally, for no reason that anyone can discern, often towards the end of a long summer Sunday afternoon, but sometimes at far odder hours, his wife can see that Hansel is restless. Eventually he will stand up and stretch hugely and say, as though completely by chance, 'I think I might wander over and see Gretel.' Or, 'Have you any messages for Gretel? I'm just going to pop across and see how she's doing.' And his wife will simulate a mild surprise because that is what he seems to expect and she is a good-hearted woman.

She accepts, although she does not understand, that it is like this for twins; they have a need and a sense of each other that is different from other people. She knows that his going off to visit his sister takes nothing from her and gives something to him. She knows too that, even more than other twins, Hansel and Gretel are bound together because of what happened to them when they were very young. Although she did not grow up in this village, she has heard the story. Their mother died in childbirth. Their father and his new wife tried to kill them. They ran away into ... they were abandoned in ... they disappeared into ... they were lost in the forest. For four months no one saw hair nor hide of them. The detail is uncertain, slippery with telling. But certainly, as suddenly as they had vanished, they came home – laden with treasure and brittle with fear.

So if, just occasionally, Hansel grows restless and slips off to see Gretel in her pretty little house in the forest, his wife has no problem with that. It is so much better than the equally occasional screaming, sweating nightmares. Sometimes she will invent a message, or give him some small object to take with him; always she will send her love, and always before leaving Hansel will kiss her affectionately.

And so it is today. His eldest daughter brings the baby round after Mass and they all eat together in merriment; but after the meal he feels that tug at his heart and he cannot settle. He dandles the baby, bouncing her on his knee, while she crows and grins widely. 'Gretel, Gretel,' he coos to her, hoping it will dull the tug and let him stay. But eventually he gets up, gives the baby back to his daughter, smiles at his family, says that he thinks he will go over to Gretel's. He does not notice his wife shake her head minutely at his daughter, who is about to suggest coming with him. He kisses both women and goes out.

In recent years he has marked the path to Gretel's house with white stones. It is a little joke, and he does not know if she has noticed. He watches for them one by one, and at the same time he looks at the trees which are just reaching the fullness of leaf canopy, darkening from early bright gold green to full rich green, so that less sun is finding its way through to the ground litter. Where the wood opens out into pasture ground there are wild roses, and somewhere deep in the hidden places he can hear a nuthatch chattering – zit, zit, zit – surprisingly loud for such a small bird.

Even as he walks his tension eases and he feels calmer. He suspects that Gretel no longer has this nagging need of him that he has of her – that she has somehow found her whole self inside herself and does not need him to show her who she is again. But he does not feel that this matters. He is happy as he walks through the forest in the afternoon sunshine.

The path curls round just before it breaks out of the trees and into her clearing, and for a moment he sees her – she is surrounded, covered in a cloud of white butterflies that are dancing around her face, over her shoulders and above her head. She is standing quite still, basking in their attention. He finds her briefly perfectly beautiful, and then he makes some accidental-sounding noise so that when he comes out into the clearing she has dismissed the fluttering flock and is standing there smiling at him. The chooks in their pen set up a cackle of pleasure and she calls, once, not very loudly, 'Hansel,' and he knows she is glad he has come.

He stands by her gate for a moment, and almost without thought reaches out for a sugar plum and pushes it into his mouth with an oddly greedy gesture for a grown man. She laughs and says:

Nibble Mouse, nibble mouse,
Who is nibbling at my little house?

It was what the witch had said the very first time, but now he laughs, the last of his restless tension draining away in the complete ease of her presence. He is fifty years old and munching sugar plums like a child again.

'Me,' he says, and they hug warmly.

In the kitchen she makes him drop scones, the batter waiting in a bowl beside the stove as though she had known he was coming. They eat them with the honey her bees have made. He notices she is putting on weight a little now, at last; it does not dim her loveliness for him. He watches her with pleasure as she moves graceful about her little house. They talk about little Gretel, about the hornbeam pollarding at the west end of the wood and about her strawberries and the white currants that are setting their translucent moon fruit along her wall.

Later they go for a walk. She puts her arm round his waist and her head leans lightly on his shoulder. There is a little party of long-tailed tits, ridiculous and agitated, bustling along ahead of them; tiny pinkish balls of feathers with absurdly long tails. They do not talk much now. It is all hushed green gold and the wind has dropped away.

There is a tiny rustle, almost too small to hear, and across the path there is a ripple, a wave, a rope shaken by invisible children. It is a weasel and her two kits, in a line, crossing the path ahead of them; elegant, wicked killers with big dark eyes. The mother weasel pauses, stares at them, her white underbelly vivid on the forest floor; and then they are gone.

When Hansel looks at Gretel he sees that she is crying; silent tears run down her cheeks and she does not move to wipe them away.

'Gretel,' he says very quietly so as not to break her stillness.

'I killed her,' she says, in the same whispered tone. 'I killed our witch. I pushed her into the oven and I killed her dead. She was like a weasel, wild and fierce and free, and I killed her.'

'You had to,' he says, 'you had to. She would have killed and eaten me.'

'Would she, Hansel? Would she? I try to remember and it is all like a story. Are they true, the stories? Are they ever true?'

'Sometimes they are true,' he says with great gentleness. She turns and lays her head against his chest; they stand in the sunlit wood and he holds her. 'Here is a true story. Once upon a time there was a brave little girl; she had a foolish brother, a weak and pathetic father, and an evil, cruel stepmother who certainly wanted to kill her. But in terrible fear, in the raging of danger and sadness and terror, she kept her head. She rescued them both. That is a true story.'

'And the gingerbread house? Really? And a forest that big? We know it is not that big.'

'I don't know,' he says, 'I've never known. But we were away for months and we survived. Perhaps we dreamed the witch, I don't know; perhaps we made her up so that we had some sort of story to tell. It was a dark place, a dark time and we were somewhere so bad we had to tell a story to make it bearable, to allow us to come back into the sunshine. That is what the stories are for.'

'Oh,' she says, 'thank you.' She pulls away and walks on a little and he follows her, watching her spine move as the weasels' had, flexible, graceful, lovely.

When she turns back to him she has stopped weeping, but she still looks sombre.

'You see, sometimes now I think I may be turning into our witch. I live in my little house and put out sweeties for the children. I hope they will come along the path, but when they do I sometimes feel cross or ragged with the disturbance. I wouldn't like it if they killed me and then went home and boasted about it.'

'Don't worry,' he says. 'I will not let them kill you. It is my turn to protect you now. I have grown less foolish.'

She puts her arm back round his waist and they follow the little path round towards her house.

He is shaken, because he has told the story and believed the story for years. He is shaken by her pure honesty and by her quiet, lovely life. He tries to sound adult and thoughtful,

'Anyway, whatever really happened, we did learn a lot, didn't we?'

Suddenly she laughs and says, 'Well, we learned never to use breadcrumbs to make way markers with, because the birds will eat them.'

'Gretel,' he remonstrates. And then, 'OK. That was not my best moment.'

She looks slyly at him, her shadowed moment melting away now, just as his do when they are together. 'I've noticed your white stones,' she says. 'I like that.'

When they reach the gate he leaves her. He can feel that she needs to be alone now, to be silent and settled. She goes through the gate and then turns and watches as he walks across the clearing. Just when he reaches the edge of the trees she calls, 'Hansel!'

He turns and looks back at her.

'Come again soon.' She has to raise her voice so he can hear her.

'Yes,' he says, 'of course.' Then he waves and sets out for home.

5

July

Great North Wood

One hot July morning I set out to find a hidden forest. It was perhaps the oddest of my woodland walks, and, strangely, seemed to bring me closest to at least one aspect of what I was searching for – the roots of the fairy stories. I went with Will Anderson, the ecologist, to see what we could find of the Great North Wood.

Once upon a time the whole country may not have been all forest, but there was certainly forest where now there is not. This is most noticeable around big cities which expanded fast in the eighteenth and nineteenth centuries, moving out beyond their traditional walled boundaries and spreading into areas which had been wooded or farmland, and which had, historically, supplied food and fuel to the cities before there was easy transport, by canal, rail and then road, and eventually by ship and aeroplane, which could bring these necessities quickly and more cheaply from further away. There is a complex relationship here between the rising population of a city, the comparative values of land for production and land for housing, and the development of transport infrastructures, but wherever you choose to begin the circular calculation, you end up with less forest and less productive agriculture and more roads, railways and domestic housing surrounding the historic urban core.

During the Industrial Revolution, London grew faster than any-where else in Europe. In 1674 it had a population of half a million, which doubled over the following century and a quarter. All major cities in Europe expanded in the nineteenth century, but in London the growth rate exploded: in 1801, when the first national census was taken, it was just over 1 million; but by 1900 it had risen to 6.7 million. It is difficult to realise just how rural many areas, which are now densely populated, were until comparatively recently. East of the City, where London now extends for miles into Essex, there was until well into the nineteenth century little more than a few villages and a great swathe of market gardens, small dairy farms and coun-try lanes. One way of measuring this change is to see how many new parish churches were built in any given area during a specific period – the old churches, more than adequate to serve their local populations, had to be supplemented in a massive church-building boom to accommodate (and control) rapidly expanding popula-tions. In 1851 Henry Mayhew, a writer and journalist, published his carefully researched *London Labour and the London Poor*, a very moving description of the plight this vast new population. The response to his book makes it clear that the educated and literary classes, living just a few miles away in the City and West London, had simply not realised how fast the East End of their own city was growing and under what pressures of poverty its population was living. The pressure was cultural as well as economic: these new residents were first- and second-generation immigrants, not only from overseas, but from rural communities all over southern England and beyond. Victoria Park in Hackney, like other similar green spaces, was an early response to what was seen as deprivation, and the establish-ment of the green belt (still under pressure today) was a later attempt to address the same problem.

The cumulative effects of the Agricultural Revolution of the eighteenth century and the Industrial Revolution of the nineteenth led to a massive shift from rural to urban life, and with it, to an extensive loss of countryside around towns and cities. One large and conspicuous loss of ancient woodland in southern Britain in the modern period has been the disappearance of the Great North Wood.

Once upon a time there was a swathe of ancient oak forest on the raised ground south of the Thames, about four miles south of the city of London, covering the area which is now Dulwich, Sydenham, Penge, Norwood and parts of Croydon, and running as far north as Camberwell. The Anglo-Saxons seem to have named it 'the North Wood' to distinguish it from the even larger woods to the south across the Weald. During the reign of Henry VIII there were dense woods either side of the main road from Brixton to Streatham, and therefore also the usual steady stream of complaints that felons and other miscreants escaped from London and hid out in the forest, preying on travellers and endangering law and order. This forest was similar to forests all over the country: a mixture of thick wood, heath and farm land, with stock, especially pigs, grazing within the woods. Being so near to the large and growing capital, the forest was always going to be vulnerable to pressures for building materials, fuel and land itself, and in addition, the Crown extracted a great deal of timber for use in the royal dockyards at Deptford, nearby on the Thames. When Oliver Cromwell seized the forest from the Archbishop of Canterbury – its hereditary owner since the Conquest, when William I gave it to Lanfranc, his first Archbishop – there was still 830 acres of forest, but fewer than 10,000 oak pollards. Inevitably, by the mid-seventeenth century, it was a forest in decline. Nonetheless, the absence of any old churches or other medieval or Tudor structures within the area strongly indicates that it stayed wild and under-inhabited until surprisingly late.

In *The Journal of the Plague Year* (published in 1772, but carefully researched), Daniel Defoe, who lived not far away in Tooting, commented:

> And as I have been told that several that wandred into the
> country on Surry side were found starv'd to death in the woods,
> that country being more open [unpopulated] and more woody

than any other part so near London, especially about Norwood
and the parishes of Camberwell, Dullege and Lusume
[Lewisham].[1]

One notable feature of the North Wood was its long association
with gypsies – who had a regular summer encampment there, on
Gypsy Hill, no less. It is not clear when they started this regular
annual settlement, but in August 1668 Pepys' diary records:

> This afternoon my wife and Mercer and Deb went with Pelting
> to see the Gypsies at Lambeth, and have their fortunes told; but
> what they did, I did not enquire.

And thereafter their presence was recorded regularly; for example,
Byron, as a schoolboy nearby, often visited the gypsies in Dulwich
Wood, until they were driven off by police during the enclosures of
the early nineteenth century.

The gypsies intrigue me. We know there were gypsies in Epping
Forest too in the nineteenth century, because the poet John Clare
slipped out of his lunatic asylum to associate with them; they were
prevalent across the whole country, and, indeed, all of Europe. They
were clearly distinguished from vagrants, tramps and 'felons', and
never seem to be associated in the public's mind with the robbers
and other dangers and of the woods and highways (although in Jane
Austen's *Emma* (1816), some gypsies do scare Harriet). They tell fortunes, have a strange, almost fairy-like identity, and are recognised
frequently as being 'different', exotic, and at home in the forests and
other wild places – but they never appear in the fairy stories. Not in
Grimm, not in Perrault: they steal no children, scare no travellers,
make no prophecies, spin no spells and sell no fairings,[2] although
other characters do all these things. In the Mediterranean and
Eastern Europe, Roma are much more visible within fairytales and
legends. But the Roma did not arrive in northern Europe until the
sixteenth century, which suggests that the basic corpus of fairy stories is genuinely medieval. Contemporary books that use fairy story

devices and themes, like Kenneth Grahame's *The Wind in the Willows*, do have gypsies, but Tolkein's Middle Earth does not. However, there were definitely real gypsies in the real Great North Wood by the seventeenth century, and there is still an oak tree growing in the middle of a housing estate to mark the spot where Margaret Finch, 'the Gypsy Queen', once had her house.

Up until the middle of the eighteenth century, the Great North Wood still covered a good deal of ground – it is over three miles long on a map of 1745, with an additional mile or so tacked on to the north-east boundary and named 'Oak of Arnon' (now called Honor Oak) – but its decline was fast thereafter. As late as 1802, 'Matthews the hairyman', a hermit, lived in the wood in a cave, or 'excavated residence', but the long string of enclosure acts led to massive deforestation throughout the country, and the Great North Wood was no exception. The countrywide increase in the value of agricultural land was underscored here by the expanding population north of the Thames and the consequent need for more productive land to feed them as well as more residential land to house them. Thus, gradually, in a series of individual acts from 1797, the whole area of the Old North Wood was enclosed and much of the remaining forest cleared.

Then, in 1806, the heirs of Lord Thurlow, a major local landowner, broke up his estate and sold it piecemeal in quite small lots to prosperous Londoners for domestic housing. This was a very early example of profit for 'developers' and caused considerable concern and outrage. Nonetheless, the sale was successful and a whole new class of people became landowners, albeit on a small scale. To build themselves appropriate homes, these new suburbanites grubbed out yet more forest to replace it with gardens – even, curiously, with 'wild gardens' designed to look like superior forest.

In 1886 Thomas Frost recalled that, in his childhood in Norwood,

> the hamlet had consisted of about a score of farm-houses and cottages scattered at considerable intervals along the lanes that intersected the woods ... the greater part of the ridge was

covered with thick woods of oaks and hazel ... the lower
northern portion, sloping towards the valley of the Thames,
was a rushy waste, upon which two or three small farmers
grazed their cows and their geese.[3]

But only a decade later, John Corbett Anderson, in his history of the
area, summed up the situation bluntly:

It must have been a fine sight to have witnessed the great forest
of Norwood as in wild grandeur it appeared in days of yore ...
The district once covered by the Great North Wood, and
which, within the memory of living men, consisted only here
and there a dwelling, embosomed amid oaks or scattered
around open commons, has now become an extensively
inhabited region, locally divided into Upper, West or Lower,
and South Norwood.[4]

Now virtually nothing of that original wood remains – although
there are fragments within the nature reserves of Dulwich Wood
and Sydenham Hill Wood. The Great North Wood has vanished
like a dream or fairy story.

Except that Will Anderson does not think it has vanished – rather,
it has become hidden and secret. And so, one summer morning, we
went to look for it, taking an irregular looping walk through the
backwaters of Dulwich, Sydenham and Norwood.

For me, though, in a very real way, this expedition began before
that. It began with spending a night at the home of Will and his
partner, Ford Hickson, a house that, despite being in central south
London, is like something from a fairy story. The Tree House, an
ecologically state-of-the-art house which they built in 2004, is
designed to honour the ancient forests and woodland. The very
small plot they have constructed it on it stands within the shadows
of a great plane tree, and the house itself mirrors a tree, with a wonderful single tree trunk supporting the spiral staircase up the centre,
a ground-floor kitchen as the roots nourishing and feeding the life

within the house and an airy wood-beamed room at the top, whose balcony opens almost within the canopy of the real sycamore tree and whose ceiling trusses mirror the high branches and spaces of timber trees in a forest. Given how many fairy stories begin with the protagonists spending a night up a tree in a forest and seeing from that height a 'small light' far off through the woods which they then follow to find their adventure and destiny, it seemed utterly pleasing to sleep in that nest and wake to the green light of the leaves.

We set out for the forest on a red London bus down Lordship Lane to Dulwich Common. The first clues to the lost wood became evident almost immediately. They are there on the map in the place names: Norwood itself is simply a contraction of North Wood and thus still bears verbal witness to its roots. Over and over again the pleasant suburban place names are clear giveaways: Woodside, Honor Oak, Herne Hill (the herons' hill), Gypsy Hill, Selhurst ('the homestead in the wood'), Forest Hill. At Thornton Heath there is a place called Colliers Water – this is not derived from an unexpected coal mine, but was where the charcoal burners once drew water to damp their kilns.[5] And street by street, estate by estate, the forest is preserved in the names.

But Will said we could find more solid evidence than that. We began walking down Cox's Walk (I would like to persuade myself that this too is named after an apple orchard, but I have no evidence at all for that) along an avenue of big oak trees, like a country house drive, and before long we discovered an abandoned railway cutting. Here there were signs that the forest was regenerating – the cutting was overgrown with straggling young trees, as well as weeds, brambles and all the charred evidence of children and vagrants camping out. It was strangely encouraging to see how quickly the wood was reasserting itself. We crossed a bridge over the railway from where Pisarro, the impressionist artist, had painted his picture of Lordship Lane Station in the 1870s. It is a charming picture and not devoid of trees, but in it you can see clearly up the line to the station. Now that has changed – the wood is too thick to get even a glimpse of the station, though perhaps at night there would be a twinkle, as in the fairy stories. Like the characters in the stories, we would have been hard put to force our way through the undergrowth to reach the source of the light.

Shortly after 1900 there was a sinister shift in woodland ecology in Britain. It is called 'oak change': before the twentieth century, oak trees regenerated from acorns inside woods – under maiden, pollarded or coppiced oak, there was a constant supply of oaklings coming on. They were cut in large quantities for house building, and there never seems to have been a shortage. Now we cannot even reconstruct Tudor dwellings properly because they require quantities of young oaks that are simply not available. Acorns still germinate and grow well on the edges of woods and free-standing on open ground, but they no longer spring up and flourish among the older trees. No one seems quite sure why this happened, although Rackham believes it was caused by a new-to-Europe mildew, *Microspherra alphitoides*, which arrived from America in 1908 and is now more common in Britain than in the United States. This is the cause of the white silvery bloom one sees commonly on oak throughout the country. Now oak often invades disused railway tracks on the edges of woods, as free space in which to flourish, but I saw no young oak here among the ash, holly, birch, rowan and willow, despite the dignified line of oak trees above the cutting. Perhaps it is too dark and shadowy, for oak is essentially sun loving. Indeed, some people think that it was the decline of coppicing and the consequent thickening of the canopy, cutting out so much light to the forest floor, that caused oak change in the first place, although the experimental reintroduction of this more traditional form of forest management does not seem to have reversed the change.

We came up from the cutting and into an area which offered us an even more pleasing image of the wood's determined survival and return. Here we were walking along a slope, below what, not much over a hundred years ago, had been a row of smart villas. They had been built originally with large gardens running down the hill but, too big to maintain, the gardens have been slowly abandoned, and the wilder wood has taken advantage, sneaking back into places from which it had been exiled. Just as previously forests have crept over Bronze Age field systems, Roman buildings and medieval farms, here they are doing the same again. Throughout the rough woodland there were traces of brick garden walls, terracing, buildings, even what was obviously once a folly, a fake medieval summer house, now decayed and breaking up, ivy clad – and probably looking far more like the romantic Gothic ruin it was meant to represent than it ever did under the care and attention of owners and gardeners in its heyday.

Of course, even in the highly unlikely event that this whole area were to be left entirely alone for the next two hundred years it would not turn back into recognisable ancient woodland: everything has changed too much. Not just oak change, but the whole infrastructure: the water table in the South-East has fallen; pollution and acid rain have changed the atmosphere; there is no longer the simple extent of woodland (the larger a piece of woodland is, the more diversity can develop, and this affects both flora and fauna; conservationists have increasingly recognised the need to create corridors linking one species-rich site to another so that there can be at least some movement between them to the benefit of each). The fauna has changed radically; originally there were wild boar in the Great North Wood, and beavers and wolves. There were also domesticated animals – a great many pigs, for example, foraged freely in the woods. In the Domesday Book woodland was sometimes measured by the number of pigs it was sustaining (rather than by acreage or number of trees). In Chapter 11, I will come back to some questions about conservation, re-establishment and the dreams of wildwood. What Will and I were looking at and for was not original wildwood, or even revivified ancient woodland; it was something new, and we do not really know what will become of it. But just as the stories change and grow and draw strength both from their ancient roots and from new influences and aspirations, so there is a deep energy in woods (and in all plant growth everywhere probably), corroded and corrupted if you like, but biding its time, lying in wait, sneaking back whenever it gets the chance. What we do know from many sites throughout the country, though few are as complex as this, is that fresh woods growing on ancient woodland sites are different from those planted on brand-new sites. At the very least, these sites are places where trees like to be.[6]

Perhaps this mysterious, changing, responsive, but always vital pattern of forest re-growth and emergence offers a good image for the way fairy stories change too. They change across cultures – the 'Cinderella-type' story is the same in African cultures (including the deep malice of stepmothers – although in central southern Africa the stepmother is usually a polygamous second wife) as in European ones, but the specific details are very different. They change through time as well – the Grimm brothers wanted their stories more 'innocent' and more Christian; recently, Disney has given us a 'post-feminist' Beauty who loves her Beast initially for his library as much as for his luxurious house and lavish meals; pantomime needs ugly stepsisters for its own farcical cross-dressing ends. The stories, like the forest, change but continue.

Before long, Will and I emerged from the trees and arrived in Peckarman's Wood. Peckarman's Wood, as is not difficult to guess, was once a real wood – it was a managed coppice for centuries, but like so much else around the area, it became redundant and was finally grubbed out, not for agricultural land, but for housing. Now it is a charming 1960s enclave of delightful arty little houses, each almost, if the imagination is given a loose rein, a potential gingerbread house, except instead of being isolated deep in the forest, they are huddled together intimately, each with its little garden. Since it was probably designed for much the same sort of people as the older villas were – prosperous spill-over from the 'Great Wen' to the north seeking something more romantic and 'natural' than overcrowded noisy streets and dense urban housing – it is fascinating to see how much smaller gardens are now that their owners expect to have to maintain them themselves without gardeners, and how much closer to each other the middle classes expect to live than our similarly prosperous great-grandparents did.

At the bottom of Peckarman's Wood there is a high hedge and a secret little gateway. We went through it and into the heart of Dulwich Wood. Here, judging from the old map, we were probably walking through a patch of the original Great North Wood. Certainly the experts tell us that some of Dulwich Wood (and a few other small outcrops elsewhere in the area) were never grubbed up or destroyed, but remain in tiny patches, and as new visitors, we found it impossible to tell. You have to have time to study woodland carefully and through the seasons to know square metre by square metre how close it might be to semi-natural forest. Obviously this does not apply to a neatly fenced couple of acres on top of a moor in Scotland – but here, we know there was wood before 1600 (ancient woodland); we know that much of it was grubbed out; we know that, with the gardens and the building work and all the other changes to the area, some of the trees here are certainly not original but we also know that woods keep their secrets well. Later in the day, after lunch in a pub garden surrounded by tall trees, we walked alongside Farquar Road, where a community group are re-establishing the 'old woods', and it was rather lovely – wild and convincing looking, with little secret twisting paths. But neatly along the wood were the ruins of old basements – lines of brick up to half a dozen courses, with gaps marking out rooms and once-domesticated spaces. Between the old original wood and the new re-established 'old wood' there had been a street of Victorian homes, presumably with tidy gardens and neat gateways. The steep slope up from the present road had been cut back in places to accommodate the houses. Now grass and wild flowers and even trees were pushing through and breaking up old floors; there were white butterflies busy in the flourishing undergrowth barely ten metres from the modern street. When I was a child we played a game in the woods in which we marked the floor plan of a house in stones and sticks, leaving blanks for doorways and windows. Above the outline the details were filled in by the imagination, but sometimes even the fireplaces were carefully delineated. What we saw here were house plans like those, but they were solid and sturdy, though, helped by local humans, the woods were winning.

Will had been right – the wood was still here, but secret and baffling, hiding and disguising itself like the protagonists of the fairy stories.

One of the things that has always drawn me to fairy stories is their sense of secrecy. Many of the most resonant tales for me are about secrets and silences and hidden truths. It was this that first alerted me to the deep connection between the forests and the stories. Like the stories, the forests guard their secrets and hide their treasures; I believe the stories took the particular themes they did because their original tellers were living in the forests. In any thick wood you will be surprised; there is a sense of the hidden and the surprising because you cannot see what is coming. You cannot see the sky, or at least not the whole of it, which, I think, is why people are so frightened of getting lost in the woods; even if one does not consciously steer oneself by the sun and the horizon, the impossibility of holding them in one's line of sight is disorientating. Under the canopy, even in a reasonably clear forest, one rather literally cannot see the wood for the trees: the solid vertical rise of tree trunks cut across any long view, 'the view is truncated'. The tangled web of lower scrubby branches and undergrowth, especially in high summer, makes paths crooked and hides what is ahead. Fallen trees and sudden sodden patches force diversions, pushing you like Little Red Riding Hood off the proper path. You come across unexpected things – the lovely clearing, the little waterfall, the ruined wall, the magnificent ancient tree, the pied flycatcher skipping black and white on an oak branch, a cloud of butterflies feeding – and once, for me, the real treasure of globe flowers, the huge bright *troillius europeaeus*, seen as a brief flash of gold ahead of me and then, after a few moments' pursuit of the invisible, there they were, huge, shining, vivid yellow, right at my feet. Or equally, of course, you stumble on the dead fox,[7] the rubbish dump, the ancient wrecked car or the wicked grinning fungus – suddenly, at close quarters and as a surprise. Often when I am walking in the woods my dog will suddenly stop, sharply alert, head up, paw raised and staring fixedly into a dense thicket or patch of bracken – she knows there is something lurking, but I cannot see it. The sense of secrets, silences, surprises, good and bad, is fundamental to forests and informs their literature. In fairy stories this is sometimes quite simple and direct: Hansel and Gretel get lost in the woods, and then suddenly they come upon the gingerbread house. Snow White runs in terror through the forest and suddenly stumbles upon the dwarves' cottage; characters spending scary nights in or under trees suddenly see a twinkling light – and they make their laborious way towards it without having any idea of what they will find when they arrive.

And very often this sense of the unexpected, this 'suddenly', is transferred to the narrative itself. The classic fairy-story plots frequently depend on secrets, on things being hidden and needing to be found. One of the things that is most regularly disguised is the true identity of a character; in this sense (though not in others), fairy stories have a very modern understanding of personality, of individual identity: inside each of us is a core 'real' self. Your social role, public appearance, background, how people regard you, even your class do not affect this – they are just 'false conditioning', and in the end the truth will out, the secrets of the heart will come to light. Many of the stories are about this untangling of the inner self from the webs and weavings of secrets and deceit. The protagonists themselves may not know the truth, or they do know it but cannot reveal what they know, often because they are bound into preposterous promises which they dare not break.

At one level these secrets are simply a plot device to spin out the tale. During a journey through a forest, the heroine of 'The Little Goosegirl'[8] has her identity stolen from her by her evil maid, who takes away all her possessions, including the prince she was en route to marry, and then binds the real princess to a promise not to tell anyone. Obviously, if the princess had arrived at the prince's palace and simply announced the truth – 'I am really the princess, and this wicked maid frightened me into pretending I wasn't. You can send messengers to my mother to check this out' – there would have been no story. As it is, the teller is able to spin a long and rich tale of virtue oppressed involving a complex plot which enables the truth to emerge without the princess having to break her oath. This serves the double end of making a good story and proving the honour and merits of the princess. (She is lucky, of course, in having the unusual assistance of not simply a talking horse, but one that can go on talking even after it has been beheaded.)

Similarly, the sister in 'The Seven Swans'[9] is bound to silence for seven years in order to save her brothers from enchantment. Without this condition there would be no second half to the story – she would get on with her complicated sewing task (she has to make each of them a shirt out of starwort – a forest flower interestingly also known as stitchwort), liberate her brothers, and nothing much else would have happened. Unable to speak, however, she becomes involved in a long and rather horrible 'adventure' in which she sacrifices her own children for her brothers' redemption and which ends with her on the witch's pyre. Her brothers rescue her at the last moment – the silence and secrecy has allowed seven years to pass, her sewing is finished (almost: one of the most touching things about this story, perhaps my very favourite of the Grimms' tales, is that she does not quite complete one sleeve of one shirt, so her youngest brother has to go through life with a trailing swan's wing instead of an arm), and everyone can live happily ever after – even her children are restored to her.

These stories run alarmingly parallel to the more modern narrative of childhood sexual abuse – especially in the tragic mixture of fear and guilt which is used to keep the victim silenced. The maid in 'The Goosegirl' is obviously female, but otherwise fits sinisterly into the role of abuser – a trusted person (the princess's mother is not negligent) known to the princess changes abruptly when the child is in her care alone; she bullies the girl into a promise of silence. Moreover, in the original version of the story the 'good' mother gives her daughter a strange parting gift – a white cloth with three drops of her own blood on it. This protects the true princess until she accidentally loses it. There is no explanation of this gift in the tale, and it is never restored or found – it is a secret within the secrecy of the story, but it is very hard not to read some symbol of virginity or menstruation into it; later on in this story, there is a peculiar, superficially pointless passage about the girl's terror over the sexual advances of a perfectly innocent young man.

The brothers in 'The Seven Swans' are banished and turned into swans explicitly because their father wants the daughter for himself. Is he banishing witnesses, natural protectors or potential competition? We do not know, but later the girl withdraws into the forest herself and will not speak. There is one story – 'All Fur' (or, in older translations, *Allerleirauh*) – that is explicitly about father-daughter sexual abuse; here the daughter is so horrified at her father's proposal that she runs away and hides in the forest wearing a cloak made from the fur of every kind of wild animal. She is found there, asleep in a hollow tree, by a king out hunting, and carried back to the castle – where she is put to work in the kitchens. Of course she is eventually revealed as a princess and marries the king, but her evasions and determination to keep her true identity hidden are extreme. She seems to be experiencing a powerful conflict between shame and her desire for restoration. Stories like 'All Fur' and other more oblique secrecy tales raise dark questions about all this silencing of young women that is treated as an oddly normal plot device.

Several years ago I led a creative writing residential weekend exploring modern approaches to fairy stories. One of the women on the course wrote a version of 'Snow White'. In her darkly resonant tale, the 'magic mirror' that truthfully revealed which woman was 'the fairest of all' was the King's eyes: looking into them, the 'wicked' Queen could always tell whether the King desired her or his own daughter. The stepmother's complex responses of jealousy and protectiveness become the motivation that drives the story.[10]

In many of the tales, however, the secrets are lighter hearted. In 'Rumplestiltskin' it is the heroine who has to find out the secret name of the 'ridiculous little man' (he is only that in the original – neither a gnome nor a devil) in order to keep her child safe. The morality of this particular story is extremely odd: the young woman is in a tricky situation because her father 'in order to make himself seem important' has told the King his daughter can spin straw into gold. The King only marries her because he is greedy:

> 'You must spin all this straw into gold tonight. If you succeed you shall become my wife.' To himself he thought, 'Even though she's just a miller's daughter I'll never find a richer woman anywhere in the world.'

And, uniquely, the woman is let off a vow she took freely and does in fact get her child back, and the little man is punished – one might think rather unfairly. But at the heart of the story is the secret identity of the little man, which has to be uncovered.

Or, in 'The Twelve Huntsmen', a dozen young women disguise themselves as men in order to win back the love of a prince, who has forgotten his promises to one of them. He is warned that they are female, but they outwit the traps he lays for them (stamping firmly on some dried peas so they are crushed instead of rolling about, and remembering not even to glance at some unusually attractive spinning wheels he lays out for them). Nonetheless, he finds himself more and more attracted to the chief huntsman – until one day, while he is out hunting in the forest, a messenger announces that the 'false bride' is approaching. The girl lover faints, and attempting to revive her, the prince pulls off her glove and sees his own ring on her finger. He immediately falls back in love with her and all ends happily. But although there is nothing at all sinister in this story, the disguise that seems so central is in fact rather pointless – she could just have arrived in her real persona and, if necessary, shown him the ring. The unwinding of the secret is the real purpose of the story.

So profound a narrative device does this secrecy become that in some of the stories there is absolutely no logical reason whatsoever for it, but it is there simply to hold the plot together. 'Cinderella' is a fascinating case in point. It is one of the stories that has become most distorted in its popular development, while at the same time it is probably the most successful and widely known of all the tales. But the version we know has surprisingly little in common even with the last Grimms' redacted tale, and the changes are instructive. In the first place, the 'ugly' stepsisters are not ugly, as I explained earlier – they are 'beautiful and fair of face, but vile and black of heart'; their true natures are hidden by their pretty faces. More importantly, there is no Fairy Godmother. Instead, the plot develops somewhat differently: one day, the father is going to the fair and asks his daughters what they would like him to bring them back. 'Beautiful dresses, pearls and jewels,' say the stepsisters. 'The first branch which knocks against your hat on your way home,' says Cinderella – a passing reference to the fact that he will travel through a wood on his journey. Unusually for a father in a fairy story, he does not forget or blunder and comes home with the promised goods. Cinderella takes the hazel branch and plants it on her birth mother's grave. It grows into a 'handsome tree' and Cinderella visits it three times a day. A little white bird lives in the tree and 'if Cinderella expressed a wish, the bird threw down to her what she had wished for'. When the Prince's ball is announced, Cinderella wants to go and her stepmother sets her the impossible challenge of sorting lentils from ashes to see if she is worthy. Cinderella calls on some birds, though not apparently the bird of her tree, to help her and is thus successful. However, her stepmother reneges on her promise and she and the stepsisters go off the ball. Cinderella's response is prompt – no sitting by the fire and weeping in this earlier version. She goes 'at once' to the tree and gets a pretty frock which she puts on 'with all speed' and hastens to the party. Now everything proceeds as in the version we know, except, of course, that it is Cinderella's free choice – rather than a restriction imposed upon her by the Fairy Godmother – to leave the ball and keep her identity secret. She repeats this sequence for the traditional three evenings, but far from being so stupid as to drop her slipper, it transpires that the Prince has cunningly covered the staircase with pitch so that the slipper sticks to it; she cannot stop to pick it up because he is pursuing her – and she has to hide in the dovecot.

In the original tale the slipper is not glass but simply 'small and dainty and all golden'. The slipper became glass at a double remove: Perrault, in his version, made it a 'fur slipper'; the French words for 'fur' is 'ver', and the French word for 'glass' is 'verre'. In a moment of erroneous inspiration, the English translator got it wrong – or rather, deeply, though accidentally, right.

Interestingly, the original involves a much less passive and more energetic Cinderella forging her own destiny, but it also does not make much sense. Since the tree will give her what she wants just for the asking, why is she still slaving for her stepmother? More crucially though, why does she choose to leave the ball repeatedly, run away and hide, and above all conceal her identity – right up to the very end? The assumption that a story needs a secret has, in this instance, overwhelmed the requirements of plot, motivation and character. So, although we lose an unusually active heroine, the present popular version makes a much better story. (We also lose the hideous but clever symmetrical choreography of the wedding, where Cinderella goes into the church accompanied by her step-sisters and two birds fly down and sit on the outside shoulder of each stepsister to peck one of their eyes out each; when the three come out of the church, the birds repeat this procedure, but since they are now walking the other way, the stepsisters both lose both eyes, right and left.).

There is an argument that there is good psychological sense in the Grimms' version of this story: Cinderella needs to test not herself but the Prince. She does not, following the betrayal of her father, who behaves rather worse in the original, dare to risk a 'one-night stand'. It is the Prince who has to prove his worthiness by searching for and finding the 'true bride'. But if that was the underlying message of the story, it is much obscured – partly by the Prince being bizarrely easy to deceive. He carries off each of the stepsisters in turn, and Cinderella's birds have to point out to him that their feet are bleeding where they sliced off pieces of toe or heel to make the slipper fit. In any event, no comment is passed on Cinderella's motives or intentions – this is a fairy story, a narrative form where things are surprising and secret but need no explanation of the modern causal kind.

Perhaps the new woods pushing their way onto land in South London that was claimed from them and then abandoned will similarly make 'much better woods' one day. We do not know. The point is that the woods are still trying, in little secret ways.

In these stories the women know their true identity and keep it secret – just as the dancing princesses conceal the secret palace where they go to dance their slippers into shreds. The forest is about concealment and appearances are not to be trusted. Things are not necessarily what they seem and can be dangerously deceptive. Snow White's murderous stepmother is truly 'the fairest of all'. The wolf can disguise himself as a sweet old granny. The forest hides things; it does not open them out but closes them off. Trees hide the sunshine; and life goes on under the trees, in the thickets and tanglewood. Forests are full of secrets and silences. It is not strange that the fairy stories that come out of the forest are stories about hidden identities, both good and bad.

And in many of the tales, someone's true identity is not known to anyone, even the protagonist – it is eventually revealed by events. There is no way the proud little princess could have guessed that her frog was a prince – it is hard to blame her for not wanting to take it to bed or kiss it; her father makes her do so because she has promised to and must keep her word.[11] There are a great number of stories in this vein. Inside each person, regardless of beauty or situation, there is a true self – someone is a 'natural' princess or prince or king. Their conduct in the forest, in the dangerous secret places, will test their integrity and reveal that self. Proud princesses will be taught that the despised suitor is the real prince, the proper bridegroom, the future king. Fathers and kings must be taught that the third son, the stupid one, or the beggar at the gate whom they have scorned and mocked, is really the hero of this story. Mothers need to learn that their favourite child is not necessarily the most deserving one. The neglected child will go out into the forest and come home with treasure, while the favoured child, spoiled and selfish, will be revealed as mean and ugly-spirited. Everyone should be cautious about the people they meet – they should be careful about trusting them, and careful about revealing too much of themselves too soon.

Perhaps this is why the most evocative things on our walk were the railway tunnels. Essentially, much of our route (more or less) followed the old railway line from Forest Hill to Norwood. Sometimes, as at the start, we were in or beside the railway cutting. Sometimes we diverted and lost the railway, but sometimes it deliberately hid itself, plunging underground and vanishing from sight. These tunnel entrances and exits have been boarded up of course, and it is impossible to follow them into the darkness. Around the mouths of the tunnels the re-awakening woods seem to be trying to create deeper veils – thick, spooky-feeling, tangled undergrowth; in one case a derelict tennis court – and then emerge somewhere else. For me, this vanishing path through places where ancient woodland and human habitation meet – a ruined past and a lively present – felt like a potent and moving image of fairy stories themselves.

Little Goosegirl

Once upon a time there was a wise old king who was troubled in his mind.

Something ... something was awry, he felt, and he could not work out what it was. There was an uneasiness, something rotten at the core. He could not put his finger on it.

'My dear,' he said to his wife, the Queen, 'I feel that a cold shadow has fallen on our castle and something is not as it should be. There are bad secrets in the air.'

His wife, the Queen, who was trimming his moustache at that moment with a small pair of scissors – a tender little task she always did herself because it amused her – told him to be quiet or she would nip his tongue. But later, while he was doing up the buttons down the back of her dress – a tender little task he always did himself because he loved the soft skin at the nape of her neck – she asked him what he thought of their son's new wife. They had been married a long and happy time, so they understood each other's thought processes.

'The boy seems happy enough,' the King said.

'She must be good in bed,' said the Queen dryly. 'Sometimes I do wonder if we are sensible to put all that effort into keeping the princes chaste – it just means that they muddle up love and sex.'

'But the succession ... a proper royal heir,' he protested.

'Well, yes,' said the Queen, 'there is always that. And there's no use crying over spilled milk. I believe,' she added, 'that some families nowadays let them choose their own brides – for love, you know.'

'I didn't choose you,' said the King, kissing the very place where the soft skin was replaced by her soft hair, 'and there is plenty of love. On my side anyway . . .' He nibbled a small question below her ear and she giggled like a teenager. Then they got slightly diverted from their serious conversation and, indeed, were very nearly late for dinner.

But later, after he had undone her dress buttons and loosened her stay-cords and tied her nightdress ribbon – three tender little tasks he always did himself because he loved the soft skin at the nape of her neck – and she had climbed into bed, he found he was restless and could not sleep. He did not like the new princess. He sensed something mean and dark in her, something wrong. But he could hardly write to her mother, his old friend, childhood playmate and distant relative on the distaff side, and complain that he did not much like her daughter. She was old and widowed and suffered terribly from arthritis, so that she could not even travel to the wedding for pain. The children had been affianced since very soon after their births; it had been settled in the usual way. There was nothing he could do. He was getting old, he thought irritably. He re-tied his pyjama string and joined his sleeping wife in the royal bed.

One morning, about a week later, his Chancellor handed him his daily list and he saw that the goose herd had asked for a meeting. He tried to manage an orderly chain of command, but he also believed that anyone who worked for him should be allowed to meet him whenever they wanted. He knew a number of his colleagues thought this hopelessly old-fashioned and believed that a king should hold to his dignity and not meet face to face with every Tom, Dick and Sally who fancied it.

'*Primus inter pares*,' he had said to the stuck-up young king from next door. And then, because he was actually quite kindly and did not want to rub the lad's face in the fact that he knew no Latin, he added, 'First among equals. That's what a king is.'

'Oh nonsense, Your Majesty,' said the younger man. 'That went out with the Conquest.'

The King wondered how the young king made 'Your Majesty'

sound as contemptuous as 'Grandad'. Nonetheless, he stuck to his old practice.

So now, at 10.15 a.m., the goose herd, whose name was Conrad, was shown in. The King liked the boy; he was not the sharpest knife in the box, but he was a good open-hearted lad and his family worked their fields well and he played fiddle in the village band. Perhaps young Conrad felt ready for promotion, in which case ... the King thought quickly. But Conrad seemed oddly awkward, unable to get to the point. The King was puzzled but persisted gently. There was obviously something he wanted to say. And finally, blushing slightly, he blurted out:

'It's that new goosegirl, sir, I can't work with her.'

'New goosegirl?' enquired the King, confused.

'You know, sir, the one what came with the Princess and you said should help me with the geese.'

Then he remembered: a pretty little thing, standing in the court-yard beside the Princess's great white horse, when the Princess came and everything had been busy; she had been pale, staring and very lovely. She had reminded him of someone, and he had asked the Princess who she was.

'Just some serf I picked up on the way,' said the Princess, though not entirely carelessly.

'Is she your maid?' he asked.

'Good heavens, no. She's not the sort I'd have for a lady's maid. I'll need a proper dresser, by the way. Maybe you could find her something useful to do – she's a sulky little brat, but we should be kind I think.'

She had not sounded kind, but she was in a new place and there was a lot going on and perhaps it just the abruptness of shyness. He had suggested that the girl went to help Conrad with the geese, and the Princess had seemed pleased. He had looked again at the little blanched face below him in the courtyard, and then events had moved on and he had forgotten.

'Yes, I remember,' he said to Conrad now. 'Why can't you work with her?'

'She's weird,' said the boy, 'she's too weird. She's useless anyway – you'd think she'd never seen a goose before, but it's not that; I could teach her, but she's weird.'

'What sort of "weird", Conrad? She looked pretty enough to me.'

'Oh yes, she's pretty, all right. That's not it.'

He blushed furiously and the King said as gently as he could, 'Did you try to woo her, Conrad? She is allowed to turn you down, you know. And she's only been here a se'night. You may need patience. Or she may not be for you.'

The boy blushed deeper, as rosy as sorrel flowers. 'It's not that, sir. Well, not really. I mean, I did think, sort of . . . but it's not that. But . . . she has this hair, sir – it's lovely, like a flag iris, golden yellow and all long. We take the geese out, and up into the wood meadows, and she sits down under a tree in the shade and she takes her cap off and undoes her plaits and starts to brush her hair out, and it is all sparkles and lovely. And she chats away all friendly and . . . Well, I thought, like, she'd only do that to show me, like, she wanted me to touch it. And, yes, sir, I did want to touch it. There's just her and me in that sweet high meadow and the geese and the sunshine and the flowers and yes, I don't mind saying it, I did want to touch it.'

'Nothing weird about that, Conrad,'

'No, sir,' he grinned ruefully. 'But then, as soon as I reach out a finger – no, as soon as I even look at her like I'm going to – well, it's like an icy cold wind comes off her, fierce and hard and so cold, so very cold. I can't explain. I haven't done anything bad, honest, but she makes me feel . . . I run up the meadow a bit, pretend to chase my hat, and when I come back her hair is all tight and tidy and back in her cap. But, sir, she's been crying, like. I don't want to make her cry. I can't work with her, sir, not if she makes me all wound up to touch her hair and I make her cry. That's not right. My mum said to come and tell you.'

'Your mother was quite right, Conrad, and thank you for coming.' The King's heart sank. He knew the signs.

'Oh, sir, and I forgot to say: she talks to that horse's head. Every morning. That is weird.'

'What horse's head? What do you mean?'

'You know, sir, that horse that came with the Princess – lovely white thing. We were all that upset when she said to cut its head off.'

'The Princess said to cut the head off her horse? Why?'

'I don't know, sir. No one knew really, but the girl, the goosegirl, she asked the groom who chopped it to nail the head up in the archway and she talks to it every morning as we go out and every evening as we come in. And it always sighs and says back to her,

"Oh, if your mother knew

Her heart would break in two."

I don't know why, but I think it's weird and I don't like it.'

'I can see that, Conrad. Now you run along and I'll have a word with her later today and then we'll see.'

'Thank you, sir.'

'No. Thank you.'

The King felt terribly, terribly weary. He wanted to go up his room and snuggle his head into the Queen's soft neck and have the world go away. But he sent for the girl.

'What's your name?' he asked her. 'Who are you?'

She looked frightened. 'I can't tell you,' she said. 'It's a secret.' After a pause she added, 'I promised, I swore it under the open sky.'

'Well,' said the King gently, 'it is good to keep promises, but it is not always sensible to make them in the first place. I think this was a foolish promise.'

But the goosegirl only shook her head and stayed mute. The King saw the tears in her eyes. He reached out a hand to comfort her and felt, as Conrad had felt, the ice cold wind of terror that came off her and chilled him to the heart.

'I think,' said the King, withdrawing his hand, 'I think we should both go and talk to your horse.'

'His name is Falada,' she said in a whisper, and then she smiled, like spring sunshine. He knew at once who it was she had reminded him of. Her smile was the living mirror of a small girl, his old friend, a childhood playmate and distant relative on the distaff side. He knew. He exclaimed:

'Oh, if your mother knew

Her heart would break in two.'

'That's what Falada says too.' She looked more confident suddenly, and happier.

'I believe we can always trust animals who condescend to talk to us,' said the King.

So the two of them walked out and stood under the mossy archway where the horse's head hung. Falada sighed and muttered again,

'Oh, if your mother knew

Her heart would break in two.'

'Falada,' said the King solemnly, 'I believe this sweet child is the true bride. Because she is a natural princess she cannot break a promise she made, an oath she took, however foolishly, under the open sky. You, however, are not a princess, you are a dead horse, albeit a magical one, and I, as a king, first among equals, charge you to tell me what happened on the road through the forest.'

So Falada's head told the nasty tale of how the false bride stole the true bride's gold cup and her silk dress and her talking horse. And the other more important things too: her identity, her childhood, the pure white cloth with the three drops of blood on it that her mother had given her on parting to keep her safe, and all the things we do not speak about under the open sky.

And when the story was told the King said, 'Thank you. We must right this wrong.'

Falada replied,

'When her mother hears this thing

She will laugh and she will sing.'

The girl was smiling now, but the King remained serious.

He said gently, 'You are a sweet child. You are innocent, whatever happened, and you will be vindicated. You do not have to marry the Prince, though I hope you will want to one day. But no one will touch you until you ask them to. And no one in my kingdom, peasant or princess, will ever again have to marry a stranger. In your honour and always, women will marry if they choose, when they choose and where their hearts and their intelligence lead them. I promise.'

And he kept that promise.

6

August

Staverton Thicks

The oak woods at Staverton are the forests of childhood, the forests of dreams. Here perhaps more than anywhere else I have ever been, the forest of the imagination materialises, becomes actual; here perhaps more than anywhere else I have ever been, a smallish piece of ancient deciduous woodland opens into the world of magic, the place of fairy story that we inhabited as children and lost, I had thought, for ever.

Staverton Thicks and Staverton Park are two contiguous woods in eastern Suffolk; in fact it is difficult for a new visitor to distinguish between the two, although technically the Park is more 'open', its canopy never fully filled in by the leaves of the ancient trees, while in the Thicks, as the name suggests, the trees are close enough together to form a continuous green roof overhead.

Staverton contains over 4,000 ancient oak pollards, some certainly at least four hundred years old. Many of the trees are 'stag headed', reaching out gnarled naked limbs above their green crowns. These 'antlers' are signs of age, but not of disease or decay: 'stag head is a normal process of retrenchment by which a tree reduces its commitments and grows a new smaller crown'[1] (just as many very old people get smaller, wizened, but without losing health or energy). Many of the oaks at Staverton, still in good health, are hollow, or have huge branches drooping to the ground and re-rooting themselves in the damp leaf mould. Close around the oaks, and even growing inside their hollowed trunks, there are holly trees which seem to be both hugging and strangling their hosts. Some of these hollies are among the largest in Britain, up to 70 feet (20 metres) high, and there are unusually huge rowans and birches too. Between the trees are the fallen and decayed branches and boles of other ancient trees, now rotting silently away. Staverton is famously rich in lichens and invertebrates, and in high summer the ground is thickly covered in bracken with intermittent clear grassy spaces.

The magic here is very deep, because the mystery is very real. Even at the level of natural history, Staverton poses riddling questions: Why do hollies, notoriously drought sensitive and so more likely to flourish in the wetter west, do so spectacularly well in what is the driest corner of England? What causes the strange melding of the different tree species, almost unknown elsewhere? What circumstances have made this ground so friendly to trees, but so comparatively poor in ancient woodland flowers? Why is Staverton Thicks here at all?

In the opening chapter I suggested that many students of fairy story and folk lore have spent their time looking for the similarities between stories from different cultures and have therefore too easily missed the specific details of difference and particularity. Oliver Rackham argues that the same thing happens with students of ancient woodland, and uses Staverton as an example:

> Research and understanding include looking for resemblances,
> but conservation is about protecting differences. It is important
> to keep an open mind and be prepared for unexpected
> categories. Staverton Park, to the *National Vegetation Classification*,
> is a specimen of W10: *Quercus robur-Pteridium aquilinum-Rubus
> fructiosus* woodland, of which there are thousands of other
> examples, and a rather poor specimen with few species of
> herbs. True but trivial: the point of Staverton is that it is one of
> the biggest collections of ancient trees in Europe: oaks of vast

bulk and surrealist shape, giant hollies, giant birches, trees that are part oak, part holly and part birch, and a hundred years' accumulation of dead wood. Besides its unique qualities as a habitat, Staverton is a place of mystery and wonder; it has a peculiar effect on first-time visitors who have no foreknowledge that the world contains such places.[2]

Staverton has this profound effect on almost everyone who goes there. George Peterken, one of our most eminent woodland experts, considers it as near to primal woodland as anything else in the country.[3]

I went to Staverton in August, which is the right month to go, because it is the month of childhood – the month of the long summer holidays, when adventures beckon and the days feel endless and carefree. The bright gold-green leaves of early summer have deepened into a rich heavy green, the canopy is dense and the shadows deep and cool. My sister has lived less than thirty miles away for over quarter a century and is the sort of old-fashioned mother who takes her children places, makes them play outside and believes in adventures, but she too had never been in Staverton, nor even knew it was there to go to. Part of the mysteriousness of this place seems to be that although it is easily accessible and ought to be famous and much visited, it guards its secrecy, like any fairy world. I have met surprisingly few people who have even heard of it.

So on a hot summer morning, she and I and one of her five children, with Useless and Rubbish, their two dogs, set out to find the wood and have a picnic there. From the outset it was a somehow childlike, fairy-tale day. To start with, in a fit of more-than-usual incompetence, I did not have and she could not find the relevant Ordnance Survey map, so we had to look *for* the wood before we could go in and look *at* the wood. We had only the vaguest idea where it was, but did know that Staverton Thicks are near Butley, out on the sandy dry plain between Ipswich and Aldeburgh, and that they stood somewhere within Rendlesham Forest, an extensive coniferous plantation. East of Woodbridge, with the forestry on one side of the road, we could see, across pleasant green fields, the darker green bulk of deciduous woodland. We pulled the car into a lay-by, under warm pine trees dappled with sunshine, and plunged into the rough wood on the other side of the road, heading, we hoped, for the Thicks.

Then there they were, the first magical thing to happen that day. In fact there is a perfectly good track, with a gate and an interpretation board, into and through Staverton Thicks, and if we had had a proper map or had even driven another 100 metres further along the road we could not have failed to find it. As it was, we re-enacted one of the most curious and deeply evocative tropes of fairy stories. In fairy stories the characters get lost going into the forest. For three days Hansel and Gretel 'kept going deeper and deeper into the forest. If help did not arrive soon they were bound to perish of hunger and exhaustion.' But when they have triumphed over the wicked witch and are ready to go home they find the path perfectly easily; 'when they had walked for a few hours the forest became more and more familiar to them and finally they caught sight of their father's house'. Over and over again this happens – in 'The Seven Swans' the younger sister wanders through the world looking for her brothers and gets lost in a vast dark forest before she finds their cottage. But later, when the Prince discovers her sitting in her tree making the shirts that will free her brothers from their enchanted swan-shapes, he takes her to his palace quickly and easily. Snow White flees, terrified, from the servant who is supposed to kill her, through a tangled confusing forest full of thorns and wild beasts, completely lost; however, once she is safe with the dwarves, the forest turns out to be positively social – full of paths, inhabitants and hunting parties. Carrying her coffin to the prince's palace presents no problems at all. It is when you are going out into the forest, not when you are trying to return home from it, that you get lost, that the forest is at its densest and most frightening.

This is unexpected because, on the whole, it is not what normally happens in real life. I have, luckily, never got seriously lost in a forest, although I know people who have, and very scary it sounds. But whenever I have felt or feared that I might be lost it has been when I realised that I was not sure of the way back again. I walk in boldly, and only when I decide that it is time to go home do I start worrying about where I am and whether I know the way back. In the fairy stories this process is reversed; and so it was for us that sunny August day in Staverton. We went in doubtfully, through some rough and tangled wood, and did not know quite where we were or what we were looking for or whether we would find it. Hours later we came out on a pleasant well-made track and arrived on the road within sight of the car.

In the meantime, we were in fairyland. Old pollards inspire a strange sense of awe. Pollarding is a woodland management technique, basically not dissimilar to coppicing; but with a coppice the original trunk of the tree is cut down to ground level and the tree then regenerates, throwing up new shoots from around the old stump; these new stems, close to each other and in natural competition for the light, grow upwards, thin and straight. When they reach the size you want them to be, which depends on what you are going to use them for – poles or charcoal or winter feed or house building, for example – you cut them back again. Gradually, as the new stems are cut back and themselves produce further new growth, the base extends into what is called a coppice stool – a huge (in very old woodland they can be well over two metres across) base which is in fact a single tree. At the same time, coppicing, by removing the shade creating branches and leaf canopy, opens up the ground to increased sunlight, which in turn allows the growth of new trees and encourages biodiversity. It was usual to coppice all the trees in a quite large area at the same time, so that immediately afterwards the space would look a bit like modern clear-felling. However, coniferous trees, with the exception of yew, do not regenerate in this way – a clear-felled area of coniferous woodland will eventually grow brand-new trees, but coppiced deciduous trees grow afresh on the old root stock. Within a well-managed wood, different areas would be cut in rotation, so that there was new timber available every year, and also there would be varying levels of sun and shade throughout the wood, allowing for movement and diversity in which different species of flora and fauna could flourish.

However, there is a problem with this technique if you also wish to use your wood for grazing stock, for maintaining deer, or (most commonly) for both. Coppicing is designed to bring on new, low shoots which provide the stock with instant and easy food. This quickly becomes counter-productive, since obviously succulent new shoots will not grow into usable wood if they are eaten. In many ancient forests newly coppiced areas were fenced to exclude the stock. In some Royal Forests the deer were let back in after a couple of years, and the agricultural stock later. But you obviously need a rather extensive area of woodland for this system to work satisfactorily. For smaller or more heavily grazed woods where the cattle and swine (and geese, and – in Scotland particularly – goats) needed to range more widely, and for the increasingly popular hunting parks, in which the deer were enclosed and the hunt itself became a more of a performance, with audience platforms and wide rides, coppicing was not satisfactory.

Pollarding was a method of tree management devised to avoid such problems.[4] Instead of cutting the tree down to the ground, you let it grow for longer and then cut it off at a level above the point a deer or cow can reach. 'Pollard' derives from the now nearly defunct word 'poll', meaning 'head', which still lingers in the poll tax, polling in elections and the redpoll – a small finch with a red forehead: essentially, pollarding is beheading a tree. Again, the tree will put out new shoots from the point at which it has been cut off; again, stripping away the canopy opens the ground underneath it to the sunlight and – where it is not overgrazed – allows new trees to self-seed into the space between the pollards. Obviously some species will pollard (and indeed coppice) better than others. As I explained, except for yew, coniferous trees do not re-grow if cut back in this way, but many deciduous trees flourish under such treatment. The best trees for pollarding are those that in a natural state put up a tall single trunk. So, for instance hazel, which is naturally shrubby with several main stems, does not make a good pollard although it does make excellent coppice. In Britain the most usually pollarded species are beeches (as at Burnham Beeches in Buckinghamshire), hornbeam (as in Epping Forest) and, above all, oaks.

Pollarding has some important effects on trees. The most significant in relation to Staverton is that it extends their lives, possibly indefinitely. Because the tree does not have to maintain so much canopy and because its branches are perpetually renewed, it stays in a 'juvenile' state. Almost all the most ancient deciduous trees in Britain were at one time pollarded or coppiced.[5] Additionally old, naturally seeded pollards are less at risk from windblow. In the now-famous storm of 1987, ancient trees were the *least* affected; being hollow or rotten appeared to make no difference whatsoever. Great swathes of Rendlesham Forest, with its 'robust' young plantation conifers, were flattened, but right in the midst of the devastation, the ancient oaks of Staverton were barely affected.[6]

But although (and because) the pollard tree lives for a very long time, strange things happen to its appearance. Because it is regularly 'wounded' by having its branches cut, water and fungi and other parasites get inside the tree, and eventually most pollard oaks are hollowed out. This does not affect its continuing life – the central core of all trees is 'dead' – but it does create homes for a bizarre range of life forms. Ancient oak trees provide habitats for 284 different insect species (or 423 if you include mites) and 324 species of associated lichens; by contrast, the introduced spruces of modern plantations harbour a mere 37 species.[7] More varieties of insects leads to more varieties of birds, and together, to wider and easier dispersal of flower seeds. The biodiversity in ancient pollard woods like Staverton (despite the fact that it has a comparatively small range of flowers) is mind boggling.

At the same time, centuries of cutting away the old growth and encouraging new shoots have led to gnarling and knotting and strange patterns in the bark; epicormic twigs (which grow out through the bark, giving oaks their whiskery look) tend to become

ever more eccentric, growing in patches and clumps and making
the tree trunks look like gnomes (or, of course, gnomes and dwarves
are whiskered and hairy because they look like ancient pollard
oaks).

But some of the most extraordinary things happen to a pollard
oak when you *stop* pollarding it. Because of the distortion and
attention it received while being managed, the new branches twist
out at odd angles, often much lower than on a 'maiden' oak grown
for timber.[8] It may develop several equal trunks from the point
where it was cut, or great branches that grow outwards, crooked
and reaching down to the ground. These horizontal branches
(together with low pollution and a damp climate) encourage epiphyte ferns, like polypody, to make their homes on the oak; mosses
and lichens and fungi flourish. The trees in an old pollard wood
become more and more different from each other, more and more
individual, more and more strange. And in Staverton there are
thousands of them.

These are the trees that as a child you once dreamed you would
climb – and for all she is twenty now, my niece is climbing them.
She is laughing at herself and we are laughing at her, but she is
scrambling up wide branches which reach down to the ground so
that she can just step onto them at ground level, and be welcomed
into her aerial castle up a magical staircase with a thick velvet carpet
of green moss. The princess whose brothers were turned into
swans must have sat in trees like these, silent and working away at
her impossible sewing; the dashing if useless future king Charles II
hid all day in a tree like this, laughing at the stupid if righteous
soldiers looking for him below. These are the trees that years ago
you thought you would build a nest or tree house in and live like
a bird, like Owl in *Winnie the Pooh* – or even, on the days you were
sulking, glare from, like the Owl in *Squirrel Nutkin*, not benign at all,
but greedy and fierce and free. Inside the hollow oaks the ground
is often dry and soft with heaps of old leaves; it smells sweet and
musty. These are the caves that you were going to run away to
and hide out in and wait for the prince to come riding along or

for an old woman to pass by and give you a gift that would make your fortune. These are the trees of magical dreams.

The wood offers more material gifts as well; along the sides of the paths, and particularly on the edges of the wood, the bracken, tall and dark, was a-dance with butterflies. None of us knew much about butterfly identification – although I have since learned that Suffolk is home to 30 of the 59 British breeding species[9] – and I do not know what kinds of butterflies they were. This made them feel more strange and wonderful somehow. There were gaudy-coloured ones with bright 'eyes' in the centre of their wings and if they were not Painted Ladies they should have been, and white ones adrift like dandelion seeds, and a gentle-looking dark brown smaller kind. And one so memorable I was able to look it up later – a Spotted Wood Butterfly (*Pararge aegeria*), dark chocolate brown with a drift of black-centred white spots across its wings, some of them cut neatly in half at the boundary between wing edge and air. They were floating and flirting in the sunshine. We invited them onto our fingers, and they walked so lightly on their fragile, slender legs that they seemed weightless.

Butterflies are lovely, silent, like angels. In the Middle Ages they were a common symbol for the Resurrection: first there is a stumpy little caterpillar, earthbound and greedy; then it apparently dies and is buried in the coffin of its own cocoon; the butterfly emerges meta-morphosed – colourful, beautiful, apparently no longer needing food (adult butterflies are primarily nectar drinking), and flying free on gentle wings. The image is better even than it first appears because something very dreadful and frightening happens inside the chrysalis. We use the word 'cocoon' now to mean a place of safety and escape, but in fact the caterpillar, having constructed its own grave, does not develop smoothly, growing wings onto its first body, but disintegrates entirely, breaking down into an organic slime which then regenerates in a completely new form. It goes as a child into the dark place and is lost; it emerges as the beautiful princess, or proven hero. The forest is full of such magic, both in reality and in the stories.

Philosophy is odious and obscure
Both law and physic are for petty wits
Theology is basest of the three
Unpleasant harsh contemptible and vile,
'Tis magic, magic that has ravished me.[10]

The magic of the fairy stories is the same magic as in woods like Staverton. The magic of trees that look like gnomes; of flowers that weren't there last time you looked; of butterflies appearing unexpected in the sunshine; of hazel catkins weathering out the winter tucked under their own twigs; of pied flycatchers, skittish flutters of black and white in the green trees, suddenly there when only days ago they weren't – now we know they were in North Africa all winter, but . . . The magic in fairy stories is ordinary, ubiquitous and unearned, like the magic of the woods themselves.

More recently, as the woods have shrunk and children have gone into them less, we have turned increasingly to a more bookish, intellectual understanding of magic – a High Art, black or white, good or evil, but a reward always of long training and arcane knowledge: Merlin, Ged, Harry Potter, the Jedi. This sort of magic is drawn from the Celtic tradition and also from the ancient Middle Eastern astronomer magicians, the magi in Matthew's Gospel who came to Bethlehem led by the star.[11] Magic in this tradition is a noble but dangerous pursuit, it can give enormous power in exchange for great labour (and, oddly, often celibacy). Even with our emerging ecological concerns, magic is emphatically not something 'natural' – it is learned, practised and priestly. It is suggestive that the 'Fairy Godmother' was introduced into fairy stories only when they became a literary, educated form: Perrault invented Cinderella's Fairy Godmother and a sophisticated scene of metamorphosis, whereas the Grimms' oral tradition was satisfied with a little bird on a hazel tree in the back yard tossing down a golden frock just for the asking. Perrault also created the Fairy Godmothers for Sleeping Beauty – originally they were just a group of 'old women' of whom there happened to be 'thirteen living in [the] kingdom'.

It is also rather noticeable that powerful men – Gandalf, Merlin – have replaced batty old women. The magicians of contemporary fantasy literature draw to a remarkable degree on myths about scientists (detached from the world in their intellectual pursuits, absent minded, socially inept and immensely powerful). The commentators who complain about sexism in fairy stories seem to overlook this – in the older tales it is most often elderly single women who dispense a peculiarly domestic form of magic.

The magic of the fairy stories is like the fat in good beef: the meat is marbled with it – you cannot cut it out and dispose of it, and it is what gives flavour and texture to the meal. No one studies magic in a fairy story from the Teutonic tradition – it is just there.

You are an old grumpy soldier without home or hope and you come down a long track through the woods towards a castle, and an old woman – for no reason whatsoever – gives you a 'little cape' of invisibility.

You are a somewhat stupid third son and your father tosses three feathers into the air to set you and your brothers off on your adventures and your feather just happens to be blown onto the entrance to a magical underworld.

You are a dispossessed princess, bound to silence by a preposterous promise extracted under threat, and your beloved horse has been taken away and killed – but for no apparent reason, it turns out to be a talking horse, and what is more, by a bit of good fortune its severed head can still speak after it is dead.

You long for a child and a frog crawls out of a pond and gives you one. (Without wanting to labour the point, frogs produce literally thousands of eggs, tadpoles, baby frogs, with exceptional and often incompetent casualness, laying the spawn in small puddles in the middle of tarmac roads if the mood takes them – a fertile image of casual fertility.)

You are a child lost in the forest and you come upon a house made of bread and cake and sugar. But oddly enough that is the *only* magic in the story – the rest is surprisingly practical and down to earth. The old woman who owns the house tries to exploit and ultimately eat you, but solely through your own labours and intelligence you outwit her, steal her goods and go home rich.

Entirely through your own disobedience and stupidity you eat a poisoned apple, given to you by a stepmother who owns a magic mirror. But it does not kill you. The dwarves who have protected you have no magical cures at their disposal; it takes some clumsy coffin bearers to shake the bite of apple out of your throat.

You are a boastful liar; you pretend you can spin straw into gold, but you can't. You are in serious trouble, but luckily a magical little man appears and does the job for you – at a price. You outwit him almost by accident; there is no magic involved on your side, but your prettiness and ambition are more powerful than any wizardry.

You are a little tailor, smug, self-satisfied and ambitious. By a casual mixture of chance and cunning, backed up by some slightly dishonest swagger and assisted by the folly, credulity and cowardice of others, you win yourself a kingdom. You get no magical help at all – you are completely self-reliant, except that among the trials you have to overcome there are some giants and a unicorn. These are from the world of magic, but you use no magic to overpower them, just native wit and a certain mental and physical nimbleness.

You yearn for a baby and you finally get one, but it is a thumbling, a tiny creature, which nonetheless has no magical powers of its own and has to use its size to advantage to make its way in the world.

You are a child who has an alarming encounter with a rapacious wolf. The only magic here is that the wolf can speak and disguise itself as an old woman.

You are a small girl whose parents have sold you (for a very low price) to a known witch, who imprisons you in a tower. Is it magic or just good luck that your hair grows so long and thick that your lover can climb up to your secret cell? The witch, despite her reputation, does no magic; the prince works no spell; you have no supernatural powers except that your tears cure his blindness.

You are a girl with seven brothers, a deranged stepmother and a possibly abusive father.[12] Here there is deep magic, for the brothers are enchanted into swans. However, their restoration does not depend on magic at all, but on a long and painful effort by you. You have to keep silent for seven years and sew each of them a shirt out of starwort.[13] There is nothing magical about your task; it calls only for a stoic endurance and loyalty. Later, while you are still labouring at your brothers' redemption, you are *falsely* accused of being a magical witch who has eaten her own babies and you are condemned to death by fire, but you do not swerve. At the last possible moment you are rescued because you have completed your voluntary reparation, and everything ends up happily.

Magical things just happen; they are everywhere, but unreliable, knotted seamlessly into the mundane world of poverty, work and the mysterious goings-on of the forest. In some stories it is hard to tell what is magic and what is not. There is luck, there is love, there is virtue, there is magic. There is the forest.

Magic is never a thing that you do – the protagonists of these stories are not themselves magical; they don't 'make magic', although they use the magical tools and chances they are offered. Although there are many stories in which there is no magic at all, there are none in which a magic worker is the principal character. Magic is something you are given, something that is done to you or around you. You do not have power in the way that the characters of higher, more noble traditions do. You may have to work very hard, and endure great pain or sorrow or hardship, but you do not do this to learn, acquire or achieve the magic that will save you. That comes from outside in a fairly arbitrary way – it is all pure gift. No one studies magic; of all the young adults who leave home to seek their fortune, of their own volition or because they have been driven out, not a single one goes off to learn magic. They go travelling like modern gap-year students, to learn about life, to escape poverty or cruelty at home, to undertake apprenticeships in useful trades, to 'learn what fear is', to make their fortunes, or for no particular reason that we learn of. The magic comes to them, without solicitation or endeavour. It is usually in the form of assistance, not solution: they have to use the magical gifts they are given, and they have to continue to work or suffer or both. There is a lesser-known light-hearted story called 'The Magic Table, the Golden Donkey and the Club in the Sack' which illustrates this point rather well. Three brothers are driven out of their home by the machinations of the household goat; they take up apprenticeships in three respectable trades – as a joiner, a miller and a turner. When they have served their time their masters give them each a reward: a table that covered itself with food, a donkey that spat[14] out golden coins, and a club that would beat people up for its owner. But the first two brothers foolishly let their magic gifts be stolen from them by a greedy innkeeper. The third brother uses his gift sensibly: he reclaims theirs, punishes the thief and makes his fortune. He was no luckier and no more deserving than his brothers, but he used his gift wisely.

A possible exception to this appears to be the 'good sister/ bad sister' stories: the good, sweet, polite, helpful sister is kind and obedient to an old lady and earns her magical reward; gold coins pour out of her mouth whenever she speaks. The bad, rude, lazy sister gets the same opportunity, but through her arrogance, idleness and unkindness she loses her chance and is punished; whenever she speaks a toad hops out of her throat. But even in these stories the magic is chancy; the 'good' sister may get given something magical, but even in that there is a high element of luck – she did not serve the old woman in some Faustian contract, she just served the old woman who happened by chance to be magical. Neither girl is given the power of magic. The old woman does not teach the good sister how to make gold flow out of her own mouth or anyone else's. No one is apprenticed to a witch, no one gains higher powers – most often they gain loads of money and usually true love as well, although that is frequently secondary.[15]

I know of no other cultural tradition that treats magic in this odd casual way. I believe it is a distinct forest magic that grew out of the experience of living in woods, where you cannot see far ahead and where things change abruptly. The desert (where the magi come from) and the seashore (where the Celtic wizards come from) are vast and dangerous. The views are long and the weather is extreme and frequently changes suddenly and dramatically. The stars revolve slowly overhead, slow enough for their progress to be pondered upon. The changes in these environments are less seasonal than they are in woods and fields. They do not carry with them the extraordinary fibrillation between same-old and shocking-new that the woods present: the rhythmic regularity of the seasons contrasting with the vibrant surprise of *this* season, of today. There are always butterflies in the bracken in August – the speckled wood butterfly is not rare, is not specific to Suffolk and is not particularly exotic (it is more neat and smart); but *this* speckled wood butterfly, today, now, preening in the dappled sunshine below a weirdly contorted ancient oak, is entirely unexpected and might not have been there. Every summer the pied flycatchers make the long journey from Africa, but *this* quick flash of black and white, *this* sudden 'pik, pik, pik' alarm call or pleasing melodious song with its repetitions and changes, this almost-certainly-a-pied-flycatcher on *this* warm August afternoon is a completely unlooked-for and magical moment which we can do nothing to create or summon or control and which comes unearned, as pure gift.

A great deal of scholarly and creative energy has been expended on fairy stories and on their improbably off-hand magic. They are wells of psychoanalytical wisdom, think Bettelheim (a Freudian) and Marie Louise von Franz (a Jungian). They are moral fables to inspire the young to be decent to the old, argues Marina Warner. They are the left-over traces of a more chthonic social mode in which animism ruled and the spirits of place were powerful and almost divine.[16] They are the political upwelling of desire and aspiration, the containers of dissent and potential rebellion for the oppressed poor. They are the invented semi-fascistic expression of an arrogant nationalism by two bourgeois linguistic scholars. They are a coded cultural tool for sexism. They are pre-modern, pre-rational, pre-scientific, pre-Enlightenment delusions suitable for the simple minded and superstitious, and therefore for children.

The fairy stories may indeed represent all these things, but in Staverton I realised something else – something very simple and primal: their magic is the magic of the forest. Staverton itself is always there, a mediocre example of 'W10: *Quercus robur-Pteridium aquilinum-Rubus fructiosus* woodland'. Today, now, we are walking in Staverton where none of us have ever been before and there are oaks of vast bulk and surrealist shape, giant hollies, giant birches, trees that are part oak, part holly and part birch, and a thousand years' accumulation of dead wood. It is 'a place of mystery and wonder; it has a peculiar effect on first-time visitors who have no foreknowledge that the world contains such places'.[17] It is the magic.

In the fairy stories, the usual providers of magical assistance are not in fact human at all – they are the natural inhabitants of the forest: most often birds and trees, but also flowers and other plants, fish, frogs and toads, animals, both wild and domesticated, and also the sun and the moon, streams and ponds. I began to feel that the fairy stories are like pollard oaks: they grow from natural seeds in the woodland; then they are attended to, both tended and managed, and used for all sorts of useful and lovely things, and they live for a very long time. They go back, bits die back, new bits branch off in crazy directions; they get mixed up, confused with other trees ('part oak, part holly, and part birch'); they provide a rich habitat for all sorts of life forms with a wide diversity of purpose and plan.

While we were in Staverton Thicks, along with all the other magical things that happened, we had an encounter with a witch. A nasty witch, not a little old wise woman. She emerged from a building on the other side of a river – it did not look quite like a house, more like a pavilion or stable or even possibly a gingerbread cottage. I have no idea what it was. She started to screech at us. We were to go away, at once. We had no business to be there. We were off the path. Seen through the trees, contorted with anger, gesticulating, wild, a real witch. And suddenly I could not remember the access codes and laws for England. In Scotland, of course, since this was not 'domain land' (someone's house and garden) and there had been no posted signs telling us why we could not be there, we would have had clear rights.

(Except we had the dogs off their leads, which the access law does not really allow.) The English law is more confused and confusing. Then she shouted a stupid thing: we weren't allowed to be there because it was an SSSI – a Site of Special Scientific Interest. Of course it was; it should be – but SSSI status has nothing whatsoever to do with access law. More often people are confused in the other direction: they think that because a place has a public designation like this it must instantly be accessible (in the legal sense.) It is not.

I do not know if this was aggressive landlordism and she simply did not want us in her private wood, even though we were clearly neither poaching nor stealing firewood. It was August – there were no ground-nesting birds to worry about. She may have been the local madwoman. She may have been right. It did not matter, in Staverton, in the thick bracken, with the ancient pollard oaks laughing at us, and the sun playing games with the green leaves and dark branches – she was a witch and added somehow to our gleeful mood. Like children we skipped away, pretending to go back to the path, but not really.

Then we had a picnic, sitting on a huge fallen trunk under a huge ancient oak.

In 1528, the Chronicler of Butley Abbey recorded that the monks had taken the Queen of France to the 'Park of Staverton' and there they had eaten a meal *sub quercubus* ('under the oak trees') *cum Joco et Ludo* (quite literally, 'with fun and games'). The chronicler added that it was *satis jucundis* – 'great fun'.

Fairy stories grow out of woods like this, ancient, weird, unexpected, surviving against the odds, but also luxuriant, tricky, lovely – fun and games, great fun. Deeply, innocently magic.

The Seven Swans' Sister

Once upon a time there was a young woman with a fierce integrity.

She sat all day on the wide branch of an ancient oak tree. She had worn away the thick moss where she sat, making a rough bark saddle, but to either side of this bare patch it was green and soft, and the epiphyte polypodies sprang crisp and strong around her. She wore a linen slip and her bare feet dangled down, her slender ankles crossed and her toes relaxed but pointed, her head bent over her work and her long hair loose and stirring in the breeze. From below, looking upwards, a passing traveller could have seen that the soles of her feet were leathery, stained and cut from going barefoot through the forest. When evening came or her fingers were too chilled for sewing, she clambered down and slept in the soft dry cave that was the hollowed oak trunk, on a bed of soft leaf mould.

She never spoke or laughed or sang. She never cried or shouted or swore. Sometimes in the cold of winter she sniffed or coughed or sneezed, but that was involuntary and did not count. She had aligned herself to the silence of the forest, the deep energetic silence of growing things, of seasons turning and of the soundless music of the stars. In spring it was lovely; in summer it was happy; in autumn it was fruitful; and in winter it was grim. Some would have called it clinical depression or 'survivor's guilt' or even autism. She called it love.

In the late spring months, from April through to June, she did not have much time for sleep: at night she would go out into the broken moonlight, which cut weakly through the thickening leaf canopy, and wander down the forest tracks gathering starwort.

Starwort, which is also called greater stitchwort, *Stellaria holostea*, is a common plant of the woodlands, and affectionately known as Milkmaids, Wedding cakes, Star-of-Bethlehem, Poor-man's buttonhole, Adder Mint and Poppers. The flowers are shining white and have five deeply lobed petals like narrow hearts, and golden stamens. It has brittle, straggly stalks and thin leaves, and supports itself on other plants. She kept great heaps of it in her tree cave and turned it carefully week by week through the rest of the year to keep it from rotting; as it dried it smelled sweet and sunny, like hay meadows, and its seed heads exploded sharply when ripe.

At first she had thought that she needed to make her brothers' shirts out of starwort petals, sewing together the silky hearts with tiny precise stitches, perhaps using strands of spider's web. Soon, however, she realised that this was impossible. Like all the *Stellari*, like most wild flowers, the blooms drooped and faded as soon as they were picked; by morning they were gone. Instead, by careful experiment and clear-eyed observation, she discovered that she could strip off the thin leaves, dry the long hairless stalks, then steep them in the little pools of the stream that flowed through the forest, and weave them wet on a tiny loom made from a piece of curved bark. It was tiring, tricky, endless work, and she wished that in her childhood she had learned more useful skills, spinning like the spiders, working like the ants.

Very occasionally, not more than a few times a year, usually at dawn or dusk on calm early autumn days, she would hear a deep throbbing music, the bell-beat of mute swans' wings. She would run out of her shelter and look up to see them through the branches against the pale sky, orange beaks protruding, long necks stretched straight out and the huge wings thrumming the air. If there were a group of seven, flying as an arrowhead, a wedge of power, her heart would lift. But swans are short-sighted, and they never seemed to see her or turn from their magnificent passing. Tears would well in her dark eyes and a great loss and loneliness possess her; but she would steel herself, clear headed if soft hearted, and return to her weaving.

Mostly, however, she enjoyed her own company, self-sufficient and contained, as many children brought up alone are, especially those like her who have grown up in a large, bare castle with a depressed mother and a father with too little self-control. She knew he loved her, fiercely and deeply, but she could never be confident, never assured or serene in his love. As a child, she did not know why. She was richly treated, given playthings, and later books and music and pictures and a garden. She had pretty clothes and warm clothes and the best of teachers. But she had no friends and no brothers to play with. No guests ever came to the castle; there were no feasts or hunts or music or games; there was no giggling in the rose bower nor dancing in the hall – and sometimes in the night she could hear her mother weeping.

There were strange details, too, that she did not understand. Once, in a cupboard under some stairs, she found a muddy football, battered and deflated; once, in a little summer house out in the garden, she found a bag stuffed with straw and a strange pattern painted on it – a white circle inside a red circle and a back circle an inch or so across in the very centre. The bag was pierced by little holes, and wisps of straw poked through them. She did not know what it was, but when she asked her father he scowled heavily and the next time she went to the summer house the bag had disappeared. On the fell above the castle there was a herd of little wild ponies, pretty and sleek, but no one rode them or loved them; there were feral guinea pigs in the plantation around the castle, but she did not know how they came there.

But it was a calm childhood, and she grew tall and beautiful and strong; her heart was as pure as a fountain, as a deep well, as a bubbling spring, and her will was toughened on solitude and quietness.

And one day, just as she came to womanhood, she overheard some chatter. She was walking in the woods by the river and the azaleas were in flower, bright and flaunting. Down by the weir there were women washing, and the steady rhythm of scrubbing tends to loosen tongues.

'It wasn't her fault,' one said, 'it is him, the old master. He was stuck on a daughter. Most would be happy with seven sons. And they were lovely boys. But not him. I know his type.'

'Say what you choose,' said another crossly. 'I don't say it was her fault, but she was the cause. You weren't here then, but I know. She was a wee spindly bairn; they never thought they'd raise her. He sent the boys for Holy Water and they dawdled, just messing about – so he cursed them, cursed them in a fit of wicked temper. I don't say 'her fault' – I just say she caused it. And nothing has been the same since. The Lady all broken up and no fun and games to be had in these parts. And she's a silent, dull thing, always mooning about.'

'It's him,' said the first, 'he was too set on her. It's not right. Swans indeed – to turn your own boys into swans and let them fly off just because you got a baby girl. That's not right.'

Not right. She knew that this was true.

That night she asked her father. She rode out his wrath because it was right to do so. She endured his maudlin tears and wheedling because it was right to do so. She sunk into the silence of her own heart and waited there until the storm had passed over her head. She ignored his apologies, his commands and his despairing conviction that nothing could be done.

Before sunrise the next morning she left home and went out into the wide world to find her brothers and rescue them from their enchantment. Eventually, and after many miles, she learned from the swallows and the spiders and the long-legged, white-furred hare what she must do. For seven years, one for each brother, she must not speak or laugh or sing. She must not cry or shout or swear. She must sit all day in an ancient oak tree and sew seven little shirts of starwort, one for each brother.

So that is what she did. She aligned herself to the silence of the forest. It was not truly soundless in the woods – there was bird song, the dancing music of living water, the insistent hammering of woodpeckers, the whispers and howls of the wind, the roaring coughs of the stag rut and the night screams of fox prey. But all the noises floated over the deep energetic silence of growing things, of seasons turning and of the silent music of the stars, of new shoots pushing through the ground, of new leaves pushing through their buds, of fungus – overnight and suddenly – pushing out of dead wood and of badger cubs growing in their underground setts. And that huge silence absorbed the sounds and mutterings of the forest where she sat and sewed. The deep silence wound itself into her heart until there was nothing left but purity of purpose and the sweetness of love.

In spring it was lovely; in summer it was happy; in autumn it was fruitful; and in winter it was grim.

And after she had been sitting there and weaving her starwort cloth for three years she had a pile of handkerchief-sized pieces of cloth, unbleached and sweet smelling. Not enough yet for seven shirts, but enough to make her think about scissors and sharp needles and sewing thread. Then one day a king came hunting in her forest. He was a young king, both handsome and kind, although he had a mother nearly as obsessive and possessive as her father. Pausing in an open glade of oak trees, he looked up and saw first her lovely ankles and her wounded feet. Then he raised his head and saw her looking down. They each smiled at the other.

'What's your name?' he asked. She smiled.

'What are you doing here?' he asked. She smiled.

'Will you marry me?' he asked. She had lived in silence and industry for three years, so she knew her own heart. It was easier for her than for him. She jumped down in one graceful leap and he caught her in his arms and wrapped her in his cloak and took her home to his palace and married her.

Nothing changed. She never spoke or laughed or sang. She never cried or shouted or swore. Now she did not even cough and sneeze in the winter, because there was a fire in her room to keep her warm. She did not nod or point or write because she was uncertain as to the rules governing such silent speech and it seemed not worth the risk. Her mother-in-law hated her, but she could not explain or console the old woman – she could only smile and go out at night, into the broken moonlight and wander down the forest tracks gathering starwort and sit in her room by day stitching her brothers' shirts and counting the seasons, the months and the days until she should have served her time.

The sweet smiles of the Young Queen, and the hard commitment within her, the depths of the silence of her heart, and the Young King's unswerving love baffled and infuriated the Old Queen. She grew spiteful and dark. She wanted to make the Young Queen speak. She set her will against the Young Queen's will. But she could not break her.

In the end she stole the Young Queen's babies. She smeared the Young Queen's closed lips with goat's blood and told the people the Young Queen was a witch who consorted with the Devil at night and who ate her own children. But the Young Queen remained faithful to her brothers and her calling. As her father had sacrificed his sons for her, it seemed right that she should sacrifice her sons for her brothers.

The Old Queen succeeded in getting her convicted. The right to silence and to the presumption of innocence is never secure. She was condemned to be burned.

The night before she was to die she went one last time out into the moonlit forest and gathered seven perfect starflowers. As she came silently back to the palace she heard in the silence of the night the distant deep throbbing music, the bell-beat of mute swans' wings. She smiled.

When they came for her she was sewing the seven white flowers onto the neck openings of the seven starwort shirts. One sadly still lacked a sleeve, but there was nothing she could do. She had run out of time, although not of integrity. She folded the shirts carefully and draped them over one forearm. She walked out into the morning and up onto the waiting bonfire. She turned to face the silent crowd, smiled at the Young King one last time, and closed her eyes.

Sometimes virtue is indeed rewarded. There was a deep throbbing sound, a great wedge of white power, of energy and wind, the music of wings, the arrowhead of long white necks, a moment of confusion and hissing. She opened her eyes; her laughter rang out like a bell above the hissing, drumming rhythm of the swans coming in fast against the rising sun. She tossed the seven shirts high into the air and without breaking their forward flight or their perfect triangular formation, the swans caught them in their strong orange beaks. The spell was broken. The enchantment was over. The Young Queen was free and laughing, after seven long years of silence.

No one is perfect. She had not finished her task, and the seventh brother, the one whose shirt lacked a sleeve, had to limp through life trailing a white swan's wing where his second arm should have been. But even he knew that she had done her very best.

Some may have called her decision clinical depression or 'survivor's guilt' or even autism. She called it love.

She deserved to live happily ever after.

7

September

Forest of Dean

On a golden September morning I went to the Forest of Dean – it was not quite autumnal, the leaves on the trees still green and thick, but the bracken was turning, touched yellow or tan here and there in its tall thickets; the berries on the rowan and hawthorn were turning red and the acorns on the oak trees were darkening from their pale creamy green summer colour. Walking in the forest it was newly hushed; the clearest sign of the passing of summer is the reduction in bird song. Although the most conspicuous of our migrant birds, the swallows and martins, will not depart for another month, many of the woodland species – like nightingales, redstarts and wood warblers – have left by mid-September. Even the permanently resident species tend to sing far less as autumn sets in, so the woods feel quieter.

But I had not come to the Forest of Dean to admire the changing of the season or the fading of bird song, though both have a particular loveliness. I had come because under the present-day forest there are more ancient forests. Three hundred million years ago there were forests growing in wet lowlands that were gradually buried by flood residue; as they were pushed further and further down underground they were compressed and heated, and where they were protected from rotting and oxidising by acidic water and mud they slowly turned into coal. Beneath the present Forest of

Dean there are extensive coal seams. There are also iron ore deposits and other mineral resources. At least since the Romans were in Britain, the Forest of Dean has been a centre of mining – a curiously industrial forest. It still is: I had come to the Forest of Dean to meet some Free Miners.

I particularly wanted to talk to Free Miners, because they are linked to fairy stories in two specific ways, both of which feel intriguing, if a bit mysterious, to me.

The first is a more general observation – in fairy stories, *anyone* who has legitimate work in the forest will always turn out to be a 'good' character. The forests of these stories are full of baddies – witches and robbers and cruel, cunning enemies of various kinds, but they are always people who have invaded the forest, who do not truly belong there. Those whose livelihood is based within the woods however are always helpful, kind and useful to the hero or heroine. The woodcutter rescues Little Red Riding Hood from the wolf; the seven dwarves take tender care of Snow White; in 'The Twelve Huntsmen' (the only Grimms' story I can think of in which women use cross-dressing as a disguise), the merry band of hunters liberates the King from false love. These forest workers are not usually the principal characters in these stories, they are helpful and supportive secondary characters who enable the hero or heroine to gain their wealth and happiness, and in particular they protect the vulnerable. To me, this minor but consistent detail is one of the things that confirms my speculative belief that these stories originated in the forest (rather than in the villages or castles around the forest). People who work in villages – innkeepers, millers, arable farmers, tailors, journeymen, castle servants – may be good or bad; but you can always trust those who work in the woods. It is not unreasonable to speculate that the tellers of these stories and the audience they told them to were people who worked in the woods. The Free Miners of the Forest of Dean are perhaps the last remaining group of people who work in forests without being 'foresters' of any kind. To be a Free Miner, as we will see, you have to be born in the Forest itself, and most of them live in it still.

The second link to fairy stories is more directly related to mining itself. In a surprising number of stories the protagonists find their fortune by going underground. They do this by going down a steep, narrow hole that appears to be built, as opposed to falling down a chasm or a rabbit hole like Alice. In 'The Three Feathers', for example, the father sets his three sons a series of tasks to determine who will inherit. To eliminate any quarrelling, he blows three feathers into the air and each son has to follow one. The two older boys go off after their feathers 'to the East and to the West', laughing at their youngest brother because his feather just falls to the ground. But he notices that where his feather landed there is a trap door, which he opens. He finds a staircase; at the bottom of the staircase he encounters a magical toad who supplies him with everything he needs to win the competition.[1] Similarly in 'The Worn out Dancing Shoes', the soldier follows the princesses through a hidden trap door and down a steep flight of steps into a country where the trees are made of silver, gold and jewels. In 'Mother Holle' the heroine goes down a well to find her fortune and comes home again covered in gold, whereas the idle stepsister, trying the same scheme, returns coated in pitch. These are very clearly not caves like Aladdin's, nor the underwater worlds of the Celtic stories; they are artefacts, very like mine shafts, at the bottom of which treasure is hidden.

Psychoanalytical readings of fairy stories interpret these descents as either the facing up to one's own inner life or as symbolic renderings of sexuality. In as much as other worlds hidden in the dark underneath the sunlit ordinary one are almost universal in folklore and mythology, there is surely something in this. In many cultures these underworlds were the abode of the dead (all mythologies that have any concept of damnation locate hell under the earth, while heaven is above the bright sky). Visits to these worlds were dangerous, nearly always entailed long journeys into desolate places, and were undertaken at high risk and for important causes;[2] but they could also be richly rewarding, a task for designated heroes. But I was interested in the fairy stories' more modest little underworlds, with neatly shored-up entrances usually adjacent to domestic dwellings, and usually stumbled upon by accident. In fairy stories these under-worlds are usually kindly disposed towards the good characters. Across northern Europe coal has been mined on a small domestic scale within forests since at least 200 CE,[3] and as the stories were being recorded, it was proving to be the underpinning of the Industrial Revolution and new dreams of prosperity. The specificity of small shafts as opposed to natural caves or underwater caverns feels forest-born to me.

So I was very keen to understand more about the Free Miners. Their continuing presence here is closely related to the larger his-tory of the Forest of Dean, which is somewhat different from the history of most Royal Forests.

The Forest of Dean forms a southward-pointing wedge of wood-land between the Severn and the Tintern valleys. The whole forest is in fact in England rather than Wales, but until the Severn Bridge was built in 1966,[4] the lowest crossing over the Severn was at Gloucester, so the forest was oddly tucked away – part of neither Wales nor the West Country, somehow separate and independent, with a strong sense of identity and its own traditions. Although the Forest of Dean was stripped of its commons and wastes in the nineteenth century, it still has a social atmosphere which reminds one of older forest culture, self-contained, secret almost, and busy with the memories of indus-try (although in fact its inhabitants are now predominantly employed outside the forest). The villages here are not called Lover or Blissford as they are in the New Forest, but Cinderford and Coleford.

The Forest of Dean was one of William of Normandy's initial tranches of Royal Forest, but even in the eleventh century it was rather different from the other Royal Forests. It was not afforested primarily for hunting – although the Forest Law applied. William may well have moved fast to assert his rights over the area in order to demonstrate his authority to the Welsh princes, who were restive and far from fully subdued; in fact, among other acts of 'insubordi-nation', they took to claiming Royal Forests on their own behalf as a way of proving themselves the equals of any uppity new French king with fancy notions. But the real asset that the Forest of Dean

offered the Crown was its famously massive oak trees. Wherever
particularly large timbers were needed, the Forest of Dean supplied
them. They went, for example, both to York for the cathedral roof
and to London to build the Tower: these trees were worth the effort
of transporting them across the whole country. The Crown could
and did sell this remarkable timber, or give it as gifts, just as it did
with the deer and game from other Royal Forests.

This is not obvious now; if you go to the Forest of Dean the oaks
do not seem any more impressive than they are in other woods –
they do not seem it because they are not in fact either any larger or
more ancient than oak trees elsewhere. This is partly because more
of the oaks were grown as 'maidens' for their large trunks here than
elsewhere, so individual oaks have not lived as long as coppiced or
pollarded trees in other oak woods. But the absence of the vast trees
that attracted William and made the Forest of Dean famous is also
due to a ghastly, though all too common, error of 'management' in
the wood in the nineteenth century.

During the Napoleonic Wars a serious concern arose that not
enough timber oaks were being grown to supply the military, which
foresaw a future war requiring massive ship-building and refitting
(and also large quantities of leather for artillery harnesses and
infantry boots – oak bark was an essential ingredient in pre-indus-
trial leather tanning). Napoleon's blockade of the Channel showed
just how vulnerable an island which was not self-sufficient could be,
not only to invasion, but also to siege. The Battle of Trafalgar in
1805 proved that maintaining a strong navy was crucial to economic
survival as well as to national security; a shortage of oak (essential
for ship building – hence the Royal Navy's anthem, 'Hearts of Oak')
was a serious threat. In response, in 1809 about four-fifths of the
Forest of Dean was authorised for enclosure; swathes of the forest
were walled, banked in, drained and planted, mainly with new oaks.
This involved clearing existing forest and also planting over large
areas of ancient heath, wood pasture, greens and commons. And
indeed, since it takes about 125 years to bring oaks to full maturity,
trees planted in response to this anxiety would have been precisely

ready for harvesting in the defence of Britain in 1939 – only by then they were not needed. Ironically, this massive planting exercise was finally completed in 1855, the year the Royal Navy built its last wooden ship. This is a common problem for forestry – it is extremely hard to predict at the point of planting what sort of wood will be most wanted by the time it is ready to cut – even coniferous plantations take over half a century to mature.

This misplaced strategy was compounded in the Forest of Dean because it was planted with the 'wrong' sort of oak trees. There are two forms of oak native to Britain: pedunculate oaks and sessile oaks (*Quercus robur* and *Quercus petraea*). The most easily discerned difference between them is that the acorns of pedunculate oaks hang down on little stalks, while the acorns of sessile oaks sit directly on their twigs. But there are other differences too, and one of these is geographical. The sessile oak is most usual in the north and west, while the pedunculate oak predominates in the south-east. (This is why the sessile oak is sometimes known as 'Scottish oak'.) It is not clear why this should be the case, and there are exceptions in both directions where you can find the 'other oak' growing where you might not anticipate it. In the eighteenth and nineteenth centuries pedunculate oaks, for both commercial and aesthetic reasons, were regarded as the best kind:[5] in many places and circumstances they show a tendency to grow rather straighter and taller than the sessile variety, and have smaller, more uniform crowns.

Although the Forest of Dean was naturally a sessile oak wood, it was replanted with the supposedly superior pedunculate oaks. The thinking seems to have been that if the inferior oaks grew so well here, then the superior ones would do even better. But it transpired that the new trees did not grow as well as the old ones; in fact, they did not even achieve full normal growth and have never even approached the super-oak status that had been so confidently predicted. In essence, this huge, nearly fifty-year project in the Forest of Dean produced an inferior product which turned out to be obsolete before the work was finished and succeeded only in degrading a large piece of ancient woodland in the process. The moral of this sad tale is that if you are going to plant trees, you should plant local – plant as precisely as possible what has already shown that it likes to grow there. Trees do not grow singly, they grow in communities and have developed to match the environments in which they find themselves. Ideally you should be using seeds from the very wood you are wishing to extend or re-plant. Rackham expresses real concern that this lesson has still not been learned; the EU's attempts to preserve species has led to rules that require people to plant only from certified stock – but that may come from a different part of Europe altogether and not, genetically, be site specific.

As I have already described, the Forest of Dean has another valuable resource, perhaps less obviously associated with forests: it has mines. The Romans mined and worked iron in the Forest of Dean, and although the mining faltered when Rome withdrew the legions in 410 CE, it did not disappear; it has continued right up until today. By the late medieval period, the Forest of Dean was one of the principal sources of iron for the whole country. Originally iron working needed forests, because it required charcoal, which is difficult to transport. In the seventeenth century, mined coal became more popular, but iron working continued in the Forest of Dean because it also has coal seams.

Many people assume that it was the demand for fuel when industrial manufacturing became widespread that used up the trees and destroyed the woods, but this does not seem likely. The idea is based on three misconceptions: that timber trees were used for charcoal making; that trees, once chopped down, do not regenerate; and that people who made a large investment in the infrastructure that was needed to develop the mining were too stupid to protect their own interests. In fact, timber trees in an environment where it is difficult to cut large wood, because there are simply no good tools to do it with, cannot profitably be used for charcoal: for charcoal you are much better off using deadwood, small wood and the shoots from well-managed coppices. Trees do regenerate after being coppiced – that, indeed, is the whole point of it: regular cyclical coppicing, together with clearing the deadwood, produces a sustainable form of fuel with can be cut to precisely the dimensions required. There is clear evidence that people knew this, and that coppicing cycles were based sensitively on a balance between what size of cut wood was most needed locally (or nationally) and what was best for the trees and the agricultural stock that grazed the forests. Woods seem to have been most efficiently and sustainably managed in those areas where the woodland was closely related to local industry – whether that was providing bark for tanning, larger wood for house building, bundles for faggots, or charcoal – and the wood therefore had a crucial economic value, rather than solely being used for domestic fuel.[6]

In the Forest of Dean there was always a strong symbiotic relationship between the three industries of farming, forestry and mining. The famous vast oaks, grown for timber, were given space to achieve their desired height and girth, while between them there was plenty of wood pasture and heath land for the agricultural stock, and a well-balanced cycle of coppicing to provide both for domestic need and for the charcoal required for the iron working. Unlike many Royal Forests whose *raison d'être* was more closely related to the needs of deer, the Forest of Dean was 'uncompartmentalised' – the newly coppiced areas were not fenced off to re-grow protected from deer, nor were other animals kept out in order to allow the deer 'first pick' at the new shoots.

The early iron and coal mines in the Forest of Dean were small domestic industries and presumably ran in tandem with farming activities. But the miners of the Dean were highly skilled and fiercely independent. The area was geographically separate from the rest of the country and the Crown owned the Forest of Dean (rather than merely owning the hunting rights, as in most Royal Forests), so localism and independence could flourish, less afflicted by landlordism (bad barons, or later rich aristocrats) than in many places. The community developed strong traditions and customs, of which the most famous are the Free Miners.

The Free Miners of the Forest of Dean have a long and heroic history. Their present rights and privileges were formally laid down in 1838, in the Dean Forest (Mine) Act.[7] It was unusual in the nineteenth century for ancient traditions, especially rural ones, to win out over 'big business', but this is what happened in the Forest of Dean. The act conferred perpetual and well-defined rights:

> All male persons born or hereafter to be born and abiding
> within the said Hundred of St Briavels, of the age of twenty
> one years and upwards, who shall have worked a year and a day
> in a coal or iron mine within the said Hundred of St Briavels,
> shall be deemed and taken to be Free Miners.[8]

A 'hundred' is an old administrative district, smaller than a county and larger than a parish. Tradition claims the name refers to an area expected to produce 100 men at arms for the Crown's wars. About St Briavel barely anything at all is known – legend pleasingly relates that he was a forest hermit, but suggests no dates for his life, nor is there any record of him before 1130.

A Free Miner is one with the right to mine a 'gale' – a specific area of the forest – provided it is not being worked by another Free Miner. The Act in fact formalised a very ancient tradition. Although the oldest record of the miners' laws and customs dates from 1610, there is good evidence that they already had exclusive mineral rights in 1244. The 1610 document contains 41 regulations for the 'winning of Myne [iron ore] and Sea Cole [coal]'.[9] The document lays down clear principles and laws on details like rights of access and the method for defining a claim. The duties of the Gaveller (the King's representative) included the collection of royalties in cash or kind, whilst the court 'that is called Myne Lawe' allowed the Miners to be largely self-governing.

During the medieval period these privileges were not unique to the Dean miners. Edward I, who granted them a Royal Charter, granted similar privileges to other mining districts – for example, in Derbyshire. Legend claims that Dean's Royal Charter was given as a reward for the services the Dean miners rendered the King in the recapture of Berwick-upon-Tweed from the Scots in 1296. Because of their experience in mining, they provided the army with a range of skills: undermining fortifications, creating earthworks and building timber structures. They were also called upon to serve in France, at the battles of Crécy (1346), Poitiers (1356) and Agincourt (1415). In the seventeenth century a dozen of them were delegated to sail with Frobisher on his abortive search for the Northwest Passage. They were the Crown's men by feudal law, and were renowned for their mining skills, hardy nature, gritty determination and ferocity in battle.

The Free Miners of the Forest of Dean have clung on to these rights tenaciously; seeing off serious threats from large-scale mine-owners from South Wales in the nineteenth century and winning an exemption for themselves from the Coal Industry Nationalisation Act in 1946. Once registered as a Free Miner by an official rather splendidly named the Deputy Gaveller, a man may to this day claim up to three unworked gales from the Crown; he becomes the owner of the underground area and can work the minerals there. These mines have always been small. Until the 1838 act, the Crown had the right to put its own miner in to work with the Free Miners in each mine and share the profits; this individual was traditionally know as 'the fifth man', strongly indicating that these were basically little family enterprises.

There are around 150 Free Miners alive today. In 2010, Ella Mormon successfully used the sex discrimination legislation to win the right to be registered as the first woman Free Miner in history. But the whole tradition is endangered. There are only a handful of collieries still operating, plus one iron mine in the Clearwell Caves in the south of the forest, an ochre[10] mine and five small stone quarries. They are economically marginal – like farmers, but without the subsidies. There are other problems too – the insurance costs for employing and training new miners are astronomically high. In safety terms they probably should be, but in terms of preserving this ancient trade, such costs are unfortunate because they make it difficult to qualify – to work the necessary year-and-a-day underground within the Hundred. Recently there ceased to be any maternity provision within the Hunded of St Briavel; this means that, short of the recession leading the government to encourage home births on an unprecedented scale, in the future no one at all will be born within the traditional boundaries that confer the Free Mining rights.

But despite everything, the Free Miners of Dean are still at work. So I went to the Hopewell Mine in the Forest of Dean to meet Robin Morgan, now in his 70s, who has been a Free Miner all his life, working his family's traditional gale. We met for tea in Morgan's warm little hut at the Hopewell pithead between Cinderford and Coleford, in the heart of the Forest. Some time ago, Robin Morgan thought he would try some 'diversification', and opened Hopewell as a museum and created safe access into part of the old mine. This failed to make enough money, and recently he has decided to cut a new shaft down to the coal seam. He was busy with this task, and before long he handed me over to John Daniels, a friend and fellow miner, to talk to me and show me round. He left us and descended to work through a nearby and alarmingly small entry-hole, very like the one the lad in 'The Three Feathers' must have used. Robin Morgan is unusual in that he mines alone. More commonly, miners work with at least one colleague, for safety and company. It seemed clear that he worked alone because he liked to work alone ... He was welcoming, open, but supremely detached, contained within his tough body and his tiny mine. It was easy enough to imagine him down there on his own in the dark doing what his ancestors have done for centuries.

John Daniels is younger than Morgan and is one of the newer Free Miners, coming into the trade after serving in the Army. He does not mine at Hopewell, but with a partner in a different gale. He was deeply imbued with history. He could see approaching threats – he is one of the most recently registered Free Miners, and it was unclear who might come next, although he spoke of two brothers, younger men, who had opened a gale 'deep inside the forest' which they were working now. But he thought that, despite the rigours and the relative low pay, these tiny mines would always have an appeal for some people: the independence, the craft, and what he kept calling the 'real' nature of the work – the physical rather than academic skills. He believes that this sort of self-employment will have a growing attraction in an over-bureaucratised world.

'But they won't be traditional Free Miners,' I suggested.

'No,' he agreed sturdily; they would not have the right to mine, but they could still apply. 'We mine of right,' he kept insisting, but it could be like citizenship – some people had a *right* to it, but even if you did not qualify automatically, it could still be granted to you if you applied. It was a good life, he declared, but also an important one, historic and meaningful.

Then we went into the mine. We picked up hard hats with head torches and plunged into the side of the hill through a gate big enough for the coal trucks to come up. We walked down a steep-sloping but now cemented pathway. In a very real sense we went down from one forest into another. But the underworld was dark, and it was easy to understand the extraordinary physical effort that had gone into hewing it out. The old mine at Hopewell is elegantly if simply engineered; there is an economy of labour in its design. The entrance passage descends straight into the hillside, but since the coal must be transported up it in carts, pulled either manually or by ponies, the ground is smoothed and the slope very regular. At the end of the tunnel the ground levels off into a hallway, and to either side, above the floor level, there are little narrow shelves, one-miner galleries, where the coal is manually hacked out from the seam and loaded directly onto the truck standing below it. Beyond this centre point, a complex pattern of tunnels and corridors crisscross one another, like a great tree laid horizontal: the main entrance passage forms the trunk, and then larger tunnels branch off that, and ever-smaller drainage runs, galleries and crawl holes form the twigs. The complex of buildings and machinery around the entrance at the surface completes the image, looking like the vertical standing roots of a windblown tree.

Some of these tunnels link Hopewell to the neighbouring Phoenix Mine; some are fully standing height and well lined with wrought timbers; others are more basic, tight-fitted and crudely finished. These allow the miners access to the seam or drain away water in fast, cold open channels. Just as there are on the great trees outside, there are occasional mosses, lichens and ferns clinging to the walls. Daniels told me there were fish in the streams too, which have evolved to live in the dark. Because underground, it was perfectly dark; the lamps on our hats shone on rough walls and created strange shadows from the irregularities of the rock face; outside the narrow beam of brightness there was the mystery of the not-seen, a sense of other passageways, of a whole maze of an invisible world beneath the sunny forest.

Because it had been opened to the public, Hopewell has been tidied up to some extent – or at least the parts of it I visited had: there are handrails, and the water channels are clearly marked; but it still felt somehow perilous, like where Frodo the Hobbit met Gollum under the mountain, in the Goblin mines. I would not like to be in there alone.

We walked for a timeless while, and never on the same path twice. Daniels told me stories of miners and the forest that were themselves somehow timeless: of accidents and heroism, and of the long-ago fights against the giant mining companies from South Wales that wanted to exploit the coal seams more commercially, and before that of the resistance to the enclosures in the forest above, to quell which the Army had been called out in 1831. He obviously loved the mine and his life; he wanted me to know about it, generously directing me to further sources of knowledge – I should go to Clearwell, where they still mine for iron; I should talk to various other people, whose names he gave me, who knew more of the old stories, both history and legend.

Eventually, far in front of us along the tunnel, there was an almost shocking glimmer of green and gold light. It grew steadily, and several hundred yards down the hill from where we started we came to a metal gridded gate and emerged into woodland that looked even more golden and bright in the sunshine than it had before we set out.

Both Daniels and Morgan reminded me of the hill farmers up on the moor where I live, clinging to an economically marginal way of life, because they experience physically its dignity and tradition. It is their heritage and their right, and they, perhaps unconsciously, create a deep and ancient freedom. They share real and traditional skills, a knowledge of hand and body which is not much valued in contemporary Britain; they all despise the 'scribes' (the surveyors, architects, planning officials and inspectors – possibly because they feel despised by them), the book learning, and the regulations that shackle them; and all of them see self-employment as the highest ambition, preferring to trust to a risky mixture of physical skill, low cunning, self-interest and good luck than to more secure but servile labour in someone else's interest.

It is easy to romanticise the whole breed. But I believe they are both the creators and the heroes of the fairy stories. John Daniels, Free Miner of the Forest of Dean, from the Hundred of St Briavel, represented this whole history. And I found myself thinking that if I were Snow White in flight and fear, I would like to come upon a group of Free Miners, with ancient skills, a personal sense of freedom and the dignity of labour, and a contemptuous dislike of courts (kings or 'Health and Safety') and bureaucracy.

Throughout northern Europe there is a deep connection between mining and dwarves. In fact, it is almost possible to say that what defines a dwarf is that he is a miner. Not every small character in story or legend is a dwarf – 'Thumblings' are tiny, but they are human beings and the children of human beings; goblins, gnomes and small devils, who also frequent the fairy stories, are not dwarves, even when they look like them; Rumplestiltskin is described as a 'little man' or 'manikin', never as a dwarf. Like the Free Miners, dwarves are 'renowned for their mining skills, hardy nature, gritty determination and ferocity in battle'. They are hard working, loyal and frequently rather grumpy – they live in the forest and they mine for treasure. Tolkein took all these traditional qualities for the dwarves in Middle Earth, and so did BB in *The Forest of Boland Light Railway*. The most famous dwarves of all are the seven in 'Little Snow White', who 'dug and delved in the mountains for ore', although they lived in the forest.

In the more modern (and perhaps more middle-class) versions of the classic fairy stories that we tend to know now, the respect for work – for skilled labour and honest endeavour – has rather diminished. But in the Grimms' collection it is a consistent theme. The forests, villages and towns of the Grimms' tales are full of young men seeking a 'good trade' or a 'good position.' This is usually why they set out 'to seek their fortune' – magic helps, but actually hard work is the most common key to success. Skilled hard work gains you your fortune. If you go out and seek an apprenticeship, your master may luckily turn out to be a magical master and will give you a magical reward – but it is a reward for hard work and skill.

I described 'The Magic Table, the Golden Donkey and the Club in the Sack' in the previous chapter, but it is only one of many similar stories. In 'The Two Brothers' the small boys, by accident, acquire a magical ability to produce two gold coins every morning; terrified by this, their father abandons them in the forest, but – despite the fact that they are not poor – they apprentice themselves to a huntsman, who, being a forest worker, is of course kind, thoughtful and honest. Eventually, through their hunting skills and forest lore rather than their gold, one of them marries a princess and becomes King.[11] In 'The Thief and His Master', a father apprentices his son to a robber – with surprisingly favourable results. In 'The Poor Miller's Apprentice and the Cat', the 'simpleton' hero wins a mill, a beautiful horse and a rich bride through faithful seven-year service to a cat. Even in the deliberately funny tale 'The Boy Who Went Forth to Learn What Fear Was', the initial impetus to the youth's prosperous adventures was his father's determination that he should learn a decent trade because he was so stupid.

The importance of work applied to girls as much as to boys. In 'Mother Holle', for example, as I related earlier, the heroine is forced down a well-shaft by her cruel stepmother. She arrives in another world, and eventually returns, coated in gold dust. But the reason for her success was that she took service with an old woman, and 'attended to everything to the satisfaction of her mistress and always shook her bed so vigorously that the feathers flew about like snow-flakes. So she had a pleasant life; never an angry word and to eat she had boiled or roast meat every day.' So when she goes home, she has earned her reward. Her stepsister, on the other hand, is idle; she accepts the old woman's offer, but 'on the second day she began to be lazy and on the third still more so, and then she wouldn't get up in the morning at all. Neither did she make Mother Holle's bed as she ought.' So the shower of pitch, 'which clung fast to her and could not be got off as long as she lived', was a fitting payment for her failure.

A significant number of the women in the fairy stories are self-employed, independent and skilled. They often have a relationship – positive or negative – with spinning. Although most women could and did spin domestically, if she became good at it, it was one of the few ways a woman could become financially self-sufficient. (Midwifery was an alternative career.) At her trial in 1431, Joan of Arc was immediately inflamed by the suggestion that she worked as a shepherdess: on the contrary, she snapped, she was a highly skilled spinster.[12]

To be honest, there are a few stories in which the heroine – and it is always a heroine – succeeds by getting out of work and into leisure. However, these stories are always triggered by the unreasonable demands of more powerful individuals, and they are nearly always humorous. 'The Three Spinners' is a nice example: an 'idle' girl is trapped by her mother's stupidity and the greed of the Queen into having to spin a vast quantity – 'three whole rooms full' – of flax, even though 'she could not have spun the flax, not if she had lived till she was three hundred years old and had sat at it every day from morning to night'. She is in despair when three strange old ladies come to her aid. They are particularly ugly: 'the first of them had a broad flat foot, the second had such a great underlip it hung down over her chin and the third had a broad thumb'. The deal is – and there is always a deal – that they will spin the flax for her and in exchange she must invite them to her wedding, introduce them as her aunts and invite them to sit on the top table. All goes well. The Queen is so delighted with the young woman's diligent labour she announces: 'You shall have my eldest son for a husband even though you are poor. I care not for that; your untiring industry is dowry enough.' The wedding is arranged; the girl keeps her promise and the old women arrive, 'strangely apparelled'; her fiancé is startled that his bride should have such 'odious friends', and questions them about how they came by their peculiar features. They reply, by turns, 'By treading,' 'By licking' and 'By twisting the thread' (the three core actions of spinning with a wheel). On hearing this, 'the King's son was alarmed and said, "Neither now nor ever shall my beautiful bride touch a spinning wheel." And thus she got rid of the hateful flax-spinning.' This is one of the sillier, shorter and more pointless of the *Märchen*, and it reads to me like a women's joke story, rather than a profound moral lesson.

Work is always good. When the dwarves first saw Snow White asleep in the cottage, they responded with a generous delight. '"Oh heavens! Oh Heavens," cried they, "what a lovely child!" and they were so glad that they did not wake her up but let her sleep on.' However, the next morning, they make their position very clear: 'If you will take care of our house, cook, make the beds, wash, sew and knit, and if you will keep everything neat and clean, you can stay with us and you will want for nothing.' Skilled work learned and performed diligently is a source of dignity and well-being in fairy stories; the dwarves epitomise that dogged commitment, particularly as they are self-employed rather than waged.

In *Uses of Enchantment* Bettelheim suggests that, in these stories, becoming a king or queen is not about political power or even power over others, it is about independence, freedom to manage one's own life and not be under the control of someone else. Because he sees all fairy stories as being directed at children by adults, he therefore sees this standard resolution to the stories as a metaphor for becoming a grown-up. I agree with his initial observation – the kings in the stories never seem to perform any monarchical or demanding duties – but I think he has missed the point: the idea is that profitable self-employment is the most desirable state, and that skilled hard work is what will gain it for you.

After I parted company with John Daniels, I left the car and walked through the woods, which grow close around the mine. I knew I was walking over the dark tunnels in the autumn sunshine. Here the trees were close together and had a dense green canopy, through which I could see very little of the sky. The undergrowth was thick too; within less than a hundred yards I could longer see the road or the mine head. It was nearly as quiet as it had been underground. I became convinced that there was a symbiotic relationship between this sort of mining and the forest that enfolds it. Free Mining rights died out on the open peaks of Derbyshire and elsewhere. Perhaps the mines need the forest, and without the trees to hide the mines and to protect the privacy and independence of the Free Miners, such traditions cannot survive. Deep in the forest you can escape the gaze and control of the 'management' and the necessary contemporary rules and regulations; going underground, you can be free to make your own life through courage and cunning. Even when the forest above you is reordered, replanted and tidied up in ways which turn out to be contrary to, and not as successful as, the old free forest where the trees grew huge and magnificent, you still maintain your right to carve out your own life by skill and hard work. Free Miners mirror the heroes of fairy stories. And both are imperilled by modernity.

The Seven Dwarves

Once upon a time there were seven dwarves.

One. Two. Three. Four. Five. Six. Seven.

Once upon a time there were seven dwarves. They lived together in a small house a long way from anywhere, high in the mountains. Montane forests are dwarf forests; the trees here grow short and gnarled – scrubby juniper, wind-warped birches and skinny quivering aspen. As the track climbed upwards out of the sweet woodlands below, the rocks broke through the surface, grey and rough faced, the trees became more widely spaced and the grass and moss and lichen between them was tussocked and boggy. The winters were long and dark here, and the hare put on white coats to camouflage themselves from eagles in the snow. It was harsh craggy forest, with its own fierce beauty and here the dwarves had built their little cottage, as snug as they could make it and with long views over the world from the front door.

But as much as the forest where they lived was dark and demanding, the forest where they worked was far more so. For these dwarves, as dwarves tend to be, were miners, and each day they put on their iron-toed boots, hefted their picks and shovels, opened one of the round trap doors they had made in the mountainside, and went down and down into the underground forest where their treasure was buried.

Because, once upon a time, there were other forests. They were very different forests from the ones we know now. There were trees, but not the trees we know – there were *Equisetales*, *Sphenophyllales*, *Lycopodiales*, *Lepidodendrales*, *Filicales*, *Medullosales* and *Cordaitales*. There were plants, but not the plants we know – no flowers, no seeds, no lignin, no osmosis, strange fleshy growths. And, so long ago that the continents were still travelling and meeting and dancing with each other and tossing up mountain ranges in their dangerous embrace, these older forests fell in great swathes into new shallow oceans, and the warm water and the soft ooze covered them so they could not oxidise and they turned into black coal seams.

Dwarves mine for jewels: rubies, opals, sapphires, emeralds, amethysts, garnets and diamonds.

Dwarves mine for minerals: iron, tin, feldspar, lead, silver, copper and gold.

But what dwarves love best is coal.

Mining for coal is dangerous, dirty work. But in the underground forests, coal teaches the dwarves precious lessons: responsibility, attentiveness, loyalty, solidarity, honesty, strength and freedom.

And so, in the power of these hard-earned virtues, the seven dwarves lived happily enough in their little house a long way from anywhere, high in the mountains.

One. Two. Three. Four. Five. Six. Seven.

And one summer evening, with the sun westering in a ruby red sky, the dwarves stomped home to their neat little house after a long day's work – tired, hungry, and eager for beer and music. Almost before they were inside they could sense something misplaced, disrupted: a smear of mud on the mat; a couple of dry leaves adrift on the floor; the tidy stools misaligned; the spoons not perfectly straight; the rims of glasses smeared; a streak of blood on the cloth; the counterpanes rumpled. Not quite enough to call for comment or defence, but enough to make them wary, to make them glance around the house and inspect each orderly familiar detail. And so, before long, in the farthest corner of the farthest truckle bed, pressed for safety right against the wall, her face turned away from door or window, they found a little girl asleep.

There is something innocent and vulnerable about anyone watched while asleep. It induces a mood of tenderness even in the toughest, roughest characters. (It probably helped that this little

girl was not the clichéd golden-haired pink child of too many
romances and fairytales: her skin was as white as snow; her lips as
red as fire; her hair as black as coal.) So they tiptoed away, in as
much as dwarves can tiptoe, and ate their supper quietly and took
their beers out into the sunny evening to drink, and they did not
sing at all lest they should wake her.

She came to them as flowers came to those other forests and
changed them for ever.

The next morning, after she was washed and tidied, she told
them that she had run through the forest all day. 'Go,' the huntsman had said, 'just go.' Young as she was, she knew that he would
rather the wild beasts kill her than do it himself. Like so many
well-meaning but wage-slaved men, he was kind but not brave.
That frightened her, as it should indeed, and she fled. Forests are
not gentle places, never have been nor ever will. She ran blindly
and in fear. By the time she found their little house she had run
through thick forest for hours – her face was cut by brambles,
stung by nettles; her hands and arms were raked by dead wood and
grasses and briar; her face was bitten and stung and swollen-eyed
and covered in mud and blood. So they did not recognise her
beauty that first night, nor for a long time afterwards.

And there was the panic fear, the terror of the wild wood to
soothe. Fear cramps up children's faces, makes them look peaky
and often sly, it narrows their eyes, thins their lips and sours their
temper. Forest and mine are the same like this, so the dwarves
knew what to do. They bade her welcome, kept the house particularly tidy and were playful with her. They took her out into the
green forest to find strawberries and nuts and mushrooms. They
took her to small bubbling streams and splashed in waterfalls and
they taught her the prettier names of the flowers: Lords-and-ladies,
Golden Rod, Herb Robert, Yellow Archangel, Solomon's Seal,
Woodruff and Goldilocks Buttercup.

"Look," they would say.

"Take a little stick and dig and you can eat the pignuts that grow
under this lacy flower."

"Look. Suck the base of this tubular petal and see where the bees get their honey."

"Look. You can be like a squirrel and eat these hazelnuts."

"Look. With your pretty nails you can split these stalks and make a daisy chain."

"Look. Now this fern is just a monk, with his bald knobbly head; soon he is a bishop with a beautiful crosier; and at last he is an angel, see him spread his feathered wings."

"Look. You can plait these reeds and make sandals, cool for hot little toes."

"Look. A ladybird has seven spots. Perhaps you are a ladybird and we are the spots."

The ancient woodlands are lovely and generous if you go quietly. She was a child, and children heal easily from that pain and fear. Her scratches and bites and bruises all healed, and so did her fear of the forest. But still she did not grow lovely. Far away down through the forest in the castle her stepmother could ask the mirror, daily if she chose to, and the mirror, which must always tell the truth, would say truthfully, "You. You. You oh queen. You are the fairest of all. You."

The dwarves could see she was *pretty*. But if you spend the hours of bright daylight in the dark you learn that pretty is not enough. Coal is not pretty. Coal is beautiful. And her hair was as black as coal. They wanted her to be beautiful.

So, being wise, the dwarves put her to work. The best medicine for fear is rigorous discipline applied with great affection – hard, slogging, difficult, skilled labour, ideally in the service of others. Especially if the child is a princess and has been raised idle.

They gave her a broom and made her sweep, though she whined about it.

They gave her a brush and made her scrub, though she grumbled about it.

They gave her a knife and made her chop, though she moaned about it.

They gave her hard soap and made her wash, though she pouted about it.

They gave her a trowel and made her weed, though she sulked about it.

They gave her a pot and made her cook, though she bitched about it.

They gave her coal and made her keep the fire – raking and riddling in the morning; tending through the day; damping down at night, though she sobbed about it.

Being made to work makes a child angry, and anger breeds courage and hope. At first she was pathetic, useless and desperate to please; then she was both disagreeable and self-pitying, moaning and lamenting and pettish; then she was wonderfully, blazingly furious; and then, all of a sudden, she was brave and whole and lovely. Beautiful. The fairest of all.

And in changing her, the dwarves changed too. Of course, as they were miners, they were used to dealing with the outside world. Once a year they had always harnessed their seven sturdy pit ponies to their seven wagons and taken their coal to the city to sell, and come home with beer, tobacco, sugar, milled flour and shiny new pans and pewter tankards and crisp linen sheets when required. But now they needed toys and coloured crayons and clothes for her to wear and they had to learn how to find them for her, so they had to talk with other people. They wanted her to have good manners so they had to become less surly. They wanted her to be happy and they wanted her to be admired so they took to going to fairs and markets and even, occasionally, parties. And, illuminated by their own kindness and her loveliness, they discovered that people could be kind and helpful and that not all the world's jokes were cruel.

So that, for a while, they were all very happy. Eight not seven.

Seven is magical, strange; a prime number; indivisible and unbreakable; lucky and dangerous.

Eight is an orderly, elegant number, a Fibonacci number – the poised spiral of the snail's shell. Eight is still the same when it is turned upside down. Eight is the visible celestial spheres – the sun and moon and planets all dancing together.

One. Two. Three. Four. Five. Six. Seven. Eight. It has a different rhythm. Eight is a resolved octave, a perfect scale; they all sang together in the green summer evenings and they were very joyful.

The trouble was they cured her fear too well. She became too bold to be careful. The dwarves heard the village gossip now and they knew that, down in the valley where the cows were fat and the pigs glutted on beech mast, the wicked stepmother was still looking in the mirror, which must always tell the truth, and asking who was the fairest of all, and learning that the child lived. They warned her and she laughed at them. She was growing more beautiful every day and more high-hearted.

Perhaps the dwarves should have taken her down the mine with them for her to learn to respect the dark and feel the sturdy power of caution and self-protection.

And perhaps, as she became a woman, she needed other women and the dwarves should have known it. Another woman to pull her stay-laces tight and admire her tiny waist; a woman to braid her hair and pin it up with fine-toothed combs; a woman to share sweet things with her like women do. There are things that even dwarves cannot teach a growing child.

Perhaps – just perhaps – she recognised her stepmother and was rash enough to want to try again, to seek out that lost love, to return to childhood and do it better. Stupid; stupid in her beauty and her courage and her greed for life.

Envy looks like a little emotion – petty and insignificant – but it is as deadly as the fungi carried by the elm bark beetle. It suffocates like stay-laces pulled too tight; it penetrates like the tines of fine-toothed combs; it poisons like an apple from the tree of knowledge. In the end the bitch-witch killed her. She died of the Queen's envy and her own stupidity.

The dwarves found that they had changed, that love had changed them. Even though her hair was as black as coal they could not bear to take her back underground, back into the dark, into the other forest, and bury her there. They kept her in the light, in a glass coffin, where the sun could kiss her though they could not. They loyally treasured her in death as they had freely treasured her in life.

Until one day a prince came by and revived her as the dwarves had failed to do. And they were generous enough and humble enough to be delighted.

They were invited to the wedding. And the grateful prince gave them the privilege of hot justice.

So they brought up coal and iron from the mines and lit a fire, a hot furnace, hotter, hotter, until it smelted the dark ore and released the metal. They forged it up all through the night before the wedding and hammered out the iron shoes. The wicked step-mother needed punishing so they made the shoes red hot.

We do not tell this part of the story any more; we say it is too cruel and will break children's soft hearts. But the dwarves know their tough little hearts yearn for justice. Dwarves know about heavy feet; they stomp and stamp in the dark dance of retribution, which we are all too scared to use. The dwarves made that wicked woman put on the red hot iron shoes; and then they made her dance until she was dead.

They did not try again. They will not try again. The dwarves have all gone back underground, delving down deep into their own more ancient forests, different forests without flowers, without blossom or fruit.

One. Two. Three. Four. Five. Six. Seven.

She was their gold. Their falcon. Their globeflower. Their birch tree. Their dappled trout. Their diamond. Their fallow doe.

Their sweet hot coal.

8

October

Ballochbuie and the Forest of Mar

Driving to Braemar from the south is a bit like entering into a fairy story. In so many of the tales the characters set out on long journeys, following the road up and across mountain and moor until they finally descend through thick forest and arrive in a village with a castle or palace where their fortune and future is to be found. North of Edinburgh, the A9 runs all the way to Inverness and finally to Thurso on the north coast. At Perth the A93 turns east off this great trunk road and, like a branch, pushes its own way northwards, out of Perthshire, where the deciduous trees are famously large and fine, past Blairgowrie and Bridge of Cally, where the road is gated to stop idiots getting stuck in drifting snow, up the desolate and lovely Glen of Shee, and out onto the high moors and craggy mountains. Somewhere north of nowhere the road crosses into the vast Cairngorms National Park, a huge chunk of granite mountain, the wildest place in Britain, home to five of the six highest hills in the country, and eventually it runs down again through lowering forests, into Braemar on Royal Deeside. The Cairngorms are cut by two big rivers, the Dee and the Tay, each with its own deep valley, collecting water from innumerable tributaries, and flowing out into the North Sea. Braemar is in the more southerly of the two, the Dee, and here Queen

Victoria supplied the fairy-tale palace when in 1856 she built Balmoral, her Scottish fantasy home where she could play romantically at being a Jacobite and, later, pursue her odd relationship with John Brown, her forester.[1] She and Prince Albert particularly loved the ancient woods of Deeside. Perhaps they reminded him of home – Scots pine (*Pinus sylvestris*) is common throughout Germany, but in Britain it is indigenous only in specific parts of the Scottish Highlands.[2] Deeside represents a specifically romantic image of Scotland, with the huge wildness of the hills dropping steeply down to the forested valleys, a lot of surface rock, fast rivers, waterfalls, ruined castles, and heather and red deer which, in cold weather, can come down to the roadsides in large herds. And here there are also some of the remaining fragments of the great Caledonian Forest.

'Caledonian forest' is now a technical term for a particular type of rural habitat – high woodland dominated by Scots pine, accompanied by birch, rowan, juniper and heather; home to pine martens, capercailzie, black grouse and other species – of both flora and fauna – not found elsewhere in Britain. Within the historical era it has been home to wolves and wildcats.

But the Great Caledonian Forest, which is commonly supposed to have spread over millions of acres of Scotland, is also a forest of myth and magic. It existed in story, in the imagination, and in the pages of medieval romance: here Merlin wanders in his madness, lamenting the folly and the violence and corruption of 'civilisation'; here there are monsters and dragons and unnamed, unimaginable perils awaiting the brave of heart; here hermits dwell, using the forest as their predecessors had used the deserts further south;[3] here wolves prowl through the long dark winters 'seeking whom they may devour'.[4] Part of the mythology is that this great swathe of uninhabited forest ever existed at all: the 'millions of acres' are now contested – much of the Highlands, as we discovered in the twentieth century, is too far north, too peaty and cannot even usefully support the 'easy' conifers after draining, peat clearance and planting. After the ice withdrew and the blanket peat moved in, a very great deal of the Scottish Highlands could not (and therefore did not) sustain woodland. Rackham argues that there is now *more* native pinewood in Scotland than there was three hundred years ago.

The myth of the immense forests of Scotland has been given additional imaginative leverage by a nationalist sensibility that claims that the trees – those that weren't burned in Viking raids, or cleared to extirpate wolves and brigands – were 'stolen' (like 'our' oil) by English entrepreneurs working under the protection of cash-strapped absentee landlords after the defeat of Bonnie Prince Charlie. This pervasive belief is based on the unfounded theory that fire and logging destroy such woods and they cannot regenerate. In fact, in every location where there is evidence of eighteenth- and nineteenth-century commercial logging, there is still pine forest in good heart.

There are somewhat under a hundred patches, some of them very small, of genuine ancient Caledonian forest, and they are very distinct from more southerly ancient woodland, or from the oak forests on the west coast of Scotland. Scots pines have some characteristics not shared by deciduous trees. You cannot coppice or pollard them; they are killed by being cut and do not regenerate on their old roots; they re-grow as new individual trees from seed and tend not to do this under their own canopy, but to the sides of existing stands. This means that pine woods have a strange habit of wandering – instead of the neat boundaries between trees and moor or field, the pine woods crawl across the hill sides, changing the shape of the land. Over longer periods of time this adds to their atmosphere of mystery, and incidentally puts a rather spooky twist on the haunting prophecy that 'Macbeth shall never vanquish'd be until great Birnam Wood to high Dunsinane hill shall come against him'[5] (although presumably not an irony that Shakespeare can have appreciated). Scots pine is also fire adapted, and, on century-long cycles, flourishes best if it is burned out. Nonetheless, these pines are individually very long lived and can become as warped, gnarled and complex as their deciduous relatives – and they do it without the assistance of pollarding or any other management system. Even the straight, tall, middle-aged trees are strange looking: they have heavily scaled grey trunks, like dragons' hides, while their upper branches are smoother, more delicate and pinky-orange. They carry their round-topped umbrellas of foliage very high, and put out few low branches, so any long view in these woods is cut by hard grey vertical lines, almost like giant telephone poles, creating an odd, rather sinister atmosphere. Another specific effect of Scots pine forest is brought about by pine's ability to root on apparently vertical rock faces, or in tiny clefts well up the hillsides, which are here steep enough to be cliffs. At Mar Lodge, a National Trust for Scotland property slightly to the West of Braemar, they say a nineteenth-century earl shot pine cones from cannon up onto his vertical cliff faces to seed the clinging, impossible trees:[6] they hover above the valleys, brooding, inaccessible and sublime, simultaneously truly wild and highly improbable.

Caledonian forest is also woodland at its most frightening and forbidding. The terror of the wild feels closer here. The glens that hold these woods tend to be exceptionally lovely in a romantic style, with green fields or lochs, smooth at the bottom, and wild open moor and hill above; but the woods themselves can feel grim by contrast, separating the two spaces sternly. In such woods it is never properly silent; old pine trees creak and moan even in quite gentle winds, and there are always rushing streams just out of sight, and a sense of chill in the air. With half an ear I catch myself listening for the wolf pack; for the brigands and the desperate clans cleared from their homes two hundred years ago; and for malevolent wood spirits who may punish the unwary visitor savagely. Indeed, as it is October, I do hear as evening falls the strange hoarse bellowing of the red deer rut – a sound as weird and unlikely as any imaginary ghost howling its grief.[7]

For me, these forests expose a deep unease, a chthonic fear; Caledonian forests are what Freud called *heimlich unheimlich* – they are uncanny. Inside most of us post-enlightenment and would-be rational adults there is a child who is terrified by the wild wood. It was, as I described in Chapter 1, in a different piece of Caledonian forest, Glen Affric, that I first recognised that forests gave me the same sets of feelings and emotions that I get from fairy stories. One reason I wanted to come to Braemar was to try and understand this strange connection better.

The English language has a large number of words for 'fear' – a quick skim through Roget's online thesaurus offers me this list of fifty nouns (I am not persuaded it is complete; it certainly omits dialect and many slang terms):

Fear: alarm, apprehension, abhorrence, agitation, angst, anxiety, aversion, awe, chickenheartedness, concern, consternation, cowardice, creeps, despair, discomposure, diffidence, dismay, disquietude, distress, doubt, dread, faintheartedness, foreboding, fright, funk, horror, jitters, misgiving, nightmare, panic, peril, perturbation, phobia, presentiment, qualm, quivering, reverence, revulsion, scare, suspicion, terror, timidity, trembling, tremor, trepidation, unease, uneasiness, worry.

There is also a further selection of adjectives, of which I am only including those without an obvious direct connection to one of these nouns:

aghast, diffident, dire, eerie, fey, fell, ghastly, haunted, nervous, spooky, shaky, uncanny, weird.

None of these words mean precisely the same thing as any of the others. I wanted to explore for myself more precisely which sort of fear it is that I experience in the forests and in the stories.

There is the straightforward physical fear of hurt or harm – the fear you feel if the tide is coming in and you cannot find the path up the cliff; if you are walking on a narrow path at the top of a cliff; if a man with a gun or dog with bared teeth is rushing at you; or if you are in a car with an alarmingly bad driver who wants to go too fast: the basic instinctual fear of actual danger that brings on the flight-or-fight surge of adrenalin and to which courage is the natural antidote, the most useful response. This is fear, or peril, or, in its milder form, alarm. Quite closely related to this is the anxiety, anticipation, or trepidation – a sort preview of the gut fear that I can experience in advance of a potentially dangerous and frightening event. These are not what I experience in forests and certainly not what I experience curled up by the fire reading fairy stories.

A more promising contender for forest fear is 'panic', because the name itself originates in the woods. Classical Greek mythology defined panic as a specific kind of terror induced by Pan, the God of wild places and especially of woods and forests. His cries could make the strongest nerves crack and drive people to madness. Panic is somewhat different from other fears – it induces extreme irrationality, rather than triggering the more normal, well-adapted fight-or-flight reaction; it is 'infectious' and spreads quickly and very dangerously through groups of people. It seldom has a clear cause – it is not fear of something alarming or threatening, it is primal terror. I have once experienced panic as an adult, although not in a wood, and it is a distressing and disagreeable sensation, partly because of the complete collapse of rationality and the intensity of its physical force, but again there is little panic of a recognisable kind in the fairy stories. The characters are seldom attacked by this sort of fear. Perhaps the nearest there is to a description of such a possessing, physical terror is of Snow White's flight through the forest after the huntsman agrees not to kill her as he has been instructed to do by her stepmother:

> The poor child was all alone in the huge forest. When she
> looked at all the leaves on the trees, she was petrified and did
> not know what to do. The she began to run, and she ran over
> sharp stones and through thorn bushes. Wild beasts darted by
> her at times, but they did not harm her. She ran as long as her
> legs would carry her.

She has just escaped from a hideously frightening circumstance – caused not by the wild, but by her own family, and she is very young – but it is helpful to notice that this is unusual. By way of contrast and much more typically, there is no indication at all of panic when Hansel and Gretel become lost, although they are frightened:

> They walked the entire night and all the next day, from
> morning till night, but they did not get out of the forest.

They are lost and scared, but there is no panic.

Characters constantly run into grave danger in the forests – they are lost, homeless, hungry, and above all threatened by dangerous human beings – robbers, witches and, most often, the evil machinations of their own families. But they do not tend to respond with this panic fear, leading to senseless flight. In fact, in the classic fairytales, the forests themselves are not presented as particularly scary.

In the delightful story 'The Boy Who Went Forth To Learn What Fear Was', there is a stupid son who is unable to understand what people who are frightened are talking about. He thinks to himself, 'They're always saying "It gives me the creeps!" But it doesn't give *me* the creeps. It's probably some kind of trick that I don't understand.' He is sent out into the world, and tells everyone he meets that he wants to learn to be frightened and will pay anyone who can teach him. Various people therefore send him off to very scary places – he spends a night at the foot of a gibbet with seven dead criminals hanging on it, and eventually visits a haunted castle full of demons and ghosts of various truly horrible kinds. His literal interpretation of events – which leads him to outwit gruesome ghost cats and dogs, have wrestling matches with dead men and play bowls against the Devil using skulls – means that he never runs away, and always defeats these opponents who all fail to scare him in the least: he deals with them with a cheerful insouciance and punishes them in a forthright manner. This behaviour finally wins him both a fortune and a princess. The point here is that even though on several occasions he is walking through a forest, no one ever suggests that a sojourn in the forest will itself teach him what fear is. It is human beings, and particularly dead ones, that are frightening.

Although the issue is explicit in this case, it seems to be the usual narrative approach; it is not, in these stories, the forest itself that is frightening, but what other people may do to you in the forest. I think there are two possible reasons for the absence of fear associated with forests. First, and simply, these stories were told by forest people to whom the woods, although dangerous, were not unknown or alien places. There were concrete and actual dangers in the deep forest, but these were problems to be dealt with, rather than terrors emerging ferociously from the subconscious. There is a real difference between the quality of fear induced by dangers one can readily identify and that caused by events that are primarily mysterious. I have cried out aloud in terror at the flit of a white ghost in a night wood, but the moment I have identified it as an owl, it has become beautiful, welcome and even exciting. The absence of panic fear in the fairy stories seems to me one of the strongest indications of their forest origin – because, let's face it, even in the daytime, even within a mile or so of a road and with an Ordnance Survey map in hand, forests can be fearsome.

The second reason feels more complicated. The stories are certainly full of horrors, although always horrors to be overcome either by courage or by humour. But consistently the dark side of the forest emerges from human malevolence. In these stories it is human beings who are cruel, savage, greedy and violent. It is usually robbers, fathers, witches, stepmothers, and more generally thoughtless or mean-minded people who constitute the danger and threaten the well-being of the protagonists. In a remarkable number of stories, the forest is the place where you escape *from* potential harm. It is 'at home', in your house – or in someone else's – that you are most at risk in a fairy story. This is simple realism, and just as true for children today, as we should remember.

Yet, nonetheless, quite separately, there is a darkness, something fearful, about both the stories and the forests.

In *The Wind in the Willows* Kenneth Grahame gives a convincing account of forest fear:

> Everything was very still now. The dusk advanced on him steadily, rapidly, gathering in behind and before; and the light seemed to be draining away like flood-water.
> Then the faces began . . .
> Then the whistling began . . .
> They were up and alert and ready, evidently, whoever they were! And he – he was alone, and unarmed, and far from any help; and the night was closing in.
> Then the pattering began . . .
> And as he lay there panting and trembling, and listened to the whistlings and the patterings outside, he knew it at last, in all its fullness, that dread thing which other little dwellers in field and hedgerow had encountered here, and known as their darkest moment – that thing which the Rat had vainly tried to shield him from the Terror of the Wild Wood.[8]

I think, as Grahame clearly does too, that the fear is of a quite different kind from the simple physical reaction to danger – or the anticipation of it and of a different kind to the violent irrational response that panic represents. It is a fear that, curiously, is better expressed in the adjectives from my list than in the nouns (I wonder if this is because this sort of fear is so nebulous, so hard to pin down and define, that it has never taken on the concrete solidity of a noun):

> aghast, diffident, dire, eerie, fey, fell, ghastly, haunted, nervous, spooky, uncanny, weird

This is the fear of things that are associated with magic – the simple, age-old fear of the supernatural, whether it is good or bad, threatening or promising, positive or negative.

The word 'weird' does not simply mean 'strange', it means the power of or agency of fate, of predestination. The Weirds are the old women who not only know what will happen in the future but can control it, can make magic. Uncanny is defined as:

> not quite safe to trust, or have dealings with, as being associated with supernatural arts or powers. Partaking of a supernatural character; mysterious, weird, uncomfortably strange or unfamiliar.[9]

In Chapter 6, I spoke about the ordinary, almost mundane magic of the woods and how that infiltrated the stories. But even the most benign magic is not safe, cannot be safe, because it is unfamiliar, spooky, weird and eerie. The woods are chaotic and wild; life goes on unseen within them, and for every lovely globe flower, springing golden in a small patch of sunshine, there is a death cap – *Aminita phalloides* – shiny, olive and yellow, just as pretty, but deadly poisonous, lurking under the oak trees. And in the stories, for every kindly old woman who gives you a useful gift, there is a very similar one who may gobble you up, put you under an enchantment or imprison you in a tower. All magic, even good magic, all spells, even kindly benign ones, carry the fear of the uncanny with them. Such magic is complex, twisted, strange, and should be feared.

And perhaps we are more vulnerable to this fear than earlier audiences for these stories were. They knew the forests better than we do; they knew the stories better too – and as the stories show, there is a strong antidote to the sinister effects of the supernatural – ferocious retributive justice. One element of fairy-story morality which we have entirely edited out of contemporary versions is that Justice itself is a harsh, even savage, power. The stories are full of 'cruel and unusual punishments'.[10] G. K. Chesterton comments that from fairy stories he learned 'the chivalrous lesson that giants should be killed because they are gigantic'.[11] Wicked characters do not simply lose out, with toads leaping from their mouths instead of jewels, or the despised younger son gaining the wealth or the princess the wicked brothers had unsuccessfully schemed for; they

are, in addition, punished for their pride or greed or unkindness
with extreme savagery. They are forced to dance themselves to
death in red-hot iron shoes; they have their eyes pecked out by birds;
they are put in spiked barrels and thrown down mill races; they are
cooked to death in their own ovens.[12] There is less mercy in human
justice than there is in the forest itself. Surprisingly few characters
are hurt at all, let alone eaten, by wild animals compared with the
number who are punished terminally by their communities. This
might be a sensible attempt to create a distinction between punishment and bad luck: it might be foolish, but it is not wicked, to get
lost in the forest, to get drowned in the river, to get eaten by a wolf
or to fall down a cliff or pothole. Only the evil get punished. I think
this is in part a response to the eerie, perilous nature of the forest –
bad people, those who use the fey atmosphere of the forests to their
own wicked ends, must be stamped out; they are not ordinarily dangerous but uncanny, weird, unnatural.

For me at least northern pine forest brings this issue of fear to a
head. At a sensible, rational level I believe that the way the stories
address the wild woods here is about our true relationship to the
wild: animals and the forest itself will support and care for individuals, but only if they face their fears and confront the wildness. But
when I am out under the gaunt pine trees with their heavy heads of
black-looking needles, like a storm cloud; when I sense them hov-
ering overhead, high up the apparently inaccessible cliffs; when their
moaning and creaking sounds like pain; when the stags are roaring
somewhere unseen above me and the early dark of the north comes
down unexpectedly, I can sense the fear beneath these sensible
thoughts and feel simple relief that the track will take me back down
to my car any time I want it to.

I went over the Grampian Hills and down into the valley of the
Dee to explore some of my own terrors. At first it was hard to see
what I was looking for: Deeside, and the whole country around
Braemar, is very beautiful. During the eighteenth century the
Highlands of Scotland began to attract tourism. In 1769, T.
Pennant published his *Tour of Scotland*. Of Deeside he wrote:

The rocks are exceedingly romantic ... immense ragged and broken crags bound one side of the prospect; over whose grey sides and summits is scattered the melancholy green of the picturesque pine, which grows in the native rock ... a vast theatre which is covered by extensive forests of pine: above the trees grow scarcer and scarcer, and then seem only to sprinkle the surface; after which vegetation ceases ... the great cataract foams amidst the dark forest ... I measured several [trees] that were ten, eleven and even twelve feet in circumference and near sixty feet high ... having it is supposed seen two centuries.

This must, from his itinerary, have been Ballochbuie, one of the more extensive tracts of Caledonian forest, although he does not name it. In 1848 Queen Victoria made her first tour of Deeside and was impressed by the 'beautiful woods'. She and Prince Albert added the Ballochbuie wood to their Balmoral estate in 1878 to protect it from a threatened logging project. Ballochbuie is therefore, like Balmoral, the private property of the Mountbatten-Windsors rather than part of the Crown Estate. This meant that it never came under the control of the Forestry Commission, and has been less affected by commercial plantation than much Scottish woodland. Ballochbuie, like Staverton, is therefore as near to 'original' or wild wood as anywhere in Britain, despite Victoria's addition of a wrought-iron bridge to allow her to paint views of the 'great cataract' of the Garbh Allt Burn.

Ballochbuie is heavily conserved. The ancient pines (called 'grannies') are fairly wide spaced and surrounded by younger generations and by reaches of heather and rough grass, with bracken and blueberries or groves of birch and rowan. The resurgence of Scottish national identity since the late twentieth century has made the northern forests a particular concern; and, without getting complacent about it, there is good headway in preserving and enhancing these distinctively Scottish woodlands.

But there is a real threat to Caledonian pine forests; the danger is not from commercial exploitation, but from deer.

The issue is simple: red deer are on the increase and they destroy woodland. They reduce the ground coverage and the range and variety of flowering plants, and in particular they devour young trees, their favourite forage. Pine woods regenerated well when they were grazed by cattle in the eighteenth century, but less well after the red deer population started to expand in the mid-nineteenth. Throughout the forests of Braemar the shortage of younger trees, from about 1850, is conspicuous. There are too many deer to allow for natural regeneration without human intervention.

It is extremely difficult to find a strategy which is effective and will assure this kind of forest a long future. Fencing areas for regeneration works in the sense that young pine seedlings are indeed establishing themselves in the experimental enclosures in Ballochbuie and at Mar Lodge across the valley. Unlike oak change, there is no suggestion that Scots pine has altered or weakened its germination capacities: simply, the very young and tender trees are being nibbled off by too many deer. But deer fences need gates and tracks through the forest to allow for their maintenance; they need to be constantly monitored and repaired. In addition, fences stop the movement of *all* animals, not just deer. This creates problems, as for example with two species of bird that are unique to pine forest terrain – capercailzie and blackcock, both rare, both blundering night travellers, and both ground nesters. They have shown an alarming tendency to crash into deer fences and break their necks. Both are endangered species and need the regeneration of the pine forests to survive. We tend to think of 'forests' or 'woodlands' as places for *trees*, with everything else being somehow secondary, but it is whole habitats, not individual trees or even species, that we need to conserve. On what possible grounds, and by what means, can we choose between blackcock and deer – other than that the needs of the blackcock are more pressing at the present moment?

The obvious answer is to shoot the deer, and then eat them, as was the custom in woodlands for centuries. Some historians believe that systematic poaching was how deer populations were managed in earlier times[13] – and certainly the fairy stories treat the hunting-and-eating of deer as entirely normal, even when, as in 'Brother and Sister', the deer in question is a small boy under enchantment. (He brought this on himself to some extent by a failure of self-discipline: he drank from a stream although he was warned it would turn him into a fawn.) But we have put deer on our 'good animal' list and there is a powerful tendency to wax lyrically sentimental about the animal. People become deeply agitated about any pro-posed culling.

One response to the deer problem has been to suggest reintro-ducing wolves. Because there were once wolves throughout the UK, the British government is obliged by EU regulations to give consid-eration to this project, and the discussion has rumbled on for years now. But if the purpose of reintroducing the wolves is solely to manage the deer, it would seem more honest and less risky to kill the deer directly. Reintroductions do not have a very good reputation – starting with rabbits and moving through grey squirrels and mink in the animal world and taking in rhododendrons and some other deliberately imported plants, those that have been successful have also thrown up considerable 'collateral damage'.[14]

Wolves are the stuff of fairy stories – the name and shape of the terror of the wild. There were lynx and bear in Scotland, as well as wolves, as indeed there still are in the vaster forests of Eastern Europe, Scandinavia and the Baltic states. A vicious and ultimately victorious fight against the wolves of Britain was fought through the Middle Ages: unlike the loss of most species, the extirpation of wolves was deliberate, planned and triumphant. Wolves induced terror in the British psyche and had to be destroyed. Wolves are the psychological embodiment of what the fairy stories knew and what we want to forget, or at least ignore: nature is indeed red in tooth and claw, and nowhere more so than in the terrible forests.

In the abstract I like the idea of wolves, but walking in the steep glens of Ballochbuie, where grim pine trees lower from inaccessible pinnacles, where ruined steadings and broken walls bear witness to the tragedy of the Clearances, and where the forests meander slowly across the landscape, I find a strange interior relief in not having to keep even an inner eye or ear out for them.

They feel, as I walk here, like one fear too many. I had come to tackle my sense of terror through another phenomenon of the forests – much smaller, more commonplace and absolutely real – which can also give me the same strange shiver of fear as the dream of wolves and as the fairy stories themselves, a sense of being in the presence of something eerie: fungi.

So after I had walked through the spooky creaking woods of Ballochbuie, I crossed through the little town of Braemar and up a side glen to Mar Lodge, a rather bizarre grandiose house built in its present form in the 1890s as a 'holiday home' for Princess Louise, the Princess Royal, Queen Victoria's daughter who was married to the Earl of Fife. It now belongs to the National Trust for Scotland. I went to walk in the forests there with Liz Holden, who lives in a farmhouse at Mar Lodge.

I have promised Liz Holden that I will not write her into this book as a witch – though I will say that her oat biscuits would make a more tempting little house for me than any gingerbread would. Indeed, it would be hard to imagine anyone less witchy in terms of almost all the stereotypes, but she is engaged on deeply uncanny fairy-story work. Liz Holden did her first degree in anthropology, but claims she was 'hijacked by fungi' after seeing a red cage fungus (*Clathrus rubra*) in a Devon garden.[15] And over the last twenty years she has become an expert in fungi, a 'mycological consultant' – not an academic, but a field naturalist (and now, I am glad to say, a lecturer and teacher).

After the biscuits in her farmhouse, below the forest and looking out across the flat, glacier-carved glen, we went for a fungus walk. The Mar Lodge estate is crisscrossed by little tracks and roads, and we set off initially in the car. Later we left it and walked in a looping meander through the ancient pine woods. They were conspicuous for their variety: there were areas that have been deer-fenced to encourage regeneration; places denuded of trees altogether; clumps of birch and rowan; swathes of very rough ground with long, ragged grasses and thick bracken, now golden tan. There were also patches of dreamlike pine forest, with the trees running up almost vertical braes above fast burns flowing pure and clean and laughing over stones, swirling into small still pools, embedded in moss and ferns; and from the rises above the burns, sudden long views over the wide valley floor would open out. Autumn was in full golden force, with rowan and birch both turning bright yellow.

And everywhere there were fungi. Holden talked and taught and pointed and saw. By the time we returned to the car I had not learned to see fungi – but I had learned how much I did not see, how much I miss every day and what a loss that is to me.

Fungi are of course by no means confined to Highland pine forests, or indeed to forests at all. We all have contact with them without qualms on an almost daily basis: the rising of bread, blue veins in cheese, penicillin, wine and mushroom soup are all dependent on fungi. They flourish everywhere, from damp cellars to open grass fields. We tend to notice them most in the warm damp weather of late summer and autumn, but in fact they are around at all times of the year in various forms and quantities.

I am not sure why they feel so strange, except for the simple fact that they are strange; and their strangeness feels close to the uncanny in the fairy stories. When you come upon fungi in the woods they have a magical otherworldly appearance, enhanced by the improbable variety of forms and colours: fungi like jelly, like coral, like brains, like tongues flickering out of alder cones, and even, with the weird earthstars (*Geastraceae*), like aliens from space. But this cannot be the whole story, because there is just as much variety and strangeness in flowering plants, although they never arouse this dark unease.

Perhaps their spooky strangeness grew when, as children, we were warned against them, and rightly: several British toadstools are fatally toxic and many others are very bad for you indeed. At the same time, many of them are not merely edible but delicious – free food, if you get it right. But like the good and bad characters encountered in the forests in the stories, it is singularly difficult to know which are which. This possibility of disastrous error is part of the sinister atmosphere that surrounds them: *Gyromitra esculenta* (the false morel), for instance, is deadly poisonous, but in appearance and fruiting season it has 'wickedly' copied the true morels, a famous culinary treat.

Or perhaps it is because, like the magic in the stories, fungi seem to appear without warning and then disappear equally suddenly. They pop up, fully formed and beautiful, where you did not anticipate it, and disappear as suddenly, as though by magic. Additionally, they sometimes appear in formations that seem 'designed' rather than natural, as though a conceptual artist has been out in the night arranging them in 'fairy rings', patterns so precise as to appear engineered rather than spontaneous.

And for me, even since my walk with Liz Holden and my purchase of not one but two recommended guides, I can never identify them with confidence. I cannot pin them down, cannot say what I have seen, cannot crack their secret code.[16] They remain darkly mysterious.

And the more I learn, the stranger it all seems. Fungi used to be classified and treated as plants, although rather odd ones – but mosses and ferns and horsetails are 'odd' too and they remain comfortably 'plants'. In 1969 fungi were hived off and given a scientific 'kingdom' all of their own.[17] One major difference between fungi and plants is structural – where plants use cellulose to provide form and stiffness, fungi use chitin, the same tough substance as the exoskeleton of insects is made from. Moreover, fungi do not manufacture their food by photosynthesis.

The visible toadstool is in fact only the fruit of its fungus (just as an apple is to a tree, producing and dispersing the seed – or spore in the case of fungi). The bulk of the fungus is normally hidden underground and is called the *mycelium*. It is made up of fine hair like threads called *hyphae*, and it is these that you sometimes see as a web of white strands under broken bark on a dead piece of wood. A mycelium may be tiny, forming an organism too small to see, or it may be massive – perhaps comprising the largest living things in the world.

Fungi have three vital functions in forests. First, there is the symbiotic partnership mycorrhiza have with individual trees, as I discussed in the first chapter. Second, once the tree is dead, or even diseased, the relationship changes and the fungi become aggressors, crucial in breaking down and recycling dead organic matter – without fungi, we would be living in a vast woodpile, stacked up yards deep over much of the surface of the world. And third, they are there in the ancient woodlands to remind us how beautiful and uncanny the forests are.

There are surprisingly few direct references to toadstools (for good or bad) in the fairy stories, although I for one am certain that if you wanted to poison half an apple to rid yourself of a stepdaughter, a small slice of *Amanita muscaria* – fly algaric – might work very well. It causes delirium and coma, a good possibility for Snow White's apparent death.[18] Nonetheless, the atmosphere of the forest, the sense that strange things, both beautiful and dangerous, can happen at any moment and without warning, is mirrored in the life of the forest fungi. Fungi constantly remind us that there are other forms of life than the obvious ones; there is the human and the wild and the 'something else' – magic or mushroom.

It is on this connection between 'nature' and 'culture' that Liz Holden has been working. In 2003 she published *Recommended English Names for Fungi in the UK*, sponsored by the British Mycological Society, English Nature, Plantlife and Scottish Natural Heritage. The Latin or scientific names are – as the reader may have noticed – not easily manageable for most amateurs, and because fungi are so often elusive it is hard to keep track of them. Holden took on the job of creating English names for British fungi. Obviously no one can make these compulsory, but most modern field guides to mushrooms and toadstools are now using her list.

As Richard Mabey so richly illustrates in *Flora Britannica*, many British wild flowers have local informal names, in addition to their 'proper' scientific Latin ones.[19] Because it is so much easier both to see and to care about something you have a personal name for (particularly if the name 'matches' the plant in terms of its shape, behaviour or other actual feature – snowdrop rather than *Gallanthus*; bluebell rather than *Hyancinthoides*), wild flowers tend to attract attention, affection and care. But when it comes to fungi, unfortunately 'there is a paucity of vernacular "folk names" even in Welsh and Gaelic from which to draw inspiration'.[20] Earlier I spoke about the tragic loss of words describing nature and the folk stories in the new edition of the *Oxford Junior Dictionary*; Holden's project moves in the opposite direction, providing new names to reclaim something of the old tradition. Among the sources for inspiration that she used, she included:

> Folklore and legend e.g. elfcup, elfin, dryad, fairy, fairy ring, Goliath, Medusa, St. George, King Alfred, Knights, Shields, Cavaliers and Roundheads have all found a place in this nomenclature. Word play and humour have been included wherever possible. Names such as Crowned Tooth, White Knight, Funeral Bell, The Flirt, Strathy Strangler, Dogend, and Nettle Rash hopefully reflect this.

The names should be 'distinctive and lively in order to engage public interest. They ... should avoid too many negative associations ... care should be taken not to introduce names for poisonous species that could infer edibility.'

Holden's work, with adults and primary school children, taking people out to walk in forests where they can learn to see and not be frightened, naming, telling, showing these magical life forms, seems to me the sort of conservation project both the woods and the fairy stories need. For all the uncanny horror of the wild places, there is the balancing – the naming and seeing and telling of stories (as dark as death caps, as scary as witches butter, as jokey as crowned tooth) about the forests, so that people can go there with their eyes open and see the deep magic and not feel too much of the uncanny terror.

Rapunzel

Once upon a time there was a beautiful princess.

Her beauty was without question – it would have flamed before the whole world if I had let it, and every time I climbed up the tower it flamed for me, blazing more brightly than the morning. And whatever they may say, it was not just that extraordinary hair – that was a mere embellishment, an extravagance of ornamentation where none was needed. She was beautiful in her deep bones and graceful as a beech tree. There's an old saying in these woods: 'every beetle is a butterfly to its mother'. But I was not her mother and when I speak of her beauty, I speak of what undid me. I would deny it if I could, but she was beautiful.

'Princess' I admit is more subjective. She was always a princess to me, although out there in the more judgemental and foolish world she was a daughter of the underclass, her father a petty thief without imagination or flair, and her mother a selfish, self-indulgent, vulgar trollop. Of course I should not say such things, but I am too old and sad for caution or kindness. They sold me their child for a handful of salad greens because that woman wanted them now and would not wait. If they had had normal neighbourly good manners he could have knocked on my door and asked for a bunch of rapunzel and I would have given it to him for free. He tried to steal it and he got caught and he sold his unborn child to protect his own scurvy skin. And in that tawdry bargain she became mine – my beautiful princess; for, as Solomon taught us, any mother who would freely put her child at risk is not the real mother. I was her real mother and she was my true princess.

I did not even plan it. I went, as neighbours do, to see the new child. I even took the silver coin to slip under the baby's pillow, to welcome her and help her family, as we do in these woods. I had not planned for my heart to leap out of my mouth and gobble the baby up. I fell in love there, for ever – a thing I have never done before. Nor since.

I picked up the child, as you do, and muttered some admiring words, as you do. Her skin was so soft against my cheek, like wind-flowers, cool and delicate. But I think, or at least I believe, I was joking when I said, 'Of course, she's mine. You promised her to me. Remember?'

'Yes, yes,' they both squealed. 'Yes, take her; yes, of course.'

They say I am a witch and that they were afraid. But I am not a witch. I am a woman with different desires.

Even then I was shocked, and I have become more shocked since, but I wanted her so much and they wanted her so little. I laid her against my shoulder, warm and sweet. I said, 'You need not fear about her well-being, for I shall take care of her like a mother.' And then she was mine.

I took care of her like a mother. Or like I think a mother should; we women all have our own ideas about that. I could not nurse her of course – there were no spells for that back then – but I was tender to her in every other way I could imagine. I taught her to read so that she could be free in her heart and mind; I stuffed her pillow with Sweet Woodruff, Lady's Bedstraw, so that she slept to scents of fresh-mown hay and almonds, sweeter and less useful than silver coins; I took her to play in the beech woods, because her hair was the colour of beech mast, and I taught her the names of all the flowers and the birds.

I brushed her hair. When she was small I brushed her hair every day, morning and evening. Later, as it grew longer and thicker, I was obliged to surrender to it, there was not time in a day to brush it twice; before the end there was not time in the week to brush it twice.

In my dreams I am still brushing her hair, brushing and braiding and binding her hair – her lovely, tendrilling, conker-

coloured, wanton hair. Brushing and braiding and binding. It was
the colour of beech leaves in autumn; there were reds and golds
in it like Slender St John's Wort in high summer and deep gilt like
Bog Asphodel on the moors. It twined like honeysuckle around
my fingers, my hands, my arms, my heart. Brushing and braiding
and binding her hair. Singing as I ran the brush through it:

Rapunzel, Rapunzel
Let down your long hair.

Bright morning,
The birds all sing,
Rapunzel, Rapunzel
I'm brushing your hair.

One, two, three
Like the Holy Trinity,
Rapunzel, Rapunzel,
I'm braiding your hair.

She was a delightful baby, and then a lovely child; but long before
she was a woman – even before she was truly a girl – her beauty
began to blaze in the sunshine. It was not just her hair – that was
a mere embellishment, an extravagance of ornamentation where
none was needed. She was like a beech tree, tall and slender and
graceful, with long fingers and green eyes and a crown of golden
hair. She was beautiful in her deep bones and in her windblown
gestures. I let myself forget that beech trees are shallow rooted and
therefore vulnerable to wind damage and storm-fall.

Her beauty was disturbing; if we walked in the woods, the roe deer
would emerge from hiding to watch her; the foxes would grovel at her
feet, confused because her hair was the same colour as theirs, and
they would walk alongside her, admiring; even the wild birds would
alight on her shoulders and the frogs surface on the ponds and puddles to gaze at her. The wild rose bushes put up long shoots and

clambered through her bedroom window to admire her asleep. That was fine and proper; but her beauty ruffled the tenor of the village too; and young men, like dogs after a bitch on heat, hung around my gates as her father had done and the rapunzel they wanted to steal now was not green and cheap but golden and precious.

One day I caught a pimply youth trying to cut off the tassel of her hair below its binding. He was a sneaking thief, but he did not get my treasure. I took her into the forest where she could be free. I took her into the forest where she could be safe. I believed they were the same thing. I was wrong, but I did believe it. I took her into the forest where I could keep her hidden.

It was not a tower. They chose to call it a tower, which sounds grim, like a dungeon. But I called it our Belvedere; when she was little she called it the Tree House, and when she was older she called it the Folly. It was not a tower and I did not mean it to be a dungeon. It was a lovely playful little house, high in the trees and looking over a nearly perfect glade in the wood; high enough to see across the tops of the beech trees as they ran down the steep valley side to the river. To perch high in the beech canopy is a lovely thing, and to look down into a clearing in an old wood is a thing to be desired. Below her was the everlasting procession of snowdrops, then bluebells, windflowers, ransoms, cherry blossom, wild roses, crab apples and dark dusty sloes. A little waterfall dropped into a deep pool at the top of the glade and sparkled as a stony brook across the green grass, with ferns and kingcups and horsetails along it. So it was indeed a Belvedere and a Tree House.

But it was not a tower, even though it had no door. I could not be there all the time and she had to be protected. And each morning I would walk into the forest, taking good care that no one followed me, and come out from beneath the beech trees and into the green glade, singing for pure joy:

Rapunzel, Rapunzel
Let down your long hair.

And she would let it down, all twenty ells of it, and I would climb up, up to her nest, and we were both happy.

I thought we were both happy.

But ...

She was innocent to the point of stupidity, which was my fault.

And she was romantic to the point of self-abnegation, which was her fault.

I do not know and I will never know just how long it went on for. Longer, I suspect, than I like to think. She was as sly as her father and as self-indulgent as her mother and she did not even have the courage to tell me. I only found out by a stupid foolish thing she said.

So there we were, happy and free and safe and together, I thought, and living in the beauty of the woods. And one morning I was brushing and braiding and binding her hair, weaving daises and four-petalled tormentil into each autumn beech leaf strand. When I finished, she stood up, with her hands against the top of her buttocks, suddenly awkward and heavy. I noticed, but without assigning any meaning to it. And she said,

'I need a new skirt. This one is too small. I seem to be getting fat.' After a little pause she added, 'Please' because I was always strict about good manners.

I knew. I knew at once. The wanton little bitch. I had the clothes off her in a twinkling. There's no mistaking: 'getting fat' indeed. Her nipples were already darkening and the bulge below her navel unmistakable. In a white heat of what I thought was justifiable moral outrage I beat her and then I threw her out, as any decent woman would. There was no place for this in my house and I was not prepared to tolerate it. Before I banished her for good and all to a cold and desolate place I cut off her hair with a carving knife. It was mine and I wanted it.

When she was gone I felt chilled to the bone and, for the first time in my life, old. But I fired myself up on wrath and waited for her tom cat to come prowling round the Folly. As the evening came and the sweetness of bird song faded into soft dusk I heard him come through the trees. He stood below the window and in a strong and confident tenor, he sang my song.

> Rapunzel, Rapunzel
> Let down your long hair.

The gall of it. I taught him a surprise lesson in good manners and humility. He limped away back into the forest, blind and defeated. I did not care. I felt a warm thrill of triumph and then a great long-lasting weariness.

I do not know why I behaved that way. I do not know. There could have been a different and prettier story – for me I mean. There was, I have learned, a prettier ending for them. They found each other in the end despite my best efforts. She had her twins, she cured his eyes and they lived happily ever after. I do not know why I acted like her birth parents – I stole her hair and I sold my love too cheap, for a moment of rage, for the short-lived flower of spiteful anger. I was a fool.

I still keep her hair. Though the flowers I wove into it have faded and crumbled, it is still lovely.

In my dreams I am still brushing her hair, brushing and braiding and binding her hair – her lovely, tendrilling, conker-coloured, wanton hair. Brushing and braiding and binding. It is still the colour of beech leaves in autumn, with reds and golds in it like Slender St John's Wort in high summer and deep gilt like Bog Asphodel on the moors. It still twines like honeysuckle around my fingers, my hands, my arms, my heart. Brushing and braiding and binding her hair. Singing as I run the brush through it:

> Rapunzel, Rapunzel
> Let down your long hair.
> Bright morning,
> The birds all sing,
> Rapunzel, Rapunzel

I'm brushing your hair.

One, two, three
Like the Holy Trinity,
Rapunzel, Rapunzel,
I'm braiding your hair.

I keep it, all twenty glorious ells of it, coiled like a snake in the
Folly in the forest.

9

November

Kielder Forest

It was an unusually bright and pleasant morning for November. Adam and I sat over our coffee watching the birds on the bird feeders in the garden of the Bed and Breakfast where we had spent the night.[1] The dense plantation of conifers at the eastern end of Kielder Forest rose above us behind the house, and looking north, we could see over the river and across the wide valley to more dark close-planted trees. We were waiting contentedly for Max McLaughlin of the Forestry Commission to come and collect us for a tour of the forest.

Between the house and the river was the road; we had come in from the east on it, and it continued westward, along the side of the reservoir and into the heart of the forest. It felt just like the beginning of a fairy story. So many of them start with the hero or heroine leaving home on the edge of the woods and setting out on a road through a forest, to meet new people and learn new things and have an adventure.

The day before, Adam and I had come down the lovely A68 from Edinburgh and crossed into England at Carter's Bar, with the vast views along the western shoulders of the Cheviots. This is one of the emptiest places in England: isolated high hills with the occasional patch of woodland along the river valleys. Traditionally, this vast swathe of wilderness between the Tyne Valley and the Scottish Lowlands was unproductive and under-populated, mainly managed for grouse shooting and sheep farming: it is desolate, fierce country.

Historically too it is a wild place – the Roman legions encountered so much trouble and unrest in this region that it led to Roman Empire's first retreat: they pulled back from the Antonine Wall (which ran approximately from Edinburgh and Glasgow) in AD 162 and constructed and heavily fortified the new Hadrian's Wall, to the south of us now. Later the area was disrupted by continual armed forays between England and Scotland, along a disputed unsettled boundary. Cross-border incursions of a broadly official kind were common throughout the Middle Ages; consequently, castles and fortified bastle houses dot the district. Later this was the Border Reivers' country; marauding bands of cattle rustlers, professional kidnappers and generally lawless brigands dominated both sides of the border from the thirteenth to the sixteenth centuries with their destructive raids, called ridings, and their fast-shifting alliances and treacheries.

Onto this fierce, and fiercely beautiful, territory in the early 1920s the newly formed Forestry Commission imposed the largest artificial woodland in Europe: Kielder Forest. There are 250 square miles of it; from Hadrian's Wall it runs almost broken for 30 miles northwards, across the border and into Scotland,[2] and east to west it is more than twenty miles wide. Commercially, it is the Forestry Commission's most successful 'wood factory' as well as its most extensive, and it produces nearly half a million cubic metres of felled timber a year: a major industrial site in the middle of nowhere. Roy Robinson, one of the first Forestry Commissioners, was so proud of it that when he was given his peerage in 1947 he chose the title of Baron Robinson of Kielder Forest and Adelaide. (He was an Australian and the only one of the seven original Commissioners who was not from the standard 'country estate, public school, Oxbridge' background.)

And this is why, through a darkening wintery afternoon, we were driving over Carter's Bar and down into Northumberland. We were going to visit Kielder Forest to try and understand more about the Forestry Commission and its relationship with ancient woodlands. It is impossible to think seriously about woodland in the UK without looking at the role of the Forestry Commission over the last century, though quite what that role is feels hard to determine. If woodland itself is the heroine of this fairy story, is the Forestry Commission her wicked stepmother, her wise king, her rescuing prince, a dark witch or a wise animal? Until the last few years the Commission has been the principal villain of most conservation and preservation discourse. It stands accused of planting excessively on its own land, suitable or unsuitable – in retrospect, it is hard to tell whether the planting within old woodland or the attempt to create forests in places quite unsuited to any trees at all did the most environmental damage. At the same time the Commission is also accused of encouraging private landowners to join in and of squeezing extravagant tax concessions for the rich out of successive governments. In this version of the fairytale, the Forestry Commission was said to be economically deceitful and incompetent; to have wantonly destroyed old woodland; to have restricted access to wide reaches of the countryside; to have totally failed to live up to any of its original remit; and, both through its own actions and by subsidising private landowners, to have desecrated the wild places of Britain (and particularly Scotland) with square-edged unnatural-looking clumps of forestry which litter the hills and look more industrial than natural.[3]

Although actually many of these accusations, especially perhaps the last, are hideously true, more recently the frog has been turning into a prince. The Commission has undergone a transformation – visible in the policy changes it has made since the 1990s.[4]

I think there are, and indeed should be, serious questions to be asked about any organisation which owns, manages or controls over 12% of the land surface of a country, which is publicly funded but unaccountable and unelected (the Crown still appoints the Commissioners), and which is both the regulatory authority over and a business rival to all other commercial forests. Nonetheless, and especially since the 1990s, the situation is more complicated than this.

A good deal of the complexity is a direct consequence of the history of the Forestry Commission itself, which, like royal afforestation in the eleventh and twelfth centuries and enclosures in the eighteenth and nineteenth century, has profoundly changed the nature and meaning of our forests.

The Forestry Commission was established by legislation in 1919. During the 1914-18 war there had been a fearful realisation that there were insufficient timber reserves in the country and that this was partly because of the neglect of forestry in the previous century and partly because of a lack of strategic planning. In 1914 less than 4% of the timber used in Britain was home grown; about half was imported from Russia, and the rest from the Baltic, Scandinavia and Canada. This supply was critically threatened by German attacks on merchant shipping. At the same time, the construction and shoring up of trenches, as well as the building of barracks, encampments, transport infrastructure and so on, massively increased the need for timber: it has been calculated that *each* soldier deployed on the Western Front used up five trees. This crisis inspired the then government to set up the Commission with overall responsibility both for direct forestry development work on its own estates and for advising and regulating privately owned woodland. Although it was created to secure the nation's supply of this crucial commodity, it was argued simultaneously that there was a handsome profit to be made out of well-managed forestry.[5]

The new Commission needed to acquire plantations and was therefore given a budget to purchase appropriate ground; to prime that pump it was handed control over all the woodlands of the Crown Estate, including the remaining Royal Forests,[6] and, therefore, as I have explained, a large part of the remaining ancient woodland across Britain. This created a second, internal conflict of interests: the Commission's primary duty was to increase timber yield and do so at a profit; this was inevitably in conflict with conservation. In its early years the Commission was keen not just on planting commercially within ancient woodland (not usually a very successful strategy, and one which tended to destroy old woods without generating useable or sustainable new timber), but also on clear-felling old woodland and grubbing it out to create new plantations.

The Forestry Commission did not invent plantations. The earliest recorded deliberate planting of trees other than orchards or in gardens in Europe is from the first century AD. In his massive Latin work *De Re Rustica*, the author, Columella, discusses planting chestnut or oak coppices alongside vineyards, to provide stakes for the vines.[7] His text appears to treat the idea of creating deliberate and extensive plantations as a part of normal agricultural activity, so it was probably already a regular practice. It certainly continued to be so: Oliver Rackham records seven references to plantations in Britain before 1500 (there were presumably more), and other European countries show a similar development. For example, there are records of plantation forests in south-western France as early as 1500, primarily for commercial purposes, but also to meet direct domestic needs. There were managed plantations of cork in Portugal and poplar in Italy.[8] By the seventeenth century several writers, particularly in Britain and France, were beginning to advocate plantations to landowners for their 'pleasure and profit'.[9] Sadly, these two aspirations have not proved reliably compatible and the tension between them has bedevilled British forestry ever since.

Through the eighteenth and nineteenth centuries, planting, both within old woods and on new (usually ex-agricultural and common) land, continued steadily. Plantations, in terms of area, overtook ancient woodland surprisingly early – by about 1720 in Ireland, 1800 in Scotland,[10] 1820 in Wales, and 1870 in England (with the exception of Essex, where it has not happened yet). So initially the Forestry Commission appeared simply to offer economy of scale and leadership. But the Commission has never quite worked as planned, or achieved the goals it set itself. And these goals have kept changing. Over the course of what is now almost a whole century, the Commission has had six successive and incompatible priorities, without ever officially abandoning any of its previous core objectives; these have been, in chronological order: assuring a national timber reserve; halting rural population decline; saving imports; creating jobs (specifically for the unemployed during the Depression); making money; and, most recently, protecting wildlife habitats and providing public amenity space.

We do not yet know about the last of these, but all the others have proved, in one way or another, illusory. Forestry has not provided jobs to the extent that was anticipated – mainly because of technological advances; we no longer need a strategic timber reserve because there is no more call for pit props, military trench supports or railway sleepers – even the use of matches has declined sharply, and in any case, the sort of timber we can grow commercially is never going to free the country from the need to import; and plantation forestry does not in fact make much money either for the nation through the Commission or for private owners – except via tax incentives. This financial aim proved perhaps the most destructive: in the years after the Second World War the Forestry Commission became almost grandiosely ambitious. Forestry gobbled up land between 1950 and 1980 to the extent that this period has become known as 'the Locust Years'. At its peak in the 1970s, new planting in Wales, Scotland and northern England was consuming more than 0.15% of the total land area per year. Over half a million acres (240,000 hectares) of what is now Highlands and Islands was planted; 20% of Dumfries and Galloway was put under forestry. Overall, 17% of Scotland is now forested, and the vast bulk of that is non-native conifer plantation divided fairly evenly between the Forestry Commission and private ownership. Some of this was so far north, or on such unpromisingly peaty ground, that it inflicted great environmental loss without even offering any true potential for profit. It looked horribly ugly to many people – a neighbour of mine, a tenant hill farmer, when consulted about a proposed wind farm on the high moor here, said that they could do what they liked – it could not possibly be worse than the forestry. When he was a boy the moors were completely treeless, but the plantations had so changed the views and the ecology of the area that wind farms seemed unimportant to him, except that, once constructed, they would not get in the way of the sheep, as the trees do.

During the 'locust years', in addition to the destruction of ancient forest to accommodate this brutal planting programme, the Commission, in what could be described as imperialistic enthusiasm, managed to do some other pretty terrible things to the landscape – a sort of collateral damage: polluting watercourses and changing drainage systems; ploughing in antiquities without proper documentation or research; seriously degrading limited and precious habitats like blanket peat moor; destroying habitat, particularly for birds. The Locust Years radically altered our rural landscapes for ever.

As yet another complication, the Commission holds, on a single mandate, at least three different sorts of land: the industrial plantation forest, which was explicit in its original remit and which was always – and still is – meant to be commercially viable; assorted parcels of ancient woodland or semi-degraded ancient woodland – some of them, like the New Forest, large – which need protection, management and development; and large stretches of land on which no trees can be grown at all, because they are too high, too stony, too peaty, too boggy or too steep. The original purchasers of the Commission's estates did not take this last element properly into account. Apparently believing that, in earlier times, the whole country was solid forest which had been stripped away by mismanagement, they seem to have thought that it could be re-planted without much difficulty. The Commission now owns a huge acreage of what are often the wildest parts of Britain despite the fact that these areas have nothing to do with forestry at all. In addition, more recently there has been considerable pressure on the Commission to provide access and organised leisure facilities for large numbers of wildly assorted visitors, from hill walkers to primary school groups.

In short, the Forestry Commission as a whole has a more or less impossible task.

I came to Kielder to try and understand the goings-on of contemporary commercial forest. I was of course especially curious because, as I have suggested, the fairy stories tend to represent anyone who works in the forest, who has proper legitimate business there, as being 'good' rather than 'wicked', and I wanted to see whether this might still be true and what it would mean if it were.

We saw little of the forest, though, as we arrived. It was dark by the time we left the village of Bellingham and turned westward. The only indication of the changing environment was the strange striped carpet that the headlights picked up on the road. In the autumn the larch needles turn brown, like deciduous trees – a fairly unexciting colour while they remain on the branches – but when they fall, and especially when they are lying on road or track, they turn an extraordinary shade of rich red. You do need a fair number of larch trees to generate enough needles, and this is one of the compensations of plantation – those glowing stripes at the sides and down the middle of a road, with the two contrasting bands of black where car tyres have pushed the needles aside.

We reached our destination in darkness and settled in for the night, without much sense of where we were – but the bright morning revealed the wide stretch of trees, and before long we found ourselves in Max McLaughlin's Land Rover, with Max McLaughlin and his spaniel, setting off to see the forest.

McLaughlin was a gift to me from the Forestry Commission. When I first wrote asking some questions for this book, they invited me to Kielder and provided me with a tour guide, and this was he. Max McLaughlin has a job with a fairy-tale title: he is a Forest Harvester.[11] Forest Harvesters work on the commercial (rather than the leisure and amenity) side of the Commission, deciding about the felling schedules and organising them. In particular at Kielder, McLaughlin is the Forest Harvester in charge of 'continuous cover'.

Continuous cover forestry husbandry is an attempt to square a circle: to create woodland that serves the new amenity and ecological agenda without totally abandoning commercial timber production. The basic idea is that you select and fell enough trees from within a patch of standard forestry to create space between the trees and allow sunlight in, and thus encourage seeding and forest-floor regeneration, but leave enough trees standing to maintain the overhead canopy, both to generate new seeds and to provide more complex habitats.

In a 1999 study of harvesting management techniques, the Forestry Commission concluded:

> The current attraction of continuous cover forestry lies in the belief that this approach is suited to an era of multi-purpose forestry where environmental, recreational, aesthetic and other objectives are as important as timber production. In particular, continuous cover forestry is seen as a means of reducing the impact of clear felling and the associated changes that this produces in forest landscapes and habitats.
>
> It does not mean abandoning stand management or timber production. Indeed the felling of trees and the harvesting of their timber is essential in continuous cover forestry to manipulate the stand structure to promote natural regeneration and to provide revenue to offset costs of meeting multiple objectives.[12]

Although there had been some discussion of continuous cover husbandry in Germany in the 1920s, the predominant method of timber management in Europe throughout the twentieth century has been 'patch clear felling':[13] cutting all the trees in a given patch of forest down to the ground at the same time; leaving the site to rot down for a bit, and then replanting it with the trees close together and in straight lines. All the trees within the patch will be the same species and the same age, which makes harvesting them relatively straightforward. Clear-felling provides some clear advantages – a large volume of timber available at a single place at a single moment offers economies of scale; the felling process does not endanger remaining trees because there aren't any; and the ground disruption of the heavy modern felling machinery is reduced because they do not have to go into the given area very often.

However there are also real disadvantages. The principal one, now that amenity access has become so central to the Commissions vision, is that stands planned for clear-felling do not make attractive woodland. The visual impact of recently clear-felled ground is even less charming – it tends to look like a scene of protracted trench warfare, littered with dead wood and ragged weedy vegetation; moreover, it is very difficult to walk through, so forest visitors do not like it. The whole clear-felling cycle is antipathetic to natural regeneration and therefore to the variation of species and age, which is one of the most attractive elements of ancient woods; and the system is destructive of natural habitats. Many woodland birds, for example, are extremely picky about nest sites; lots of wildflower species need time to establish and particular conditions of sunlight or wetness to flourish, but clear-felling creates a very abrupt change in the local environment.

Continuous cover is designed to avoid these problems. In Kielder they are starting to re-develop stands of trees originally planted for clear-felling. McLaughlin's job, just like the Lord's Steward or the Verderer in a medieval Royal Forest, is to decide which trees should come out and which remain, seeking a balance between commercial viability, aesthetics and ecological diversity. Indeed, this must have been the way that the ancient woodlands were managed, where maiden trees stood proud of the coppices below them and were selected for harvesting according to the need for timber of particular sizes or kinds.

McLaughlin was generous and enthusiastic – he wanted to show us the full cycle of his work and a rich variety of forestry activities. In consequence, this was a forest walk that never turned into a walk. To cover the ground efficiently we spent a good deal of the day hopping in and out of the Land Rover and manoeuvring our way up

rutted back tracks to see different phases and types of forest management in action.

First he took us to see some selective felling in action. The lumberjacks could have been, like the Free Miners in Dean, characters
from fairy stories – huntsmen, woodcutters, carters; father and sons,
heirs to several generations of forest workers. Watching them at
work, it was easy to remember all the workers in the forests in
the fairy stories: the woodcutter who rescues Little Red Riding
Hood from the wolf, or the old huntsman who generously adopts
the impoverished twins in 'The Two Brothers': independent, self-
employed, highly skilled. But this was not old-fashioned axe and
or even power-saw felling. The lumberjacks were working with
something that seemed as fantastical as a fairy story might be, but a
very hi-tech, ultra-modern fantasy: a state-of-the-art woodcutting
machine (rather confusingly also called a 'forest harvester').

This wondrous and strangely beautiful piece of machinery is of
course one of the reasons why forestry has never been able to supply
the number of jobs predicted in the early years – the machine, com-
puter controlled, and surprisingly compact, does everything:
mounted on huge wheels like a tractor, its 'arms' reach out and hug
the selected tree in a fierce embrace; then it strips off the branches
with its integral delimbing knives; and then, without having to lay
the tree down and so damage its neighbours or disturb the forest
floor, it delicately and precisely feeds it through its arms into an
electric saw which cuts the trunk off in preselected lengths and
stacks them neatly, so that another machine – called a forwarder –
can cart the pre-measured logs to the track side for removal.
McLaughlin can thus select which trees will be removed with considerable freedom and without risking any damage to the trees he
wants to keep. The elegance, the economy of labour, and of course
the extraordinary skill required to use it at all generated a riveting
fascination, a deep mixture of awe and laughter. Delighted, we
admired the removal of several trees. Adam was enchanted, and
devised a wonderful contemporary version of Little Red Riding
Hood in which the woodcutter was replaced by a modern forest

harvester, which would capture the wolf in its own even more enormous jaws, strip off its fur, cut its bones into tidy lengths and stack
them by the roadside. Even the commercial activities of the forest
felt rich with imaginative possibility.

We left them, clambered back into the Land Rover, and drove
ever deeper into the forest; looking at different sorts of felling, at
new plantations and natural regeneration sites. And eventually we
jolted up a tiny rutted grassy track, then left the car and walked in
to see the results of McLaughlin's endeavours in a section of older
continuous cover – or, more precisely, the beginning of the results,
since trees take a very long time to establish new patterns.

I had not been prepared for how lovely – even at this early stage –
it would be. The piece we went to see was being developed from an
older plantation of conifers, so the trees had originally been planted
very close together and had grown very tall, with few lower
branches and long thin trunks. They were spruces, with their dark-
coloured needles, and the day was bright so that light was working
its way in through the roof cover, despite the thick shade. This com-
bination created a weird luminous effect. The mossy, ferny ground
appeared brighter than the overhead cover of needles, so the light
seemed to rise up from under our feet rather than pour down from
the sky. In winter sometimes, when there is fresh crisp snow on the
ground under a heavy grey sky, this same eerie visual effect can
occur, but here, in greens and golds rather than tones of white, it
was somehow oddly more fey. There was a lot of jewel green moss,
humped up, presumably over the bases and roots of the now-
removed trees, a few last blackberries and the beginnings at least of
a complex 'floor' – baby spruces, some only a few inches high, huddled in overcrowded groups underneath the trees that seeded them.
With so many of the old trees taken out, smaller, scrubbier bushes
and little birches and rowan seedlings had found their own way into
this new space. The dank drainage ditches that fill with black peat-
slimed water between the rows of mass plantation spruces had
vanished and been replaced by a sparkling little stream, and it was
easy to imagine that when more people had wandered through,

avoiding the blackberry thorns and the green humped remains of the trees, there would be a little winding path curling round the trees and away into the distance. Of course it is not, and is never going to turn into, real ancient woodland, and it would be foolish to pretend it was. But it was beautiful, and curiously reminded me of the pictures of forests in children's fairy-story books – the sort of faux naive forests that Disney enshrined in our consciousnesses with the animation of 'Snow White' in 1937: the trees wide spaced, the grass very green and flowery with small paths running across it and large numbers of highly anthropomorphised animal and birds scattered about in unnatural association with each other and the human characters.

This memory from childhood was enhanced by McLaughlin's big brown and white Springer spaniel – my father had a very similar spaniel when I was small, although this one was rather better behaved. He ran happily around us as we explored and talked, coming when called, and sitting at McLaughlin's feet, grinning as they do. Like most large spaniels, his had an extremely expressive face, and he watched his owner apparently intelligently and understandingly before loping off about his own business, snuffling about the green floor of the wood. There are surprisingly few dogs in the fairy stories, but there are a very large number of talking animals. They fall into three categories. There are the humans who have been enchanted into animal forms: the little fawn of 'Brother and Sister'; the swan brothers whose sister served the seven years of silence to liberate them; the bear in 'Snow White and Rose Red'; or the Frog Prince who rescued the princess's golden ball and was restored by her rather savage attempts to get rid of him by throwing him at the wall.

There are the stories in which animals themselves are the protagonists, like 'The Four Musicians of Bremen', a donkey, a dog, a cat and a cockerel, and whose story I shall tell my version of at the end of the next chapter; or 'The Wedding of Mrs. Fox', in which Mrs Fox has a Cat for a maid, and is courted by other animals after she becomes a widow; or the improbable story of 'The Fox and the

Horse', who conspire together to capture a lion so that the horse's owner will continue to feed and stable him in his old age. There are a surprising number of these stories in the Grimm brothers' collection, but they seem to have fallen out of fashion and are little known now. They tend to be short and humorous, indeed rather silly, tales which do not easily fit into our more elevated approaches to the fairy stories as journeys towards adult self-knowledge.

But by far the most common talking animals are woodland creatures who just happen to talk. Although very occasionally, as in 'The White Snake',[14] the humans have to learn how to understand their language, more often they just speak normally and nearly always helpfully. All sorts of animals have this skill (if that is the right word) – it is an integral part of the magic of the forests and of the stories themselves. There are talking frogs, wolves, ants, foxes, snakes, goats, horses, cats, deer and, above all, birds – of many different species. Nothing else seems to distinguish them from their non-talking relatives, except that they are treated with respect and gratitude by the wise hero or heroine. One of the stranger realities here is that there is no indication that all animals can talk; for instance, no human character hesitates to kill for food or self-protection. In 'The White Snake' the hero happily hacks the head off his own (non-speaking) horse to provide a meal for some (talking) raven fledglings; huntsmen go on hunting after talking with a deer or fox; no one is a vegetarian. It is simply that some individual animals can talk and they will always say something worth hearing.

I have no convincing explanation for this insistent narrative device, and I have never read anyone who comments on it. But watching Max McLaughlin's dog in the highly manipulated 'continuous cover' glade – where first the forest itself was artificially inserted into the landscape and now it is being deliberately (and mechanically) managed to look more 'natural', more like the forests of childhood and memory, more like an invented ideal of ancient woodland – I was provoked into questioning the interplay between the imagination and the real, between the forests and the fairy stories, and how that relationship changes. Who are the 'good' and 'bad' characters, and how do we tell? What is animal and natural; what is cultural and human? What is magical? What is imaginary? Everything happens in the forests.

Continuous cover is still a new and experimental approach to forestry, not just in the UK but elsewhere too – and, like any experiment with trees, it will take a very long time to find out if it is going to be successful. But it is also a move back to how forests were managed before modernity, when trees were coppiced or pollarded or left as maidens and then cut individually for timber, when wild and domestic animals were less clearly distinguished, when the line between work and leisure was blurred, and the idea that you grew trees for both 'pleasure and profit' did not need to be argued.

Meanwhile, across the rest of the forest, old-style (which is a very new style) commercial forestry continues, with clear-felling and replanting, and in some places clear-felling that will not be replanted but left to regenerate on its own. In the centre of the forest there is a large, long lake, Kielder Water, which is in truth a reservoir – as artificial as the forest – with boats for hire; there are camping sites; miles of forest track – for riding and off-road cycling and walking, and which include a section of the Pennine Way; a very beautiful new observatory equipped with a large telescope, and also space to use your own. There are some pieces of environmental art scattered encouragingly around; there is a castle and a village with a pub. It is all somewhat confusing – is this forest? Is this a taste of the wild? Is it in fact nothing more than a rather crude theme park intent on making a profit? Is it the best chance we have of preserving into the future some remnant of our forest roots? I do not know the answers here, but it makes me feel intrigued and hopeful to see the Forestry Commission wrestle with them.

In an unexpected way, although the trees and other natural phenomena themselves have little or no resemblance to the forests of the fairy stories, *culturally* Kielder is perhaps more like the medieval forest than the precious and beautiful little pockets of remaining ancient woodland are. A forest like Kielder is a profoundly social place as well as a wild one. In the fairy stories there is always a lot going on in the forests. People work there: the stories are full of characters busy about making their livelihoods – not just in the obvious task of wood cutting, but also mining, hunting, animal tending and farming. In the fictional forests, too, there are villages and castles. There is also a great deal of leisure in the woods of fairytales meetings and eating and socialising of various kinds, like hunting, not only for food, but also for amusement. There are fairs, and evenings by campfires and chance encounters, and a considerable amount of social play. There is learning in the forests – they serve a true educational function: foolish young people go out into the woods and come back wiser, often through positive encounters with trees, flowers, animals, birds, or humans.

The forests of fairy stories are large but, apparently, well populated. There are permanent residents: witches in gingerbread houses, robbers in dens, woodcutters at work, millers in their mills, farmers in their fields, landowners (usually kings) in their castles with their domestic servants and their families around them, and peasants trying to survive. And over and over again, there are travellers, people who do not live or have their business among the trees but who are passing through on their own quests and journeys – on foot, on horseback or in carriages of various descriptions. On the one hand the forest can be very large and lonely; Hansel and Gretel and Snow White are all lost and alone for a while in the forest – but then they all meet strangers, living and busy deep in the woods. The sister in 'The Seven Swans' settles like a bird into a tree to live out her vow of silence – and almost immediately a hunting party comes by; Little Red Riding Hood barely has time to reach her grandmother's house when a woodcutter passes by. All weddings are well attended; all inns are full of company; and if you want to christen your baby daughter, there are at least thirteen wise women living near enough to invite.

There is another fairy-story aspect to Kielder: the road goes right through the middle of it. In other large forests, like the New Forest and the Forest of Dean, there are roads of course, but they usually amble from one village to the next, with the forest broken up by farms and houses. The roads do not enter the forest on one side and go right across it for over thirty miles almost without any break in the solid wall of dark trees on either side and only a few places open enough to see the hills above the forest or the lake at its foot. You leave the wide hill country at Bellingham in the East, set off up the valley of the North Tyne, still small and gurgling over stones, and then it is all forest until you emerge into wide hill country at Riccarton in the West. If you were to drive past Kielder village in the night, you would see the twinkling lights through the trees as the travellers in the fairy stories do. It is a proper journey; once you have passed the dam at the bottom of the lake there are extremely few houses, no shops and no petrol stations on the road until you get to the other end. Off the road there are little rough tracks and paths which lead deep into the forest and eventually out onto the high moors above, but in this respect Kielder replicates the endless travels through the forests of fairytales, the road along which the heroes and heroines go out to seek their fortunes and find their adventures.

I made that journey myself the next day, heading west towards home. The castle, itself an eighteenth-century fake built as a hunting lodge, stood up above the little village, constructed for the original forestry workers (before the village was built they lived in a camp now drowned under the reservoir). The road wound through the trees, up towards the Scottish border and then down into the Liddel Valley. There were miles and miles of unbroken forestry here, enough to be impressive. In 2006, Oliver Rackham wrote:

> Forty years on, was it wise to object so strongly to blanket afforestation? Ought plantations to be scattered over the country, rather than concentrated in a few areas? Blanket afforestation intrudes on fewer views than pepper pot afforestation; it affords economies of scale for the foresters; and it allows plantation ecosystems – whatever they might be – to develop on a large scale and with a wider range of habitats and of possible sources of animals and plants.[15]

Like Rackham, in actual experience I found the enormous reach of Kielder much less intrusive that the frequent little blobs of forestry scattered around the Scottish hillsides. Driving across the open hills to the west, I started to think that all the forests in all the fairy stories are artificial: they are idealised fantasy forests in which strange things can happen and lives can be changed.

Little Red Riding Hood and the Big Bad Wolf

Once upon a time there was a man who lived alone in the forest.

He lived in the forest in a small cottage a long way up a rough track. He worked in the forest, tree felling, track filling, ditch digging, and deer killing. Power saw and rifle. On the whole he worked alone, although if there were tasks to be done requiring more than one worker, he would do his share, silently and without smiling.

Once a week or so he came down his rough track on his quad bike and went to the office to get his work schedule. He broadly followed his orders; no one could quite say that he did not do his job. His boss and his colleagues were uncomfortable around him. There was a faint shadow that fell when he arrived and that evaporated in the sunshine of his departure. They did not like him, but they never teased or bullied him. He was strange and dangerous.

Once a month or so he came down his rough track in his Land Rover and went into the village and bought supplies. Tea bags, powdered milk, sugar, probably more biscuits and less fruit and vegetables than was good for him. He never bought meat, but then most of them didn't – why pay for what you can kill for free? He looked at his feet, never received any post, and spoke to no one.

Once a year he would bring his quad and his Land Rover in for servicing. He would draw his equipment from the store as and when needed, never asking for any favours, never taking less than his due. In the winter the smoke from his stove could sometimes be seen drifting up from among the trees. Occasionally, especially when it was misty or very cold, someone would say in the pub of an evening that he had taken to coming out at night, prowling, spying;

but someone else would tell the first someone not to be so bloody stupid and the conversation would drift off again somewhere else. No one really cared enough to give a sharp, eager edge to the gossip. He was not originally from round there anyway.

Once, maybe three years back, he had not come to the meeting and he had not been to the village. People noticed. They always do. After a week or so Ken and Davie were sent to check on him. They rode up, roaring their quads, partly delighting in the day off, partly irritated, partly curious and, although they would never have admitted it, partly scared. The cottage looked dark and shabby. They shouted a bit outside and finally bashed on the door. He came out looking dreadful, obviously ill, probably feverish; but he had his rifle in his hand and he cursed them, so they fled. Embarrassed by their fear, they told the office he was sick but did not want any help. The next week he arrived at the meeting on time but he did not thank the boys or the foreman.

It was a life.

He lived alone because he liked his own company and disliked the company of other people. He felt safe in the huge emptiness of the forest and its muttered comings and goings. He was at home in the wildness of it, the secrecy. Other people broke into those secrets and into the dark places in his guts. They gave him a fierce headache, which was hatred, although he did not know that.

One night, late – almost midnight – in winter, with snow on the ground and a moon four or five days off the full, silvering the edges of heavy, fast-flying clouds, his phone rang. It was the emergency call – three rings, then silence, then another three rings and silence. After four rounds of that he answered the phone, grunting his name. Could he get down quick? There was a lost child. The voice was almost apologetic. It was Iain's stag night and so most of the boys were away and probably drunk and hard to get hold of. The voice did not quite say they were sorry they had to bother him but it was implicit, hanging there in the frowsty cottage air.

He dressed quickly, took his torch, his rifle, heavy boots, gloves, gaiters, balaclava. First aid kit. Keys to the gates. It was part of the

job, although he had never had to do it before. When he went outside the cold caught his throat and he coughed; then, standing still
in the dark, he heard a high-pitched scream. It was not a child; it
was a rabbit, taken probably by a fox. He knew it was important
that he got down as quickly as possible, before anyone started wondering where he was, but even in his haste he noticed the neat
double footprints of the roe deer along the snow on the track. He
preferred roe to the occasional big red deer that came down from
the high moor; he liked the way their heart shaped rumps flashed
through the trees as they leapt away. Their meat was sweeter and
easier to manage too.

The bike slithered on the icy track and the moon cast lumpy
shadows, making it difficult to judge the best path, but he did
hurry as much as he could. After a noisy while he saw the yellow
lights from the office and the white and red lights from the
gathering cars. He swung his quad into the car park, circled once
and pulled up next to a blue pick-up. As he switched the engine off
and there was the sudden stillness between his legs, he knew. He
knew absolutely what had happened and he was both angry and
frightened.

In the shed they called the office there was a lot of coming and
going. He stood with his back against the wall and watched the
hullabaloo. His boss was sitting at the desk looking worried; there
were four policemen, anxiously trying to get a decent signal; there
were three walkers, rather over-elaborately kitted out; there were
half a dozen folk from the village and a couple from the farms,
already – and there would be more of both soon as the word
spread. There was a conspicuous shortage of the forestry workers –
Iain's stag night was taking place over sixty miles away. In a chair
in the middle of the office there was a hideous heap of blubber and
peroxide blubbering. It was the child's grandmother. His headache
thumped at the sight of her. He closed his eyes. It was all her fault.

She was ten years old. She was wearing pink trainers and a red
anorak. She had been missing since about two o'clock, her grandmother thought. She had almost certainly not left the forest. Of

course she would be all right, but frightened and very cold. They should find her. Not wait till the morning.

His boss got up and pinned a map to the wall; took a felt-tipped pen; started marking circles, looking at his motley and inadequate forces, trying to deploy them sensibly, where there was little sense.

He forced himself to speak through the thudding of his headache. He'd go up Carsfrae, he said, up to the loch, should he? He knew that best.

She couldn't have walked that far, could she, surely? Not if she was alone. If she were alone. The bulk of the grandmother wailed. The older of the policemen looked up sharply, glanced around, his eye pausing speculatively.

He pushed himself stiffly off the wall. His boss nodded at him, relieved that someone was doing something vaguely useful. He went out again into the night.

He took his quad up through the trees. Under their cover the forest was very dark, infinite pools of blackness retreating uncowed before his headlights. After about twenty minutes' riding he stopped at the loch side. Out from under the trees it was much brighter; around the rough shore the water was frozen, glistening in the moonlight; but out towards the middle it was as black as the forest had been. A sudden fierce flit of white overhead was a barn owl on the hunt. The trees crawled up and around both sides of the water and then petered out. At the top end of loch it had proved too boggy even for plantation and the glen ran up into the hills as open rough grass and loose scattered rocks; the moon made enough light out there to see the shape of the hill line.

He switched his engine off and the silence flowed down from the heights. Behind him the trees moaned and creaked softly. He listened, listened to the nothing of the night. Then he unstrapped the rifle, slid it out of its canvas tube and loaded it. Carrying it broken over his forearm, he left the quad at the end of the track and very quietly turned and began to walk up the western edge of the loch. He knew where he was going. Where the Menzell Burn cut down along the forest edge there was a small fall, frozen into silence now, and the channel curved away there and had carved out a peninsula of broken rock. Near the water it was thick with ferns, and in summertime with dragonflies. Behind this was a rock overhang, a small cave. There was its lair.

Three years ago he had taken sick with a fever. Early one morning the two of them – a man, all beard and thick glasses; a woman, skinny with a steel peg in her lower lip and a wild intensity in her eyes – had come to his cottage.

They told him they had stolen a wolf from a zoo and wanted to set it free. But now they had got lost; their van was stuck in some mud ruts quarter of a mile away; they needed his help.

He would have told them to get lost. It was no concern of his. But Ken and Davie arrived, crashing, shouting, hefting his headache up on the muscle of their din. He signed to the two strangers to keep quiet and went out and ran the boys off. He came back into the cottage smiling, and then it was too late. He was committed.

The three of them walked through the wood to the van. The wolf was in the back, mangy, desperate, sad. He could see the sadness, deep in the green eyes that stared without forgiveness, without kindness, without engagement. The beast was restless, turning and turning in the confines of the metal box; it was as lean and strong and fierce as his headache. It was pacing round and round, beautiful and wild.

It was all folly; it was the fever, the madness of the fever and the headache and the green eyes and the sadness. With crafty skill he had lured the wolf out of the van and into the back of his Land Rover. He had pushed the van out of the mud for them and sent them on their way. Then he had taken the Land Rover up to Carsfrae and set the wolf loose. He had gone home to his bed and woken two days later uncertain if it were true or dream. Dream, hallucination, delirium. It was true.

Now as he crept up the loch side in the icy moonlight he was fierce with rage. A stupid child, a little fat spoiled poodle dragged into the forest by her foolish grandmother, ignorant, arrogant, flaunting her so-called sweetness, luring men to evil thoughts, tugging, tugging at his chest. Stupid old woman, fat and flubbery in the chair, wailing. Stupid little girl who should have stayed in town and left him alone. Left the beautiful wolf alone and free on the hillside; the wolf who hunted alone, who struggled against the world. Stupid little brat. Stupid. Stupid. Dangerous idiots. Pink sneakers and a wretched whiny voice.

But even in his rage he was silent, slipping through the trees, careful, deft in the shadows.

Beyond the end of the faint path he had followed, up where the Menzell Burn, frozen into silence, cut down along the forest edge, he found them. The little chubby girl with her clothes torn and her soft belly sticking out under her red jacket, terrified into stillness, petrified, unable to move or shout, was pressed up against a huge boulder left there by a passing glacier a very long time ago. She could not retreat any further and she could not take her eyes off the wolf.

The wolf was three metres away, watching her, crouching, tail and belly low, perfectly attentive. In the moonlight he could see that it was scrawny, too thin and desperate with hunger and grief. The cape of hair on its shoulders, which should have been heavy and luxuriant, was thin and matted into rats' tails. There was terror and sadness in it.

He paused under the shadow of the last tree. He could see that at any moment the child's fear would break out and she would turn to run. She was too stupid and ignorant to know that wolves prefer to attack from behind. When she turned it would pounce. He smiled. Waiting and watching.

Its claws would rip off the silly jacket; the weight of its leap would bowl her over; the fangs would sink into her flanks, and then, when she was down, into her neck. The wolf would be well fed for once, would slink back into the rocks around its cave and lurk there until the winter was over and there was easier ground prey and it would live another wild season, free and beautiful. And he could go home to his bed and no one would ever know.

When he looked at the wolf his headache eased. The wolf was beautiful. The wolf loved him because he had set it free.

All he had to do was nothing. Just wait. She would crack, run, scream. The wolf would kill. Serve the little bitch right – that would teach them to avoid the forest and stick to the paths and leave him in peace; not come tormenting and tempting him. They would never know he had been here, that he had found her, that he had seen anything.

But they would search until they found her bones and then they would hunt the wolf, and there would be weeks of noise and coming and going and being and doing in the forest and there would be no peace. No peace for the wolf. No peace for him. They were not free. They were not wild.

He could sense the tension in the child and in the wolf. He waited as long as he could. He watched her as the wolf watched her. He knew she had not seen him and she was ready to break. Then he snapped up the rifle barrel, raising it in a single movement. The noise made the wolf turn and stare straight at him. He saw its eyes, filled with sadness. He shot it neatly in the dark space between the two green lights.

This is what a wood cutter has to do when a girl child is endangered by a wolf.

He did not want to touch her. She made him sick. But he picked her up and carried her back through the trees to the quad. He lifted her onto the saddle and, swinging up behind her, settled her between his legs. He rode more slowly going down than coming up. He did not speak a single word to her.

He led the child in by her hand, offering no comfort. The office was still a puddle of light. His boss was sitting at his desk with a phone in his hand. One policeman was standing by the door, his cap off and a clipboard in his hand. The grandmother was still a lump of slobbery mess on the chair. Everyone else was out in the forest.

The grandmother started screaming – did he hurt you? What did he do to you? Did he? Are you? The child started snivelling. His headache started thumping.

After he had answered all their questions, they let him go. Dawn was breaking grey and grim. The moon had set. The outline of the trees was pulling away from the dark sky, coming towards him. It was terribly cold. He rode back up to Carsfrae and walked once more up to where the Menzell Burn cut down along the forest edge. The ground was frozen too hard for him to bury the wolf, so after a struggle he broke the ice and threw the body into the loch.

Then he went home and hung himself. They did not find him for eleven days.

He was the wolf.

10

December

The Purgatory Wood

On Christmas Eve I went into the Purgatory Wood.

We were in the middle of a freakish cold snap. Western Galloway is famous for its mild wet climate and we are ill equipped for snow, but December of 2010 was one of the coldest on record and the whole country was locked down under snow and ice. By Christmas Eve it had been over a week since my thermometer had registered a daily maximum temperature above freezing, and I had been six days without running water, dependent on the good will of my neighbours and a daily delivery of a 25-litre flagon on the back of a quad bike. Below the house the river was frozen so hard that I could see the paw tracks of drama: a fox pursuing a rabbit straight across the water.

Nonetheless, it was bright and sunny; it was sunny throughout the whole week, a bright cold sun shining in a bright blue sky and catching the snow into sparks of diamond. Three days before, I had woken at dawn to watch the lunar eclipse: the moon a dark shadowy red against a navy blue sky, while on the other side of the valley the still invisible but rising sun turned the sky pale gold and eggshell blue. On Christmas Eve it was very cold; the snow, which had mainly fallen over a week before, was – untouched by any thaw – still white and fluffy wherever it had not been trodden on; the air was sparkling and crisp and there was no wind.

The Purgatory Wood is a patch of privately owned commercial forestry, which fills in between Arecleoch and Kilgallioch forests, two larger stretches of Forestry Commission plantation, making it a part of the vast (too vast) Galloway Forest. At three hundred square miles, the Galloway Forest Park is the largest in Britain. And while wide swathes of the park are not under plantation at all, because they contain rich ancient woodland or seriously wild hill country, the forestry continues well beyond the boundaries of the park. At all times of year the Purgatory Wood is a sinister and unattractive place, as such plantations tend to be. Typically, it is planted predominantly with non-native spruce, and in winter spruce is particularly flat coloured: monochrome monoculture at its most monotonous. Although there are occasional stands of larch, little looks deader than larch with its needles off – the thin branches and proliferation of twigs make a dry brittle outline like tiny bird bones. The wood is very densely planted and therefore it is well-nigh impossible to walk between the trees; in places, even my dog struggles to force herself through branches that come right down to the ground, so any walker is effectively confined to the track. There are the occasional standard treeless breaks, with drainage ditches dug straight down the centre, but they tend to be boggy here, overgrown with rough tussocky grass, although occasionally I could see down them and out onto the cold white hills. The owner of the wood – an anonymous 'trust' – has, moreover, done a strange thing: it has erected neat little wooden notice boards which give the names of the farmsteads destroyed to plant the trees: Glenkitten, Miltim, Craigenlee. You walk among dead-feeling trees and dispossessed ghosts.

The Purgatory Wood not only has a sinister atmosphere, it also has a dark history. The name was adopted because the wood is planted alongside the Purgatory Burn. The Purgatory Burn marked the western boundary of the leper colony beside Loch Derry, five miles away from where I entered the forest. The care of lepers in the Middle Ages was managed primarily by the Church – the very first leper colony in Britain was founded by Lanfranc, William I's Archbishop of Canterbury, deep in the forest of the Blean in Kent in 1084 – and the monks from the Cistercian Abbey in Glen Luce, down on the coast, gathered lepers at Barlure – now an attractive farmhouse a few miles south of my home. I am unclear where these lepers came from initially. Leprosy (both 'true' leprosy – Hansen's disease, caused by the bacteria *Mycobacterium leprae* and identified in 1873 – and the various other skin complaints mistakenly identified as 'leprosy') was widespread in Britain in the twelfth and thirteenth centuries but not common, so the inhabitants of this colony must have been drawn from an extensive area. When a sufficient number of sufferers had been collected at Barlure, they were led or driven away up onto the high moor and sent across the burn. It was called the Purgatory Burn because, once across it, they could never return; Purgatory in Catholic theology is not the same as Hell – it is a sort holding place where less-than-perfect souls can be refined after death until they are fully fit for heaven. There were no forests on the peat moors then, just long stretches of high rough country, a wild, desolate terrain in which to live out a grim and desolating fate.

The track I took into the Purgatory Wood meets the Southern Upland Way as it climbs up from New Luce, and a single path crosses the Purgatory Burn and runs eastward to Laggangairn (where there is a very smart little modern bothy beside that ruined farmhouse), and then beyond it to the Laggangairn standing stones – the last vestiges of a Bronze Age stone circle, carved with eighth-century Christian graffiti left by the pilgrims to St Ninian's shrine at Whithorn; from there it leads to Kilgallioch, 'the Ladies' House', a nunnery, though whether to serve the lepers, the pilgrims or both is now unknown; and eventually makes it way past the (completely vanished) colony itself on the banks of Loch Derry, before beginning the lovely descent into the Cree Valley. But I was not going so far on Christmas Eve – not in all that cold snow, and with sunset early and the dark gathering before half-past three.

I went to the Purgatory Wood on Christmas Eve with nefarious intent. I went to steal a tree.

The tradition of bringing an evergreen coniferous tree into the house and decorating it for Christmas is of surprisingly recent origin. It seems to have started in Livonia (now Latvia and Estonia) on the Baltic coast in the fifteenth century. But it did not spread beyond urban areas in northern Germany until the early eighteenth century, and took a long time to move south down the Rhine, because the Catholic majority of southern Germany considered it a Protestant custom. (This is slightly ironic because it is now protestant fundamentalists who object to Christmas trees.)[1] The practice was disseminated throughout Europe mainly through the influence of assorted German princesses marrying widely across the continent. The Hanoverians brought the tradition to Britain.

It is not true that Prince Albert introduced Christmas trees. (In fact, Queen – then Princess – Victoria described a Christmas tree in her journal when she was 13.) This popular myth about Prince Albert's role seems to have arisen from the following odd little circumstance. In 1848 the *Illustrated London News* published a woodcut of the royal family grouped round their decorated Christmas Tree. In 1850, *Godey's Lady's Book*, a popular American almanac, published a copy of this picture, but 'photoshopped' it, removing Victoria's tiara and Albert's moustache, to make the scene more domestic for its readership. This picture was enormously influential in establishing Christmas trees in the USA (and may even explain why today American Christmas trees are different from European ones, denser and more regularly shaped than the droopier naturalistic European fashion). The almanac reproduced the picture in 1860, and by the 1870s Christmas trees had become widespread everywhere in both Britain and the USA.

There are no Christmas trees in the traditional fairy stories – partly because when the Grimm brothers were collecting them there were no Christmas trees at all, but also because the fairy stories are curiously lacking in any seasonal detail; occasionally we can guess the time of year in the broadest sense, but usually because of some detail of the plot – Snow White's birth mother, for example, is sitting in a window with an ebony frame doing some sewing when she pricks her finger and a drop of blood falls into the snow on the window sill; it looks so pretty that she prays for a daughter 'as red as blood, as black as ebony and as white as snow'. It must be winter – although even this is slightly surreal because people do not ordinarily sit with the window wide open in the cold of winter. Similarly, characters plough and harvest and hunt – all of which are seasonal activities. The seasons themselves, however, are implied but never described: oral-tradition stories must be ready for use at any moment and not tied too closely to time or place.

But the late appearance of Christmas trees in the real world and the absence of decorated trees more generally in the fairy stories feels a bit surprising, because the tradition of bringing the forest into the home or village to mark special holidays is very ancient. Flowering may was collected and brought home on Mayday; and holly and ivy were used to decorate homes for Christmas throughout the medieval period (as was mistletoe, the sacred plant of several pre-Christian religions, particularly the Druids). Both holly and ivy were quickly given Christian symbolism – ivy representing faith and eternal life (because ivy continues to grow on dead wood), and holly being a reminder of Christ's crown of thorns, the prickly leaves sprinkled with blood-red berries. The popular carol 'The Holly and the Ivy', first found in print in 1709 and probably sung earlier than that, was a replacement for a far older version which had no Christian content at all.

There are ancient customs, too, of decorating trees; winding them in coloured wool was possibly the origin of the maypole, and dancing round them was a tradition that worried the church authorities. At Joan of Arc's trial in 1431 the Inquisitors investigated in considerable detail a local custom in her area of going out to dance around a specific tree. (Joan's trial is immensely illuminating. Her judges were committed to finding something to justify her inevitable death sentence; in this passage they were endeavouring to establish that she was inspired by pagan spirits or superstitions, but similarly in their investigation into her attempt to escape by jumping out of a window, we can learn a good deal about ideas of suicide; and in other parts of the record we can see very early concepts of what would become the characteristics of Christian 'witchcraft' in the following century.) Despite this discouragement, all through Germany – and especially in Bavaria – people danced round and decorated trees, particularly lime (linden, or *tilia*) trees, but this never occurs in any of the Grimms' tales.

But whether the custom was started by ancient pagans or by nineteenth-century nobility, a Christmas tree – a real one with coloured lights, a trumpeting angel and a disparate collection of ornaments, some of which I have hung every year since I have had a home of my own – feels like a necessary part of my Christmas. At the same time I resent the ridiculous prices charged for trees, and so on Christmas Eve I went into the forest to steal one.

To be honest, my plans were neither as bold nor as wicked as this sounds. I did not take an axe, I took my long-handled garden loppers, which would struggle to cut through any living wood more than a few centimetres thick. I only wanted a very small tree.

The Purgatory Wood was planted in the 1970s, so from a commercial point of view it is nearly mature and should be clear-felled in the next few years. Like most commercial forestry of this type, it has a reasonably solid and usable vehicle track which runs in a big loop through the forest, originally for the purposes of planting, and now of maintaining and inspecting the trees and clearing the drains. These tracks have to carry quite heavy vehicles through the lifetime of the forest. On the wet steep slopes of a forest like the Purgatory Wood where the ground is naturally peaty and boggy and also full of large chunks of rock left by the retreating glaciers at the end of the last ice age, a common way of constructing such a track is to build up a sort of ridge or rampart of loose granite chips and then tamp down the surface. Obviously such a track is vulnerable to water erosion and even to being washed away by rain and flooding, so deep drainage ditches are often cut on both sides of the raised plinth, usually with pipes running through below the driving surface to carry the water under the road and off the hill. This means that you walk as it were above the level of the ground either side of you on a sort elevated causeway. Meanwhile, the planted trees are set back a bit from the track so that their roots will not damage the drainage runnels. Between track and trees then there is a strip of ground which forms a remarkable little micro-habitat of its own. It draws on both the artificial forest and the old land which was there before the forest was imposed on it. The thick trees give this little band shelter from the wind; the width of the track lets in some sunlight; the drainage cuts make it damp; and the disturbance of the ground while constructing it makes it irregular – huge boulders, for example, have been pushed aside by the original digger.

Unexpected things flourish here – mosses, ferns and fungi, but also grasses, wild flowers and scrubby bushes, and even small trees. The carnivorous plants of wet acid bog seem to do particularly well. The little spoon-shaped leaves of the sundew spread out into quite extensive patches that look red-gold because of the stiff little hairs covering the leaf surface and waiting hopefully for the arrival of a passing insect to supplement the limited nutrients in the acid soil. Each hair exudes a little drop of viscous liquid, so that in low sunshine they seem to be bejewelled by dew that does not evaporate in the daytime. Because of this:

> Early herbalists believed that by 'sipping the distilled water thereof ... the naturall and lively heate in mens bodies is preserved and cherished.' This was the origin of a whole range of potions based on the sundew's syrupy seductive secretions ... Throughout Europe it was mixed with a variety of spices to make a liquor called *Ros Solis*, which was regarded as a source of youthful looks and strength, virility and longevity. Inevitably sundew was also believed to be a love-charm, a reputation enhanced when its mysterious power to lure and entrap other creatures was eventually realised.[2]

But probably my favourite of these trackside carnivores (or part carnivores) is the butterwort, whose tiny orchid-like flowers stand singly on fine but sturdy stems well above the rosette of pale, fleshy, sticky leaves. It can apparently grow directly on wet rocks and always seems unlikely, unexpected in its refined delicacy.

There are other treats, too, along these forest bands. In Purgatory Wood there is a place where I have seen flag irises flowering with heather. And as a sudden total shock, a healthy clump of cottage peonies, violently pink amidst the sombre colour scheme of browns and greens. It has been suggested to me that these might mark the garden ground of a now-vanished cottage; but they are still startling and somehow inappropriate. The wild roses, bilberries, and, best of all, wild raspberries seem somehow more suited to the place. You enjoy all these unexpected little delights as you look down from the track, with an easy elevated view.

And, to cut to the chase, in places, usually right beside the track, little self-seeded spruces, which cannot break out into the light within the planted forest, germinate cheerfully and sit there inviting an act of minor yuletide theft. They grow crookedly and weakly, often close together or with several trunks, asymmetrical and scrubby. They have no future, and when their big parent trees are ready for harvesting the developer will arrive with vast machinery and widen and remake the whole track solid enough for the lorries to haul out the timber, and these little seedlings will be mowed down and abandoned. I am in effect looking through a rubbish dump for a little unwanted tree, less than a metre high. I search carefully for one that is reasonably straight, reasonably regular in its profile, and somehow measuring up to my idea of what a miniature Christmas tree should look like.

'Methinks the lady doth protest too much.' It is theft and I know it. As a matter of fact, Christmas tree theft is a real problem and on the increase. In the UK trees are most usually stolen already cut from retail outlets, like garden centres. It seems that most are taken singly and for personal use, but they can be a valuable haul too, almost impossible to identify and easily sold on. They are also stolen from the ground, cut down in the further corners of Christmas tree farms, or the distant reaches of plantation forest, often at night, and slipped away in 4x4s or trailers under cover of darkness. The thieves do pretty much what I was doing – slipping semi-legally onto a piece of land where it is not illegal to walk and then stealing the landowner's property. In a sense it is a kind of poaching, except that wild animals (even bred wild animals like pheasants) cannot be anyone's 'property', while wild plants (including planted ones) do belong to the landowner. This is 'illegal logging', to put it crudely, and the local version of this – for domestic use, fuel or whatever, is a small but significant part of deforestation, carbon emission growth and natural habitat spoliation. I am not entirely sure why I feel a sturdy inner confidence that it is somehow all right for me to take my Christmas tree in this way while being very strict about how any timber I purchase (for furniture or for building) is properly and legally cut.

On Christmas Eve, under a nearly untouched cover of soft white snow, and on a faintly guilt-inducing (or at least don't-get-caught) expedition, the Purgatory Wood seemed especially eerie. There is only one road access into the plantation, and that is up a long single-track country road. The gate is always kept padlocked, which, under the Scottish Access code, it probably should not be, but it is a good solid clean gate and easy to lift the dog over and then climb myself.

That afternoon it was plain to see that one vehicle had been in since the snowfall, leaving clean, precise tyre lines in the snow. There were sharp little roe-deer tracks, and either a large dog or more likely a fox had walked up the hill before I did, but overall the snow lay smooth and dense – so white in the sunshine, and flat because there had been no wind to ruffle or drift its surface. Each branch of each tree had a perfectly poised line of snow on it, and under the trees where the snow had not reached the ground, it was by contrast very black and dark. I headed up the hill about half a mile into the forest where I had previously noticed a little patch of small spruce seedlings and where I planned to cull 'my' tree. I had slightly underestimated the difficulties of selecting a tree in thick snow. One problem was that I could not see the base of the tree trunks, as they were hidden beneath the white surface, and consequently I could not accurately gauge the height or be certain that

the tree under consideration was separate from the ones that surrounded it. Another was that what, on the bigger trees, were
charming, decorative lines of snow were, on these tiny ones, heavy
enough to weight down the branches and distort the shape. Since
my conscience would not allow me to cut a tree and then reject it, I
had to get it right first time. I wandered around my little thicket
kicking promising trees to dislodge the snow and then waiting for
the branches to rise up to their natural angle; I ferreted around the
bases, clearing away enough snow to get very wet, cold hands and
to inspect the point at which the tree emerged from the ground. The
area began to look rather peculiar, as wherever I had kicked a tree
it was dark green and prickly, while those around it stayed white
with the sharpness of the needles softened by the snow; and the
ground began to look as though a flock of demented rabbits had
been scrabbling there. Finally I made my choice (not, I have to say,
entirely successfully – that year's tree will not go down in the annals
as one of my better selections; it was not quite straight and was a
little spindly) and cut down and lifted out the chosen tree.

I stood back in the middle of the track and paid attention to the
forest itself. Although it was only early afternoon, the northern sun
this near to the solstice stays low in the southern sky, so there was no
direct sunlight; but looking back down the track, I could see over the
trees and out onto the Markdhu Fell and the distinct shape of the
Corlie Craig at the top of it bathed in golden sunshine. The shadows of the dyke along the moor edge looked very black. Inside the
forest the trees seemed to stretch away for miles. Up there, the long
grass broke through the snow, creating golden patches bright under
the very blue sky, so that it looked a completely different colour, a
different world, from the blue-white shaded forest around me. It was
perfectly still and completely silent.

But although I could hear no sound at all, I was aware that something was going on because suddenly the dog, who had been
snuffling about to her own amusement, was standing rigid, head up,
quivering with attention, alert and looking straight into the blackness of the trees.

Snow has a strange acoustic effect. Sound diminishes over distance, but does not do so in a measurable way – there is a sound phenomenon called 'attenuation', which causes the distance and volume at which sound travels to vary according to the atmosphere. Noise attenuates more rapidly the hotter and drier the air is. (This is one reason why it is famously so silent in deserts – the hot dry air swallows up the sounds.) Equally, sound carries further and louder in cold, wet weather. Obviously, cold and wet do not always go together any more than hot and dry do – the calculations are complex in all weather conditions. But with snow, thick soft snow, there is a further complication because, just like a thick soft carpet or curtains inside a house, the snow absorbs the sound (rather than bouncing it back like rock cliffs or plain windows and walls do). The overall effect is to separate individual clear noises from general background murmur, so that the former become sharper while the latter fade. It also makes it very hard to guess the distance from the source of the sound to the ear.

The explosive bang of a rifle shot was therefore sudden and enormous, and seemed to come from very close indeed. It was immediately followed by a bizarre cacophony of noise: the dog started barking, high and sharp in the clear still air, and simultaneously there was a great cracking and smashing of wood. Three roe deer broke out into the open and leapt across the drainage ditch less than ten metres from where I was standing; seeing me too late, the lead deer immediately spun round to head up the track, but there was the dog dementedly barking; the second deer, trying desperately to flee the rifle somewhere behind it, and avoid both me and the dog, slipped on the track and fell. There was a flurry of panicked deer, one sprawled and struggling to get on its legs again, the other confused and frantic. The third deer found a path between me and the dog, crossed the track and second drainage channel in two huge glorious bounds, and led the way into the forest on the other side, followed amazingly rapidly by the other two and then by the wildly over-excited dog. Briefly I could see the leaping movement of their white butts, and then, as they thrust into the dark trees, snaking and pushing through the lower branches, I could hear but not see them.

The whole noisy episode was over within moments. I knew that my dog could not catch them and would return shortly, wet and panting and pleased with herself, so I felt no concern. I stood on the track with my little tree in one hand and my loppers in the other and tried to calm myself. It had been a shattering, as well as a rather magical, moment; I had been very abruptly shocked out of silence, and there is always a purely physical reaction when this happens; but I quickly realised that this was not, or was not all, that was making me scared: it was the invisible man with the gun in the forest. A thug, a robber, a maniac killer.

Afterwards I realised that this was ridiculous: in the first place, had I been attentive to what I had seen, I would have known there was someone in the forest, because there had been that single line of car tracks coming up the hill in the snow, and since I knew there was no other way in or out for vehicles, I could have worked out that whoever it was was still in the plantation. Second, whoever it was was there legitimately, because the gate had been neatly padlocked behind the car tracks, so he must have had a key. It was almost certainly one of the good guys of the forest – a woodcutter, a huntsman, a forester. Because deer are so destructive to woodland (see chapter 8), it is very normal in this sort of plantation to issue licences to competent sportsmen and encourage them into the forest to cull deer. There was no reason for me to suppose that this was anyone other than that. Nonetheless, I was alarmed.

I had a second, more rational reason for anxiety. People shoot foxes, as well as deer, in these woods. My border terrier looks at first sight remarkably like a fox – indeed, the previous summer I had yelled at her as she streaked through long grass out on the high moor, apparently out of control and off after the sheep. After a few moments of infuriating impotence as I tried to get her even to listen, let alone obey as she disappeared into the bracken, I was drawn by some small noise to look down and she was sitting just beside me looking worried: I had been shouting, ineffectually, at a fox. My neighbours are all aware of this possible confusion, and are mostly kindly and careful, but an armed stranger in the thick trees might have shot her accidentally.

But I quickly realised that this was not the source of the gripping fear I experienced then. It was the fear of a robber band, a murderous gang, or even a party of giants.

This was a different fear – it felt physically different from the true forest terror, the uncanny fairy-tale shivers I discussed in Chapter 8. That fear comes from inside, from the imagination and, I believe, from my body itself. The fear of robbers, of violence and violation comes from external sources, like this: rifle shots; stashes of old alcohol containers – broken bottles and empty beer cans; seriously abused and wrecked bothies; and the distant growl of dirt bikes and quads where there should not be any. As a matter of fact, I strongly suspect that the riding of illegal bikes in wild places and the back-hill drunken parties in ruined steadings are not usually remotely sinister or likely to lead to rape and robbery, although they are potentially hideously damaging to the forest environment – the deep peat of the Silver Flow, about twenty miles East of the Purgatory Wood, is probably ruined for ever because of the wild off-track journey that quad-bike fashion has developed from Carsphairn to Gatehouse of Fleet which routes itself through several SSSIs. But the fear is there; it is a fear brought on by hearing or seeing something aggressively human, where you thought there was nothing but wilderness. It is a particular forest fear, because people can be so near you without you seeing them. Other walkers on hill or moor are usually visible a long way away. In the densely planted forest there are no long views; there are natural sounds and things on the move that you cannot identify and some of them may be 'wild', but equally they may be human and dangerous. Without the gunshot, three deer suddenly leaping across a track in front of me would have been startling, even alarming – and the dog would have been just as deranged. A sheep in the dark, or a fox, or even a large bird encountered suddenly can be breath stopping, but the fear evaporates immediately with identification and knowledge. The sharp awareness that you are not alone, and that strangers may be very near to you indeed and no one, except the stranger, will hear you if you scream generates a straightforward and not necessarily irrational or inappropriate fear.

For me, and I expect for most women, there is an extra edge to this fear – most of the people you encounter in wild places are men; the sorts of things that create this sort of fear are strongly connected, for me, with masculinity. Yes, of course there are women who lurk about in the high hills and deep in the woods – indeed, I am one of them – but guns, hard drinking and noisy vehicles have the deep fear of rape as well as robbery attached to them.

I never saw the man with the gun that day, although I have often met strangers in the woods: men with guns, men with binoculars and cameras, men with power saws and survey rods – and none of them have ever in the flesh felt remotely threatening. But under the trees it is very dark – someone in there could be watching me, tracking me, stalking me rather than the deer and I do not know who they are or where they are or how many they are.

The fear is there and is particularly present for anyone immersed in fairy-story literature. Because, along with those who work there – woodcutters, foresters, miners, huntsmen and hermits, who are usually on the side of goodness and love – forests in fairy stories have practical as well as magical dangers. As well as wicked witches, greedy wolves or other magical perils, there are robbers, murderous gangs and human social dangers. Robbers are a very different kettle of fish in the fairy stories either from the legitimate inhabitants of the woods or from outlaws, exiles or the dispossessed. It is not always morally clear why one cunning tricky character is a hero and another a villain – except perhaps the virtue of courtesy. The tricksiest hero, the most determined heroine is always polite. Robbers are not polite – they have appalling table manners and aggressive conduct.

There are a lot of them. We think of fairy stories as being about princes and princesses, but, as I pointed out, there are only 29 (out of 210) stories in the Grimms' collections in which the principal character is a prince or princess. In fact, there are more stories –

over thirty – that feature robbers – often in gangs – thieves, and other criminal individuals. These are stories about 'stranger danger'. Your stepmother is highly likely to try and get rid of you, your father to sacrifice you selfishly for his own comfort, your brothers to laugh at you and take sibling rivalry well beyond the point of humour. (Your sisters, on the other hand, are an almost invariable resource of support, succour and love.) Your beloved's parents, your own servants, and assorted wicked old women may well be ranged against you; the Devil himself, magical animals and powerful elemental forces will endeavour to work your downfall. But the robbers are in a different category – they are nameless strangers and there is really nothing personal about their assaults; in a sense, they are simply doing their job. In 'The Robber Bridegroom', which is very nearly a Bluebeard story, except that the heroine makes no error apart from agreeing to marry a man she does not feel comfortable with, the robber's action is so impersonal that he kidnaps, kills and eats a different woman even while expecting his fiancée to supper – he is driven by simple wickedness and violence untouched by love or indeed any emotional engagement whatsoever.

The robbers are the single most serious practical, as opposed to magical, danger that that heroes and heroines have to encounter, with the possible exception of parental poverty for the young and the unhappiness of marrying without love. These robbers are not usually burglars; they do not break into houses to steal while the residents are safely in bed. They attack people who are on the road, travellers – and usually travellers passing through forests.

Clearly assaults by robbers on travellers are not confined to forests. The road from Jerusalem to Jericho is semi-desert, but 'falling among robbers' there was a sufficiently recognisable misfortune to find its way into Jesus's parables, with the story of the Good Samaritan. Travel has always been dangerous, and some of the fairy stories reflect just this simple knavery such as anyone might encounter on the road, and against which modern travellers take out insurance. When I earlier described the story 'The Magic Table, the Golden Donkey and the Club in the Sack', I did not focus on the narrative role of a rascally innkeeper who steals the table that spreads itself with food and the donkey that spews out gold coins from the two older brothers on their way home from apprenticeships. The innkeeper is thwarted by the youngest brother, whose magical cudgel which 'plays such a dance on the innkeeper's back' that he returns the two previous thefts as well. This is a moral tale about it not being enough to go out into the world and earn your fortune – you have also to be wary and clever about guarding and keeping it. This is not a story about the forest, or even really about robbers.

But the robbers who were imaginatively scaring me in the Purgatory Wood are very much a product of forests. They lurk there in hidden bands, in old houses or caves. The four Bremen town musicians are trying to escape serious threats to their lives by leaving home and going to seek their fortune. They form an association and journey through the forest to find a better living. They get lost; night comes on; they seek what shelter and safety they can, and then through the trees (as so often) they see a light; they make their way towards it and arrive at a 'well-lighted robbers' house'. Through the window they can see 'a table covered with good things to eat and drink, and the robbers sitting at it enjoying themselves'. So the four of them come up with a crafty plan to drive the robbers out and take possession. 'After this the robbers never again dared to enter the house; but it suited the four musicians of Bremen so well that they did not care to leave it anymore.'

It is, in terms of the story, totally irrelevant that the four 'heroes' are a donkey, a dog, a cat and a cockerel. These are not magical animals, they are the fairytales' usual old lags betrayed by their masters and using their wits to survive; they are the wounded soldiers, the abused children, the abandoned old women and all the other victims who do well in the fairy stories. Each of them has given good service in their appointed role and has now been rendered redundant; they seem to be animals solely to add an element of humour to the plot, and to make the abject defeat of the supposedly dangerous robbers all the more humiliating for them. The moral here is: 'Don't be afraid: the robbers aren't that dangerous;

the profit of cunning is greater than the profit of power.' One of the hidden aspects of this story, and of others of a similar genre, is that the robbers do not actually do any robbing. Although the protagonists can, at a single glance, identify them as robbers – bad guys, whose property can reasonably be taken away from them – they do not in fact do anything except live well in a non-familial and therefore anti-social setting.

The usual function of robbers in fairy stories is to provide the protagonists with a rich source of money and comfort that they can legitimately lay claim to. The protagonists cannot, for example, steal from members of their own social group – other travellers, working families, lone old women unless they are witches (who are as easily identified as robbers), or children; this would be despicable and would lose them their hero status in an instant. They may, however, outwit kings and robbers. Indeed, they should.

This is not to say that historically there were not real robber gangs in forests and other lonely places, ready to prey on vulnerable travellers. Just over the hill, barely ten miles west of the Purgatory Wood, on the Ayrshire coast between Ballantrae and Girvan, was the cave-lair of the terrible Sawney Bean. In the early seventeenth century he and his vile gang, made up mainly of his incestuously generated offspring, terrorised the neighbourhood, attacking travellers, robbing them of their possessions and subsequently killing and eating them.[3] When the local militia finally caught up with him they found his cave not just littered with human bones, but hung with carcasses being smoked over the fire.

Even earlier there was a worry that roads and paths through woods were particularly vulnerable to robbers and muggers. In 1285 some of the first legislation about this was passed, possibly in response to the murder of two travellers through the Prior of Barnwell's Wood at Bourn in Huntingdonshire.

The highroads from merchant towns to other merchant towns [must] be widened wherever there are woods or hedges where a man may lurk to do evil near the road, by two hundred feet on

[both sides]; but this statute extend not to oaks or to great trees,
if they be clear underneath. And if by default of the Lord who
may not want to level earthwork, underwood or bushes as
provided above and robberies be done, the Lord is responsible.
And if there be murder, let the Lord be fined at the King's will.[4]

Curiously, clearing the sides of tracks through the forest, as pro-
posed by this law, would produce an almost identical effect to the
cleared areas between track and trees in the Purgatory Wood, and
elsewhere, which the forestry developers have now made for other
reasons. Moreover, although no ditches as such are mentioned in the
legislation, these clearings were called 'trenches', bringing to mind
the drainage channels either side of me as I walked. I was sensible
to be a bit frightened.

But the real point about fairy stories is that they laugh at the powerful and the frightening. They diminish and belittle the danger by
mocking it, and simultaneously they encourage cunning and trickery as a way of achieving the security that is every protagonist's
desire and right. Kings are mean-minded and foolish; robbers are
cowardly and boorish – both deserve to be outwitted exploited and
to provide the fortune that the heroes and heroines need.

In this sense, the robbers are closely related to giants, who also
appear regularly in the stories. Although my own fears that afternoon focused directly on robbers, and I would have been startled in
a very different way if a giant had emerged from the forest, the two
perform almost identical functions in the fairy stories. They share a
good deal in common too: although always fierce and threatening,
and thus provoking great fear in mediocre individuals, they are
stupid and easily outwitted by those who overcome their fear. Like
robbers, giants have disgusting domestic habits, often living out in
the open air or in dens rather than houses – and they enjoy heavily
carnivorous diets. They also have hoards of loot or 'treasure', which
the hero can access legitimately; in this particular, they are very like
the dragons of medieval romance and hagiography. It is always
heroic to kill giants because they deserve it, just because they are

giants – they are too big. There seems to be something almost amounting to a rule here – the smaller the main character in a fairy story, the larger his opponent. I cannot find a story in which a prince kills or outwits a robber – that is the task of the poor but brave and cunning hero who tackles robbers with humour and insouciance. But the diminutive hero – the Little Tailor or the succession of Tom Thumbs and Thumblings, the physically weak, disempowered or vulnerable – performs the same task with giants.

In fact I probably misunderstood my own fear in the Purgatory Wood: the person who shot the rifle was the hero – I was the robber.

The Four Comrades

Once upon a time in a winter so cold and hungry that mothers cut and ground silverweed to make flour to feed their children, a farmer decided that he could not keep his donkey any longer. The donkey had served him well and faithfully for many years, but now it was weak, its knees knocking inwards like spindleshanks and its coat matted and patchy. It stumbled at the plough, was too scrawny to ride and unable to carry firewood in from the forest.

The old man decided to send it to the knackers. That's gratitude for you. 'No, no,' said his children piteously, and possibly nervously, for they knew from the old stories that kindness to animals made you rich. But it did no good. Hard frosts make hard hearts.

The donkey was not having any of that. In the night it slipped its halter and set off along the road through the forest, planning to go to the nearest city and join the circus – or even try a little street busking if nothing better came up.

As the icy dawn broke the donkey met a dog – a poor, sad, mangy thing, its claws pulled to stop it hunting and its back quarters stiff with age. It was pretty much toothless and but a weary shadow of its youthful self. It lay beside the roadside, the very portrait of dejection.

'What ho?' said the donkey, full of bravado now it had made its break from slavery. 'Smile, mate, it may never happen.'

'It has happened,' said the dog gloomily. 'Years of faithful service, all-round good and devoted canine, competent pointer, cunning retriever, energetic house guard, a bit of herding and gentle with children. And what do I get for it? Rendered redundant, no pension, no dinner and an overheard threat of murder. All the children said "No, no" most piteously, but I didn't see them feeding me any scraps. That's gratitude for you. Didn't have any options but to slip my leash and make a getaway. Hard frosts make hard hearts.'

'Well,' said the donkey, 'let's join forces. United we stand, you know. I'm off to the town – and could use a partner. Can you do any tricks?'

'I can do quite a stylish begging thing, and can die for my country. The kids like that.'

'Patriotism is not enough,' said the donkey.

So together they went on along the track through the forest and before long they met a cat.

'Bugger,' said the dog. 'Now I suppose I'll have to chase it.'

'New occasions make new duties,' said the donkey; 'time makes ancient good uncouth. Defence is the best form of defence, if you ask me. Give it a try.' In his imagination he refigured himself as a Robin Hood type wearing a Che Guevara-style beret, though it fitted oddly because of his ears.

It transpired that the cat had a similar story to tell: despite a lifetime's employment in efficient rodent management and letting the babies pull her fur, the cat had – that very morning – learned that she was going to be put in a sack and drowned in the mill pond. 'That's gratitude for you,' she said,. 'The children said "No, no" piteously of course, but they drank every drop of milk in the house and never offered me so much as a lick. Felinism is worse than sexism. I know how it is. Hard frosts make hard hearts.'

'You'd better come along with us,' said the donkey. 'Workers of the world unite; we have nothing to lose but our chains.'

'No one chains me,' said the cat haughtily. But noticing that the donkey looked peevish, she quickly added, 'Great rhetoric though.'

So the three of them together went on along the track through the forest, and before long they met a cockerel. He was far from shabby and run down; his comb was scarlet and his feathers fine and his voice loud enough to wake the dead.

'Damn,' said the cat, 'Now I suppose I'll have to hunt it. No rest for the wicked, eh.'

'Au contraire,' said the donkey. 'Give peace a chance.'

(The others were beginning to find his sententious quotations rather irritating, but live and let live was their motto.)

The cockerel's tale was a sorry one. Although he crowed piercingly each morning, so the children got to school on time and the milch-cow knew when to let down her milk and the hens when to lay their eggs, his owner had unfortunately discovered that he was gay and therefore unable, or at least unwilling, to service the flock, and had decided instead to wring his neck and boil him into soup.

'There's gratitude for you,' said the others, 'but hard frosts make hard hearts, they say.'

'It is not about ingratitude,' said the cockerel indignantly, 'it's about homophobia and sexual exploitation.'

Nonetheless, he liked the idea of being in a troupe in the city a good deal more than he liked the idea of being in a pot in the oven, so he went along with them.

So the four of them together went on along the track through the forest. They passed a pleasant enough day exploring their ideological differences and exchanging competitive stories of their personal suffering and oppression. But towards evening it became clear that they would have to pass a night in the forest, which appeared to be endless.

'Ah well,' said the donkey dramatically,

'Fair this long road, these hoary woods are grand

But we are exiles from our fathers' land.'

'Cliché,' exclaimed the others, finally infuriated, for it was getting darker and colder by the moment, and hard frosts make hard hearts, as we have learned.

Nonetheless, there was nothing to be done so they had to make the best of it, and they settled in, under, on and up a great granny of a Scots pine whose branches offered some small shelter from the rising wind. Separate now in their chosen beds, they turned inwards each to sleep in his or her own way.

'Tired nature's sweet restorer, balmy sleep,'
murmured the donkey,
'that knits up the ravelled sleeve of care.'

But before any of them could find true contentment in what the
donkey might well have called 'the tender embrace of Morpheus',
the cockerel, who was furthest up the tree, suddenly let out a surprised squawk. Through the thick woods and the thick darkness he
could see the cheerful light of a fire. His comrades were less keen
than he might have hoped.

'Typical,' said the dog. 'Now we have to get up and plod through
the trees until we come to a little house or cave and it will be a
witch's cottage, or worse, because it bloody well always is.'

'Or a robbers' den,' sighed the cat.

Nevertheless, the requirements of the narrative obliged them to
make their way towards the light.

The cat was right. It was a robbers' den, and peering through the
window, they could see the robbers looking fierce and wicked, all
gobbling down an enormous and tasty dinner.

But these four were not stupid human beings who – at this point –
always go in and ask for succour and get into trouble and the story
runs on for another six pages. They were intelligent animals nearly
at their wits' end. So the donkey stood at the window and the dog
jumped onto his back and braced himself against the horror of letting a cat scramble onto his head. She did, nonetheless, and the
cockerel fluttered onto hers, and at the word of command they began
their concert:

The donkey brayed.

The dog barked.

The cat yowled.

And the cock shouted, 'Cockadoodledoo, doodledo, doo do.'

A hideous cacophony, enough to scare any robbers out of their
minds, and these ones rushed out of the house and, as they passed
the four comrades, the donkey kicked them and the dog bit them and
the cat scratched them and the cockerel pecked their faces, and they
ran away through the forest and never dared to come back again.

So the donkey and the dog and the cat and the cockerel decided not to go to the city, but to settle down in this handsome retirement home, grow fat on the robbers' ill-gotten gains, and live happily ever after, because:

All animals except humans know that the principal business of life is to enjoy it and they do enjoy it.

There are lots of morals to this little fable about gratitude and friendship and making the best of things. I will leave you to work them out for yourself, but remember: The darker the night the brighter the song; the colder the winter the sillier the story, so they say.

11

January

Glenlee

A wet, raw January, when the dark pounces before 3.30 in the afternoon, does not feel like the time of year for stomping off to walk in the wild woods. It feels more like the time of year for curling up in front of a log fire, watching the flames and slightly dreamily reading fairy stories.

It is also the time of year when I, like all gardeners, occupy myself planning next year's garden; imagining schemes and ordering plants. So I find myself spending time thinking not so much about forests as about gardens. And thinking about fairy stories and gardens together turns my mind to the nineteenth-century romantic aesthetic in gardening which led to the development of ornamental forests and woods, artificial, but not in the sense that commercial plantation forests are artificial; to the creation of woods of the imagination, the forests of artists and of fairy stories. And I am struck afresh by the synchronicity between the rise of woodland gardens and the re-emergence of fairy stories; this new type of garden emerged, in both Germany and Britain, at almost precisely the same time as the Grimm brothers – speedily followed by other collectors – were first publishing their fairy stories. Indeed, I would argue that they came out of the same cultural movement and influenced each other profoundly. Throughout the nineteenth century

people were creating new woods suitable for fairies to live in. They
were woods that were meant to look like ancient woods – or, more
precisely, like people imagined old woods had looked.

Over Christmas Cathy Agnew, the wife of a very old friend of
mine, told me how her husband had taken his small nieces into the
wood behind their home, Glenlee, and persuaded them that fairies
lived in it and played under a beech tree. So, on a slightly less grim
day than many have been recently, I found myself driving over the
hill road to Glenlee to explore its wood that is still, at least in the
imagination, home to fairies.

Glenlee is a substantial country house built in 1823. It was
designed by Robert Lugar, a fashionable and successful architect of
the time, who was a leading proponent of the Gothic revival, particularly in Scotland and Wales. Howard Colvin, the architectural
historian, comments of Lugar that he 'was a skilful practitioner of
the picturesque, exploiting the fashion for *cottages ornes* and castel-
lated Gothic mansions ... he was among the first to introduce the
picturesque formula into Scotland'.[1] For Lugar, as he himself made
clear, the fundamental attraction at Glenlee was its location:

> The situation is most agreeably retired, and partakes much of the
> character of an English park, abounding in well-grown forest-trees,
> which seclude it, by their density, from the mountain scenery which
> surrounds it.
>
> The walks up the glen are highly picturesque, and present
> many beautiful and interesting views, connecting the rich park
> scene and fertile valley with the distant mountains.[2]

'Agreeably retired' remains true: Glenlee is a few miles north of
New Galloway, a small village at the head of Loch Ken, in the
Valley of the Dee. The whole area, known as the Glenkens, is
unusually lovely, and ecologically very rich; it is a Ramsar site;[3] the
green fertile valley is hemmed in by true 'wilderness' – the Galloway
Hills to the north and east, and the muscular bulk of Cairnsmore of
Carsphairn in the Scaur Hills to the west. The valleys of the Dee

and Water of Ken and the long twist of Loch Ken itself create a green corridor between Ayr and Kirkcudbright. Additionally, the Glenkens have extremely romantic associations – most famously, when Young Lochinvar 'rode out of the west', he rode down from his home here, to kidnap his bride across the border in northern England.[4] Walter Scott's poem about him was published in 1808[5] to almost instant acclaim. The area was also much admired by Robert Burns (1759-1796), whose friend John Syme wrote: 'I can scarcely conceive a scene more terribly romantic . . . Burns thinks so highly of it, that he meditates a description of it in poetry.'[6] So when Lugar came to design Glenlee, its romantic associations were well in place and cannot have failed to inspire his architectural concept.

Although every imaginable approach to Glenlee brings the traveller through wonderful countryside, I probably have the very best of it arriving from the west, along the Queen's Way – the road through the hills from Newton Stewart. This savagely harsh landscape is where Richard Hannay had his Scottish adventure in *The Thirty-Nine Steps* after he 'fixed on Galloway as the best place to go'.[7] It is too heavily planted with forestry now, but in places there are great rough sheets of granite so near the surface that even the most optimistic forester never tried to plant there, and there are good views of the Galloway Hills, gaunt and lowering, with the pale winter sunlight catching the remaining snow up on the heights. The wild goats have come down beside the road: they are 'feral goats' really, the now wild descendants of the goats that preceded sheep as the common domestic animal of the poor on the high farms in extreme wild places in Scotland. They inhabit the Galloway Hills, like ghosts of a lost way of life.

I find myself thinking about the goats which feature in the fairy stories. There are a good number of them, and they more frequently speak in human language than any other animal except birds. Although adult goats are often tricky and mean tempered and get the protagonists of the fairy stories into trouble of various kinds, baby goats, properly called kids, are always both vulnerable and charming in character. During the nincteenth century the word 'kid', which had previously been used to describe a young pugilist or thief, began to be used more generally (though the *OED* still lists it as 'slang')[8] to describe human children, usually affectionately. I wonder if that shift in meaning – from pugilist to child, from thief to innocent – was influenced by the very positive role baby goats play in the fairy stories. It is unusual for a word to 'improve' its standing; it is much more common – as we have already seen with 'gossip' and 'villain' – for a word to collect negative rather than positive connotations and associations. But 'kid' became affectionate and less critical over exactly the same period that the fairy stories became better known within literate society.[9]

Beyond Clatteringshaws Loch, I leave the main road for a very narrow little lane that winds down to the broad valley of the Dee, bypassing New Galloway. The landscape changes abruptly here, the land dropping steeply, although the big hills are still visible to the north. Suddenly it is pastoral; the forestry stops and is replaced by older deciduous woodland of oak, ash and rowan, all bare-branched now, with willow scrub marking the courses of the tumbling burns. This is the Garroch Glen, and it has a secret wild enchantment enhanced by its contrast with the fierce hill country.[10] Here on the steep side of the valley, tucked under the hills above it, is Glenlee. In fact the lane runs behind the house and its park, so I was looking down, through the trees, over the valley. It is still, nearly two hundred years later, very much as Lugar described it: 'highly picturesque', with 'many beautiful and interesting views, connecting the rich park scene and fertile valley with the distant mountains'.

Originally parks had been fairly open wooded areas designed for the preservation and formal hunting of deer; but various factors – including the enclosures, which broke up the necessary large areas with fences, and the improvements to guns, which made game-shooting more pleasurable – meant that this sort of deer hunting declined in popularity from about the beginning of the eighteenth century.[11] At the same time, and partly in response to this, many landowners redeveloped their deer parks as ornamental landscapes, though keeping the old name. The eighteenth-century landscaped parks are now much admired and often seen as elegant barriers against the 'natural' woodland that is supposed to have preceded them, an Enlightenment project to demonstrate human authority over nature. It is less known that, as well as keeping the old name, 'park', most of the professional landscape designers also kept old trees and woods. They distinguished clearly between gardens, which were heavily reconstructed and managed, and parks, where the plan was to enhance an already existing landscape with a few new features and the rearrangement of longer vistas. Humphry Repton (1752-1818), who wrote extensively on the subject as well as designing landscapes himself, expressed this widespread view:

> The man of science and taste will discover beauties in a tree which the others would condemn for its decay ... Sometimes he will discover an aged thorn or maple at the foot of a venerable oak; these he will respect, not only for their antiquity ... but knowing that the importance of the oak is comparatively increased by the neighbouring situation of these subordinate objects.[12]

These designers saw themselves as developing and improving the traditional deer park: in many cases they even kept the deer as ornamental features. As late as 1867 there were still 325 English parks with deer in them,[13] but while these animals were culled for the table, they were not hunted. The 'gentlemanly' way to kill deer became going to the Highlands to stalk and shoot them.

Throughout the eighteenth century the ornamental park grew in popularity – and increasingly included an admiration for woods and glades. At first this was predominantly governed by classical ideas and inspired by the fantasy landscapes of painters like the Poussins and Claude Lorraine; fine examples of this style can still be seen at Stourhead and Stowe, where carefully moulded landscapes, including trees and copses, are decorated with reproduction classical temples, columns and statuary. By the end of the eighteenth century, however, the rise of Romanticism caused a major shift in aesthetic fashion. There was a new delight in the 'sublime' and the so-called wild – waterfalls took over from formal cascades; craggy rocks from classical statuary; and 'wildernesses' from more formal arrangements of vistas and planting designs. In Jane Austen's novels the steady progress of the popularity of wildernesses can be observed. In *Northanger Abbey*,[14] written in the late 1790s, Henry Tilney, representing new and refined sensibility, is just laying out a wilderness in the grounds of his vicarage; by 1813, when *Pride and Prejudice* was published, even the old-fashioned and pompous Lady Catherine de Bourgh condescends to sit in the Bennets' 'prettyish kind of a little wilderness on one side of [the] lawn'. In the period between the two novels, fashion had moved forward. Among other signs of the times, the Grimm brothers' collection had been published in Germany.

The marked rise in prosperity and land ownership of the middle and professional class also led to smaller areas of park or garden. You need a great many open acres and a very great deal of money (not just for the installation, but to maintain the park as a sweep of non-economically productive ground) to make a good Capability Brown landscape; you need far fewer to make a grove, a dell, a little wilderness or an 'ancient' wood.

By the second half of the nineteenth century a different fashion had a rather strange effect on some of this supposedly 'natural' gardened woodland. The Victorians developed a passion for 'exotics' – plants that were not indigenous, but had been discovered in far-off corners of the Empire and elsewhere by adventurous explorers. The range of available trees and shrubs suddenly expanded radically – and among the new plants were many well suited to the new natural or woodland gardens. It turned out that a number of these did very well in Britain.[15] A large variety of new conifers was introduced – Wellingtonias, noble fir, sequoia, monkey puzzles – as well as other dark-leafed species, like copper beech, which seemed to suit the mysterious atmosphere the planters wished to develop.

Glenlee is broadly typical of its period – a large country house rather than a 'stately home', with a curved drive rather than a formal eighteenth-century avenue. The area of park land around the house is marked by a collection of particularly fine trees, in a loosely mixed arrangement of deciduous hardwoods (oaks and beeches) and 'exotic' coniferous species; behind the house the woods crowd in, appearing more dense because the ground rises sharply and the trees behind the front rows are visible in an ascending sweep.

The whole effect is pleasing and welcoming, the possible stern-ness of the house softened by a pretty flagged terrace and a semi-formal garden. But the real reason I have come here is that, behind the house, running up the increasingly steep valley side, is a romantic gorge and a fairy-tale forest in the high Romantic manner, as Lugar clearly visualised it.

Cathy Agnew and I walk along a mown grass path from the drive, past the old walled garden, and begin to climb through a shrubbery and then into the wood itself. We are wearing boots; our dogs are running free and excited by proper country smells: this is definitely a wood, not a garden. As we pass beyond the grassy shrubbery and under what would in summer be the green canopy, although at present, with the trees bare, it is an open network of branches and twigs, the path changes from grass to trodden beech mast, red-gold even in the depths of winter. The trees close in. At this point the large trees are predominantly beeches, oaks, and var-ious conifers, which of course carry their dark needles even in bottom ebb of the year, but there is an understory of rowan, hazel, holly and rhododendron. It is a small wood; at this time of year, I can usually see through the trees to the old stone wall which encloses the wood and adds to the sense of being in a secret, private little world.

At first the path leads upwards quite gently, and then, unexpect-edly, we are standing looking down into a deep, narrow ravine; and at the bottom of it there is a tumble of water, dashing through and over rocks. A substantial burn has carved itself a deep, almost ver-tically sided chasm through which it charges, noisy and exuberant. There are two wonderful waterfalls: not little dribbles, but wide white sheets of hurtling water falling over broken black rock into deep, turbulent pools. Because of the way the burn – and therefore its ravine – twists and turns, from one side of the chasm you can look at these falls straight on, and there are rustic benches to allow you to do so in comfort. Cathy says that in the very cold weather at Christmas the water froze and the ice hung silent and motionless in glassy icicles down the great granite slabs; but on the day I am there it is fast and makes a deep music, filling the glen with a sense of mysterious energy.

The path goes on climbing to the top of the wood, winding round trees and rocks. It is laid out in a narrow horseshoe shape, running up one side of the torrent, then curling round and returning down the other side. There are heaps of dead rhododendron branches obscuring the views, where they have been trying once again to curb the shrub's invasive progress; but because of the unusual mixture of the trees and the climatic conditions here, the whole wood is home to many rare mosses and lichens, and has been designated an SSSI. To assist in the conservation of these species, all the dead wood here is left *in situ*. In some ways this is fortunate because it means less maintenance work, dragging the old wood out and burning it. At the same time, this 'natural' approach of benign neglect adds a further touch of apparent wildness and romance. Down below the path, across the bottom of the gorge, dead trees that have crashed across the burn look like small bridges, thick with moss and epiphyte ferns. At the top end, the wood is boundaried by an old mossy drystone wall, and views open out onto the high moor – a startling, abrupt change in the mood and even the quality of the light. The burn enters the wood under the little road I came along in the car, but inside the wall there is a footbridge to carry the path over the burn without needing to leave the wood. It is a little wooden bridge, more rustic and quaint than the later wrought-iron one over Queen Victoria's cascade at Ballochbuie. From it I can look down onto three or four tiny islands in the burn, each standing well above the water level, with vertical square-cut sides that looked almost artificially levered into place, so perfect were they; but Cathy Agnew assures me that they were natural. Each one is just big

enough to sustain a little 'arrangement' of plants, like a tiny
Japanese garden – a single small rowan and a clump or two of ferns;
a pile of broken stones, green with moss and tan with the fallen
leaves and detritus of the wood. In the autumn, precious, delicious
chanterelle mushrooms (*Cantharellus cibarius*) grow on these rocks,
bright gold funnels with their heavily ridged undersides; but they are
more or less impossible to gather, protected by the steep-sided rock
and leaping torrents of water. Across the bridge the main path
turned back towards the house, along the other side of the gorge,
with the same views from a different angle. It is wilder here, with
more hazel trees, and their broken nut shells on the ground bear
witness to the presence of red squirrels, now tucked away in hibernation.

Glenlee has one particular magical aspect. The trees here, and
especially the specimen conifers, grow to vast heights. The tallest
European larch in Britain[16] was planted on a small, flat piece of
ground right beside the burn, its trunk rising through the ferns and
mosses, which are green even in this drear season; it soars
upwards – branchless and apparently perfectly straight; from the
path along the top of the gorge I can look down to its base, which
seems far below me, elegant and slim beside the tangled water; but
looking up, I realise I am still much nearer to its base than to its
crown. Far overhead, the branches begin, and the dark head of the
tree seems to float high against the grey sky. When we scramble
down the side of the ravine to stand beside it I become aware just
how massive and solid the trunk really is, making me feel tiny and
temporary; but from the path above the ravine, the extraordinary
upward thrust of the trunk looks ethereal, delicate, impossible. The
larch is not alone. There are two Douglas firs that are even taller,
and they probably still have a good deal higher to grow. These
conifers are of such distinction that the eminent tree historian Alan
Mitchell, of the Forestry Commission's research wing, has visited
and measured them at various times over a thirty-year period and
written about them, so they are well authenticated, should they
need it.[17]

When Lugar first admired the setting of Glenlee, the wood was here; it formed part of his picturesque vision for the house. It would then have been predominantly oak, with hazel and rowan mixed in. There are indeed a number of oaks around the house, as well as in the glen, which are evidently ancient – much older than the house or the laying out of the grounds – the sort of oak that Repton would have recommended keeping. It seems probable that the beeches were added fairly soon after the house was built. But the conifers were planted throughout the century as fashion and enthusiasm dictated. For example, the first Douglas fir imported from the northwest coast of the USA was planted at Drumlanrig (the home of the Duke of Buccleuch in Dumfriesshire) in 1848. The ones here at Glenlee *cannot* be older than that – and all the evidence is that they were planted in the 1860s and 70s.

In this sense the glen here was fortunate: it seems to have had successive generations of tree-planting enthusiasts, and over nearly two hundred years, they have developed and cared for a unique and lovely thing.

It is not wild. Red Riding Hood's wolf would be hard put to sneak through the undergrowth on swift and silent paw, never mind locate an aged granny in an isolated cottage. Hansel and Gretel would find it well-nigh impossible to get lost in this forest, or stumble upon a witch's gingerbread house (although, as a matter of fact, the land around the glen has several little estate houses, including the lodges, which were built in the Gothic style and could fool the imagination on first sight). It is not wild but it is a place of enchantment.

I have been trying to work out why these artificial Victorian woods are so redolent of the atmosphere of fairy stories, and I think there are at least three reasons.

The first is the simplest. As I have already mentioned, the two are simultaneous. The printed form of the stories was introduced to English readers and quickly achieved wide popularity and cultural reach at exactly the time that these sorts of woods were becoming fashionable. From the late eighteenth century there was a great deal of cultural exchange between the various German states and Britain – the British royal family was Hanoverian and all the monarchs had German consorts. The cultural closeness was also influenced by anti-French sentiment – first in opposition to the Revolution (which began in 1787) and subsequently in the anti-Napoleonic alliances. The Romantic movement emerged out of this cross-fertilisation; for example, Goethe (1749–1832), the great hero of the movement, was profoundly influenced by *The Poems of Ossian* by James Macpherson, both directly and in his own explorations of *Volkspoesie* (folk poetry). These poems, published in the 1760s, and which Macpherson claimed were translations from the original ancient Celtic (although this is still much disputed), not only influenced the Romantic movement generally, but more specifically inspired the study of regional folklore, directing the attention of scholars like the Grimm brothers themselves towards these sorts of works. At the same time, the German 'romantic woodland gardens' and picturesque landscapes were inspired by the earlier 'English Garden' style: Friedrich Ludwig von Sckell (1750-1823), often dubbed the 'father of German landscape gardening', was trained in England. The two impulses were closely connected to each other, as well as connecting the German and British Romantic movements.

Thus, both the idea of collecting folk tales as 'authentic' expressions of a deep and ancient sensibility and the picturesque aesthetic which informed ornamental woods like Glenlee grew out of the same historical impulse. Not surprisingly, then, the illustrations of the first published versions of the Grimm stories, and the many other collections that followed swiftly, showed forests that looked very like these woods. The influence of these illustrations on the way we visualise fairy stories is profound.

All the great collections of fairy stories have illustrations – it has become almost part of the genre.[18] The Grimms themselves were initially resistant to this idea, apparently worrying that it might undermine their scholarly and historical intention, but they were persuaded by their publisher, and from the early editions onwards the collections were always illustrated. Early German illustrators tended to go for interior scenes, perhaps influenced by the German title: *Kinder- und Hausmärchen* ('children's and house [or home] stories'). Philipp Grot Johann (1841-1892), their principal illustrator, who was explicitly proud of his work on the tales, took a subtly satirical approach; for instance, in his illustration for in 'The Devil With The Three Golden Hairs', the Devil is pictured reading the stock market report from a newspaper. But later illustrators, especially in the English translations, tended to focus more on the outside – and therefore inevitably on forest scenes. Above all, the influence on our imaginations of two illustrators – Walter Crane (1845-1915) and Arthur Rackham (1867–1939) – cannot be exaggerated. Both these artists were heavily influenced by the Arts and Crafts movement – Crane, indeed, was a founder member and worked directly with William Morris. Their forest pictures are full of twisted, gnarled trees and especially of dark coniferous evergreens, exactly like the picturesque artificial woodlands that were also enthusiastically embraced by Arts and Crafts followers, who saw in them something more 'natural' and unsullied than the formal gardens of neat borders and bedding plants or 'un-English' classical landscapes.

Walter Crane was one the first artists to define the difference between easel painting and illustration: by removing frames from his pictures and designing them as part of the text, he not only changed the nature of children's books, he was also able to insert his imaginative vision more deeply and directly into the fairy story.

But perhaps Arthur Rackham was even more influential. Rackham was an immensely successful illustrator of a wide range of books – from *Gulliver's Travels* and the Lambs' *Tales from Shakespeare* to Wagner's *Siegfried*. In 1900 he illustrated an edition of the Grimms' tales[19] with 95 line drawings, and this was so successful that the 1909 revised edition increased his contribution to 40 colour plates and 62 line drawings. The forests in these pictures are pure Arts and Crafts renderings of the picturesque: he might have made his sketches at Glenlee.[20] Although he did not abandon the 'pretty' Victorian fairies with pointed toes and delicate filigreed wings, he often broke away from these stereotypes to show much darker, harsher woodland, filling his forests with both gnarled tees and gnarled gnomes and dwarves, with anguished, suffering heroines and with a general atmosphere of the uncanny, neither light nor sweet.

A second connection, though a more complicated and intellectual one, is that both fairy stories and woods like these have been made and developed by a rather similar process. We no longer know the true origins of the stories – we know they are a great deal older than 1812; we know, as I have discussed throughout the book, that in collecting and transcribing them, the Grimm brothers changed them. They changed them formally – from an oral to a written form; they changed them subconsciously in relation to their own lives and concerns; and they changed them further quite consciously and deliberately in order to 'improve' them for specific audiences. This process has continued ever since – one of my favourite examples is the young 'feminist' heroine in Disney's 1991 *Beauty and the Beast* who loves her Beast as much for his library as for the luxury of his castle.[21] Since 1812 we have come to want our magic more difficult to perform and more spectacular in its effects; we want our heroines more active and our heroes less military; we want justice to be gentler and morals and religion to be less overt. We import, as it were, fairy godmothers and insert them like exotic trees into the old stories. We weed out the unwanted tropes like birds pecking people's eyes out or natural mothers ever being cruel. But we plant all these new details into the core of the old story – just as the Victorians planted New World giant firs, Himalayan rhododendrons and Japanese maples through their ancient woods. And when you add something brand new, something which does not belong naturally in the place you put it, you are doing some subtle magic and creating some very subtle effects.

And third and finally, such woods are works of the creative imagination, and so they do to genuine ancient woods and forests what the fairy stories do. They take the actual real forests with all their perils and pains and convert them into places for leisure and delight. These artificially ornamented woods were designed solely as places to play, in which to enjoy oneself – not just for children, but for adults too. This, as we have seen, was not true for real forests until very recently. Originally forests were not for 'amenity use', they were places of hard work, bitter poverty and contested rights. They were places of exile or flight; they were places where trees and animals and plants had to be managed, worked on or with and used; they were work places rather than playgrounds.

But the stories that came out of such forests were for amusement; telling them and hearing them was an activity of leisure moments. The real features and events and interactions of the forests were remade creatively into something far more relaxed and playful. Indeed, with the early fall of the dark in midwinter it is particularly easy to imagine that this was the season when the stories were told, to the rhythmic sounds of spindles or knitting needles. They would more readily be told than read. In old highland blackhouses,[22] each child had its own 'firestool' – simple wooden stools which were designed to be stacked and put aside during the day to make space and brought out at night to circle the fire; such an arrangement, in an ill-lit and smoky room, would encourage story telling through the winter months.[23]

Of course I also know that this is a romantic fantasy – life in the blackhouses through the long highland winters must have been 'poor, nasty and brutish',[24] even if not solitary or short, but that is all the more reason to suggest that the stories were meant to delight and entertain rather than edify their hearers.

I always find it slightly depressing to see how solemnly too many people can take both forests and fairy stories. Here, for example, is a fairly typical passage from a contemporary writer:

> The fairytale journey may look like an outward trek across
> plains and mountains, through castles and forests, but the actual
> movement is inward, into the lands of the soul. The dark path
> of the fairytale forest lies in the shadows of our imagination,
> the depths of our unconscious. To travel to the wood, to face its
> dangers, is to emerge transformed by this experience.
> Particularly for children whose world does not resemble the

simplified world of television sit-coms ... this ability to travel
inward, to face fear and transform it, is a skill they will use all
their lives. We do children – and ourselves—a grave disservice
by censoring the old tales, glossing over the darker passages and
ambiguities.[25]

It is not that this is untrue. I have made these points myself. I agree
entirely that this is *one* of the things that *some* of the stories are
about – cruelty and malevolence and serious danger. But in reality
most fairy stories are not about 'finding yourself through terror' or
working out the more problematic questions of identity. They do
not all offer a negotiation through the latency period into mature
sexuality, or the rewards of a well-developed sense of self-esteem.
They are not even about magic in any serious sense of the word. A
surprising number of them are very silly indeed – they are jokes,
elaborate teases, for fun.

In Chapter 8 I discussed 'The Boy Who Went Forth To Learn
What Fear Was' – the story of a young man so stupid that he cannot
imagine what fear feels like. Nothing frightens him. Because of his
courage, or foolishness, he wins a fortune and a princess. What I did
not tell in that chapter was the end of his story. Although she loves
him, his princess-bride becomes somewhat bored by his continuous
plaintive desire to learn what 'the creeps' would feel like, so she
finally solves his problem:

> She went out to a brook that ran through the garden and
> fetched a bucket full of minnows ... That night when the young
> King was sleeping, his wife pulled the covers off him and
> poured the bucket of cold water and minnows on him. Then
> the little fish began flapping all over him, causing him to wake
> up and exclaim, 'Oh, I've got the creeps! I've got the creeps!
> Now I know, dear wife, just what the creeps are.'

No one, surely, is supposed to take this seriously. The 'path' of this
fairy story could not be more different from the solemn pontifications

of too many commentators. It is important to remember that this is as much part of the fairy-tale canon as 'Hansel and Gretel', 'Snow White' or even 'Sleeping Beauty', which can be read, though they do not need to be, as dark allegories of the psyche. A substantial group of the stories – for example, 'The Musicians of Bremen Town', 'Riffraff', 'Clever Gretel', 'The Death of the Hen', and 'The Mouse, the Bird and the Sausage' (which I mentioned in the opening chapter) – are purely humorous. They are games – sometimes quite elaborate and well-worked-out games – like shaggy-dog stories. It would be would be hard to draw any serious moral, let alone a profound symbolic meaning, from them. The one clear intention of such tales is to amuse.

It is worth remembering that all fairy stories end happily – and very often with some sort of party, at which there is lots to eat and drink.

The ultimate objective of both heroes and heroines throughout the Grimms' collection is to find a 'cushy billet', to enjoy themselves. As I have already shown,[26] Bettelheim notices, as any attentive reader can hardly fail to, how very little 'ruling' or work of any kind any of the kings actually have to do (they never go to war, they seldom have to make serious judgments in the legal sense, and they are certainly not weighed down by paperwork), and suggests that kingship simply represented being a grown-up from a child's perspective. But if you see the stories as I do – as entertainment for grown-ups as well as children – then you can see kingship in a slightly different way: it represents being rich from a poor person's perspective. In addition to the task of monitoring their children, usually unsuccessfully, kings in fairy stories eat a lot, fall in love a lot and go hunting a lot. (They also do a curious amount of getting dressed up in posh clothes and admiring their own gardens.)

The hunting is not surprising of course; hunting was probably the activity during which rural people were most likely actually to see their monarch.[27] The woods and forests from which they laboriously drew their livelihood in effect belonged to the King in order for him to hunt in them. Royal hunting was not the trapping and netting and snaring that ordinary people practised (both legally and illegally) in the forests – it was a colourful ritual performance, often accompanied by lavish picnics.

In England particularly, throughout the historical era, the royal household developed the custom of paying visits around the country – these, frequently nearly bankrupting the local aristocracy, must have looked entirely leisured to the local poor. Great feats, pageantry, masques and concerts and hunting for the pleasure of it (somewhat inefficiently, from the point of view of supper) were the standard entertainment on offer. To be a king, in the view of the rural labouring classes – probably right up to the nineteenth century, when Queen Victoria (partly in response to the perceived 'decadence' of her immediate predecessors) invented a new vocabulary of 'service' and emblematic domesticity – was to be on permanent holiday. Even administration and diplomacy must look fairly easy to a sub-literate population whose principal work is manual and physically exhausting. As we become more and more an urbanised society we are losing touch with the continuous grinding work of agricultural life. Now we tend to have office hours; we go to work and come home to play. We have organised holidays, during which we do not expect to work. On a farm, even now, there are no days when the cows do not need to be milked or the chickens fed. The distinction between leisure and work is much more blurred and both happen in the same place. You find your amusements as and when you can – the more of them the better.

More leisure time is the clear aspiration of many of the characters in the classic fairytales. Not only are the stories themselves frequently witty or even foolish, the lifestyle they present also gives some justification to the nineteenth-century bourgeois claim that unenclosed forest and common were indeed 'a nursery and resort of the most idle and profligate of men'.[28] No one who can find an alternative wants to work: they want to become queens or kings, or at the very least to get rich, by cunning trickery, by courage, by the assistance of magic (Why spin yourself when a little manikin will turn up and spin gold for you? Why work in the fields when you can trick the Devil himself into doing your ploughing?), or by pure chutzpah. Punishment never follows from this – on the contrary, prosperity, happiness, a lover beyond the expectations of your status, and usually children are the direct reward. It is so much more important to be kind, generous with what you have and merry hearted than to do an honest day's work.

Although in many of the stories hard work is honoured and respected, it does tend to be presented as a means to an end – and the end is not having to do it any more. And in just as many stories, eating, drinking and making merry set the scene and form the content. It was not until the twentieth century that Cinderella's ball became an evening event: in the Grimms' version it was a 'festival' that ran all day for three days. Rapunzel's prince is just loafing about the countryside when he comes across her tower – and thereafter he is free to visit her daily apparently; the Little Tailor does nothing to earn his rich reward – a whole kingdom as well as a princess – except boast, somewhat falsely, of his courage and then con kings and giants and a fierce wild boar. The old soldiers sit around in pubs grumbling until they can hear something to their advantage.

Similarly, the distinction between 'child' and 'adult', like the distinction between work and play, was less rigid. The 'invention' of childhood – and its prolongation with increasing education – is a modern development, although it sometimes appears that apprentices were given many of the privileges of contemporary students. (In Tudor London the Mayday rioting – after the flowering trees were brought in from outside the city – seems to have been treated extremely casually, given the great severity with which other disturbances were handled.) On the whole children started to work much younger and were expected to behave as 'small-sized' adults, with proper responsibilities and duties, as soon as they passed infancy. When this model was replicated under industrial, rather than rural, conditions it proved immensely damaging to the young – hence the heroic moves to protect children by controlling their work hours and conditions in the second half of the nineteenth century. But within an agricultural framework, the blurred edges of work and play did not give anyone much concern: it was not children's work that worried the charitable, but their poverty in the most direct sense.

Now, just as we have divided work from play, we have also drawn a clear line between childhood and adult status, and have further separated the latter very clearly from puberty as well. In the fairy stories – and this seems to me to reflect an older community's social reality – 'play' is not confined to children: children work and adults play, and the distinction is not at all clear.

The nineteenth-century ornamental or artificial forest, planted with exotic and strange trees and flowers from distant lands, was designed only for leisure. This sense of freedom was enhanced of course by the large number of domestic servants that the owners of these sorts of woods had available to maintain them, to keep the paths clear and the litter removed. They were forests of 'conspicuous consumption' demonstrating that you could afford to have a plot of land of your own which was put to no economic use. These woods were not even hunted; they did not provide fuel for the fire or food for the table – you could just wander in them romantically. Like the fairy stories, they provided 'time out'. They were there for fun. Not surprisingly, there is only one 'artificial' forest in the Grimms' stories. It has trees of silver and gold and jewels – and it is where the twelve princesses go to dance and play all night.

I love the Glenlee woods. The trees are magnificent and slightly strange and the waterfalls an extraordinary hidden delight, and the whole ravine creates a fairy-story setting. I am not at all surprised that its owner was able to persuade a small child that the fairies still lived and played there; as a grown-up, I have had a happy, leisured afternoon walk there, despite the early dark of the northern winter. And as we come down from the little wood and back towards the house I have another 'fairy-tale moment'. I have come along a narrow path down through a dark wood and then, suddenly, I am out of the trees and in front of me is the house, its windows lit up in the dusk – big enough from that angle in that light to pretend to be a palace or castle. I am welcomed in, as travellers from the forest should be. We sit in the kitchen and drink tea and eat cake, as any traveller in a fairy story would.

Dancing Shoes

Once upon a time he had betrayed her secrets.

One upon a time he had come limping up the long track through the forest, sullen, wounded, homeless and angry. He had tricked her, spied on her, betrayed her and then married her.

She despises him, she always has, from the very beginning. She is right; she knows he is an old lag and not a king at all. So now when he wakes alone in their huge canopied bed, curtained in silk from far away and embroidered, by her, with gold and silver foliage, he feels not shocked but lonely. He feels a huge sad emptiness, which will not be assuaged by the three little princes sleeping in the nursery or by the new child who is swelling her belly now and making her soft and sweet, though not for him, never for him.

He knows she will be with her sisters – that she will have sneaked back to the dormitory, the long bare room where they lived as girls, where they giggled and teased and played and created their own magic worlds into which he had never been invited.

On his best days, when the hunting has been good, when his children have seemed sweet to him, or when he has known that his lands and his people are flourishing under his kingship, he can feel a tender pride in his wife and her sisters and their faithful if high-handed love for each other. He is delighted by their easy affection. Twelve of them, enough for any amusement, and they had grown up not wanting friends, never lonely, never needing to negotiate with the world like he has had to do since his youth.

He had come up the long track through the forest, a laid-off soldier, wounded in someone else's war, dumped as useless; a man without home, or family, or purpose. Redundant. Hating kings and their power and their riches and their easy, proud complacency. The track had led to the castle and the meagre village at its foot. He had kept company that night with a charming woman whose own son had gone for a soldier and she missed him and was full of ready sympathy and good-humoured comfort. And afterwards, as he was rebuttoning his breeches and picking the leaf mould gently out of her hair as a grateful man should, she had asked him what he would do now and he had laughed and said he hadn't a clue and didn't care much, perhaps he should have a go at finding out where the princesses went dancing at night. It was a joke – princesses and their night clubs weren't part of his world.

'Those trollops,' she said, 'that's easy. Just don't drink the wine they offer you and take this wee cloak which will make you invisible.'

He never asked her how she came by it. It was easy come, easy go with her, as he had just learned, and a sensible man never cross-questions a witch who is doing him a favour.

He took it with gratitude and did not check that it worked until she had gone off about her own business. Invisibility was not a thing to be sneered at – he could make an excellent career as a robber if he chose – but she had given it to him for a purpose, and he was old enough and clever enough to know that he had better not treat magic things too lightly, so he presented himself to the King. The gossip was that the old man tried to deter princes now, that he was tired of chopping off the heads of the sons of all his neighbours – it led to ill feeling and would leave the wide country short of leadership in the next generation. They said that he regretted his rash proclamation and was heard to bemoan the fact that a king must keep his word, come what may. But he welcomed the soldier, because there would be little negative feedback from his execution and, after all, the King had eleven other beautiful daughters he could marry off more creditably if by some awkward chance the limping fool were to be successful. So he gave him a

decent dinner and saw him settled in the small ante-chamber so he
could watch the girls' night-time antics and see where they went to
dance so vigorously that they wore out their pretty little shoes.
Then he left him to it. To them.

The twelve princesses were in high spirits. Even as he pre-
tended to sleep he was beguiled by them. They were entirely
wonderful in their bitchy humour, their open contempt for him, for
their father and for the world. They were so bold, so witty, so
unself-conscious and so affectionate with each other. They were
like his comrades-in-arms except that they were beautiful and sexy
and fearless. They scoffed at him and he adored them for it. A
single child, an orphan raised by an uncaring uncle and a much-
harassed stepmother, cast out early and sent to the wars, he had
never known this easy witty banter, this happy confidence, this
tender togetherness, this proud freedom. He followed them down
into the secret world of their dreams and wanted to dance and play
with them for ever.

And still, on his best days, that is what he wants. He does not
want to separate them. He still feels a tender pride in his wife and
her sisters and their faithful if high-handed love for each other. He
is delighted by their easy loyalty and their deep laughter. He loves
their conviction that they are special and may ignore all the rea-
sonable demands of other people if those should inconvenience
them in any way. And because they give freely when they give,
they give graciously – laughingly, they call it *noblesse oblige* and
the people call it royalty and mostly love it when they do not hate
it.

Tonight is not one of his best days. He wakes alone in the huge
canopied bed and feels a huge sad emptiness. He is lonely and he
can never say so; if he tells her how much he has given up for her
she will look at him with a haughty blankness – she will never be
able to believe that it is more fun in the inn than in the castle, that
the burdens of kingship are heavy and that he deserves some of her
attention. Her eyes will narrow coldly and he will know she is
remembering that he tricked her and betrayed her and got riches

and kingship out of it. Briefly he thinks he will go down to the village and visit his witch woman, but that is less fun now he is a king and she gives herself to him with fear and self-interest instead of casual pleasure and laughter.

But the bed is too wide for a man alone and he cannot get back to sleep. He decides he will go, again, and look at the princesses in their private place. He gets up, quietly, anxious not to rouse his servants who need their dreams to make him endurable to them; he lights a candle and goes to the chest he never opens, at the very bottom of which he has hidden his little cloak. He betrayed their secrets but kept his own – none of them to this day know how he tricked them, and although it is a long time since he used it, the cloak remains safely concealed. He feels a dark comfort in his stratagem: they keep themselves hidden from him, and now he will do the same by them.

In the chest there is a heavy velvet and ermine gown of state which he never wears, and underneath it are the jacket and breeches from his soldiering days which he never wears. He lifts them all aside. He reaches in for the cloak which is wrapped in an old rag at the bottom and feels instead something different, something harder and smaller. He knows what it is before he sees it. Slowly, knowing and refusing to know, he brings his hand into the light of the candle and, as he knows he will, he sees that he is holding a little dancing slipper. It is made of soft cream-coloured silk and is embroidered with gold and silver leaves and tiny chips of diamond, but the sole is ragged, worn through and threadbare; it has been danced to pieces.

She has been dancing again.

There is a horror on him and his anger makes him briefly, hotly brave. He looks into the chest more directly, the candle held high, and he sees there are lots of pairs of shoes, all frayed and ruined, all danced to pieces. She has hidden them where she thinks he will not find them.

In his rage he grabs the little cloak and flings it over his shoulders. Now he is invisible even to himself. He snatches up one of the dancing slippers, as evidence; he has always liked evidence, has gathered and used it to persuade himself as much as others. It vanishes into the aura of invisibility which wraps itself around him and, invisible, he storms through the castle, the old wound in his left leg aching at his pace.

He flings open the door of their dormitory, hot with a wrath he believes at this moment to be righteous. She is a wife. She is a mother. She is a queen. She is pregnant, carrying his child – if it is his child. He will cry shame upon her and upon her sisters. He will summon all their husbands and expose their wanton ways. Their hoity-toity attitude and haughty indifference will do them no good. He will burn them on a pyre in the castle courtyard and smile inwardly while the people cheer. His witch woman had called them trollops and he should have listened to her.

But the dormitory is silent, empty. Moonlight streams in the windows, bathing the room in its cold clear light. There is a chaos of cast-off clothing and tossed-about bedding, but it is all held in a silvery stillness. He is arrested at the doorway and stands leaning on its frame, his heart hushed by the beauty and peace of the long room. He is defeated.

After a few moments he sees that where the fourth bed on the left-hand side, her bed, ought to be, there is a blank space. The bed has sunk down, folded away, to allow them access to the secret passage. He comes limping up the long room, slowly, and sits on the third bed and looks into the black pit. He can just see the top two or three steps, but he knows the narrow flight goes on down and down and down, dusty and cold.

He will follow them, he thinks, he will catch them red handed and there will be no excuses, but he just sits there looking into the blackness.

He knows that at the very bottom the stairwell will open out and there will be the forest of silver trees and golden trees and the stands of trees with diamond leaves, all lit by a different moon; and there will be the straight smooth road that leads to the lake and over the lake will be the palace on the island.

He knows they will be all dressed up in silver and gold and diamonds, dancing with their dream princes; laughing and drinking
and dancing, doing standing up what is better done lying down,
and it will be so beautiful and they will be so beautiful that his
heart will melt, as it melted before, and he will lose his anger in a
silent enchantment and afterwards they will mock him for his
weakness. So he just sits on the bed, sullen, wounded, and looks
into the darkness of the pit.

He takes off the little cloak and waits, turning her ruined slipper between his hands. He will, he thinks, wait until they come
back. They can see him sitting here as they come up the staircase,
footsore and weary, their dresses in rags, their slippers danced to
pieces. They will come up the stairs exhausted but satisfied and
then they can see him here sitting like a king on his throne and be,
however briefly, afraid.

He is the King, he thinks. He is her husband. It is both his right
and his duty to bring them into line, to break their haughty spirit,
to scatter their pride in the imagination of their hearts. He has
earned this right and he has a duty to exercise it. For their own
good. For the good of their children. For the good of the State. He
practises a fine speech. He thinks it should begin, 'Ho, Madam,'
which has a royal ring to it. 'Ho, Madam Wife,' would be even
better, but he knows himself too well. He was never born to that
kind of speech. He wants to say something quite different.

'Trollops. Sluts. Grow up. You aren't little girls any more – you
don't live in fairy land. What do you know of the real forest, you
pampered bitches, of the real world? The trees aren't made of
silver and gold for most of us; the paths aren't straight and paved.
Men aren't handsome princes free to dance all night; real men go
out and they work; they get sweaty and tired and cross because that
way they can just about hope to feed their children. Women don't
have fancy frocks to ruin, and hundreds of pairs of dainty silk slippers to dance to pieces; real women stay home and stay faithful
because that way they can just about hope to feed their children.
It does not always work: rain at haymaking, no rain at sowing-time,

a wound in someone else's war – and the wolf of hunger prowls at
the door and the rats of destitution gnaw at the foundations. When
real men and women turn to each other for sex and consolation,
they don't dance elegantly; they roll on their backs and get leaf
mould in their hair.'

That is the easy bit. He rolls the phrases around his head and is
pleased with some of them. He eliminates several cruder and more
vulgar insults that spring to mind, feeling that a certain kingly hau-
teur is called for. The next part is more difficult to gauge. How will
he punish them? He will strip off their silken knickers and put
each one of them over his knee and whip their naked bottoms. He
will sit on his throne to do it. He will invite the whole court, yes,
and the village too, to watch him. It gives him a strange dark pleasure to think of their humiliation. He will send them out as kitchen
wenches to neighbouring castles – no, to merchants and millers
and doctors and priests who will enjoy making royalty suffer. He
will lock them up, each in a separate dungeon. He will have them
drowned like kittens for the adultery of their hearts. He will have
them burned for witches. He . . .

'Don't,' says a voice, 'don't do it. Go back to bed now and pretend you never knew.'

He cries out in sudden terror and looks up and sees in the pale
light of the moon that what he had taken to be a bundle of bedding
on the last bed on the right-hand side is, in fact, the littlest
princess. The one who had been once been the most beautiful of
all, the one who had always known him and seen through him,
whose shy heart was open to his. The one who has never married,
the one whose beauty faded first, who is raddled now, whose hair is
thin and dull and whose shoulder bones and ribs show through her
too-pale skin. The one he loves.

'Don't,' she says. 'Don't hate her.'

'Why are you here?' he asks. 'Why aren't you with the others?'

'I don't go any more; it hurts too much. Joy hurts too much when
it isn't real. It isn't real, you know, that forest, that dancing. It can't
harm you. Go back to bed now and let it be.'

Her eyes are huge in her bony ruined face and they catch a corner of the moonlight. He knows that she is terribly sad and he knows why. He stands up and takes a step towards her.

'Go back to bed,' she says and he walks obediently to the door, then stops. He turns again to look at her, crouched in her corner, and suddenly she says, 'Yes, you should have married me.'

'I was afraid,' he says slowly. 'I was afraid of you. You knew who I was, you always knew. You were afraid of me. You were right to be afraid. I wasn't good enough; I was just an old soldier with no right to marry the real princess. I was afraid of loving you and betraying you and hurting you.'

'Well,' she says without bitterness, 'we got that wrong, didn't we?'

She does not say, 'I love you.' She does not need to.

He leaves the dormitory and walks a short way up the stone-flagged corridor. Then realises he has left his little cloak behind. He stands still for a moment, turning the pretty, ruined dancing slipper in his hand. He goes back. She is still sitting up on her bed. He crosses the room and picks up the cloak. He puts it on, vanishes, takes it off, reappears and grins at her.

Suddenly she laughs, a sweet birdlike sound; like a robin in the winter forest.

Slowly he says, 'If it isn't real ... that forest, that palace, those princes ... if it isn't real, then perhaps we could go dancing with the others. Just sometimes. Just for fun. I could wear this cloak and no one would ever know. If it isn't real, if it's just a fairy story.'

'Yes,' she says, 'yes, that would be fun.' She laughs again and he laughs too.

12

February

Knockman Wood

February is the bottom of the year, the dead time. The winter has scoured the land; it looks naked and clean. The dark still comes early and the nights are long and cold.

Although, for once, it is not raining, there is a sharp wet wind carrying mist and mizzle, raw on my face; there was a frost last night and there is still a skim of ice on the edges of puddles and ruts; I am glad of gloves, woolly hat and gaiters. I am stomping across a small bleak plain which was once wood pasture; there are still some fine old oaks, a few ashes with their hard black buds like spearheads, and some scrubby hawthorn; away to the east there are even some cows pasturing. But there are more tree stumps, more dead bracken and more reedy bog than there should be and the trees are now far too widely spaced. In summer this is a gloriously rich habitat full of wild flowers and butterflies, but now it is grey and depressing. The track is waterlogged, and to compensate, other walkers have, in places, diverged from it and cut new waterlogged little paths, a wider and wider smear of mud alongside the main track. It is all pretty bleak.

One reason it feels bleak is that this is a woodland habitat lost more to neglect, to underuse, than to aggressive deforestation or enclosure. In that sense it perfectly illustrates the symbiotic relationship between forests and people. If you overgraze open woodland the bracken gets in; once that has established itself you no longer have useable wood pasture because neither sheep nor cows eat bracken, unless desperate. Bracken, that perfectly natural 'wild' plant, is the enemy of woodland: once established, bracken takes over aggressively, reducing the amount of sunlight reaching the earth and preventing flowers and seedling trees from germinating and developing, reducing biodiversity and renewal – and it is extremely difficult to get out. Bracken, in this sense, is like deer; without management, they will both destroy woodland and prevent its regeneration. Our relationship with the woodlands is so ancient and so complex that we cannot go back to the beginning again – the conditions of 'the beginning' no longer exist.

Of course, one of the advantages of walking in February is that there are no nettles, and not much visible bracken either. Gently the plain begins to rise, and so does my mood. Along the slope ahead of me there is the loveliest high, undulating dry stone wall. Even at first sight there is something strange about this wall; it curves graciously like a wave, not following any natural line or geological feature. It is too beautiful, too well made and far too tall to be an ordinary farm dyke. And it is not – it was constructed in 1824 as the boundary to a deer park. In a moment of sublime romanticism the then owner not only made a brand new deer park, he stocked it with fallow deer, not native to these parts. Not ordinary fallow deer either, for some of them were white. Some of them still are. I have seen white deer in the woods beyond the wall. Each time I see one, despite knowing they are 'artificial', I am re-enchanted – they seem so much the creatures of dreams, of medieval romance and of fairy stories. In several stories deer, often magical, lead princes to their true loves. In 'Brother and Sister' the children run away from their cruel step-mother and get lost in the forest, where the boy is transformed into a deer – although he can still speak. Later they find a little house and live there, with the sister taking tender care of her deer-brother. A royal hunt comes to the forest and the deer-boy cannot resist his impulse to join in the sport.[1] He is hunted and wounded by the King, who then follows him to the cottage and falls in love with the sister. They go to the King's palace and eventually, despite further machinations from the stepmother, the spell is broken and the boy restored. I love this story, partly because there is an unusual gentleness in the bond between the siblings. The girl cares for him very tenderly:

> Every morning she went out and gathered roots, berries and
> nuts for herself, and for the fawn she brought back tender grass,
> which he ate out of her hand. This made him content and he
> would romp around her in a playful fashion. At night when the
> sister was tired and had said her prayers, she would lay her
> head on the back of the fawn. That was her pillow, and she
> would fall into a sweet sleep.

It is as though the bossy busy big sister needs the little brother in an animal form before she can express her true affection – no other pair of siblings in the tales, and there are lots of them, demonstrate this intimate physical affection.[2]

I am not looking for deer today.

I am going in search of Sleeping Beauty's castle.

As it happens, I know where it is, unlike the first time, when I found it entirely by chance. On the Ordnance Survey map it is called Garlies Castle; it was built in 1500 on the site of an even older castle and abandoned in the early nineteenth century. But on a raw February day, in the quiet of the winter forest, it is Sleeping Beauty's palace. It is deep in the woods above me, and they are perfect woods for the story. They are ancient oak wood inter-planted in the early nineteenth century with beeches. The same owner who built the wall inserted these grander trees around his ruined castle and all along the southern boundary of his deer park, where they could be viewed from the new house he built to replace the castle. Now their fine-fingered winter twigs and massive grey trunks are just passing maturity and make a wonderful visual contrast to the oaks.[3]

Garlies Castle is at the northern end of the Knockman Wood, a stretch of ancient woodland which demonstrates a surprising number of the features of forest history that I have been exploring and at the same time is also part of a project which offers some vision of a way forward for our ancient forests.

The Knockman Wood is in the Cree Valley, a small river system that drains off the high Galloway Hills. Either side of the river, and particularly on its eastern bank, the land rises sharply into open moor and high hills Although the area was inhabited from the pre-historic period, it was never sufficiently fertile to justify the effort of clearing the valley sides of trees above the water meadows. A wet climate, little agricultural disturbance, steep slopes and an acidic soil is the perfect terrain for oak forest, and the Cree Valley maintained a significant amount of semi-natural forest for an unusually long time.

But in the twentieth century Galloway, as I have already mentioned, became one of the areas of the country most heavily affected by the development of plantation forestry. Nonetheless, for an assortment of reasons – the terrain was too rough, steep or wet; the woods were particularly remarkable or historic; just on the whim of individual landowners – small patches of ancient wood escaped the 'locust years'. These smaller woods were often adjacent to or even within the plantation forest, awkward little parcels of loveliness. Inevitably such a patchwork has a range of owners and contains some oddities,[4] but presently all of them are managed by the Cree Valley Community Woodlands Trust (CVCWT), whose aim is to 'develop a Forest Habitat Network that has at its core the River Cree, with riparian corridors ... from source to sea'.[5] The jewel in its crown is the glorious Buchan Wood higher up at Loch Trool, a fragment that, like Staverton and Ballochbuie, is as near as we have to untouched natural woodland.[6] The CVCWT owns none of these woods, it just manages them. In the fairy stories we have seen that it is the people who work in the forests, not the distant kings who own them, who turn out to be the 'good' characters; so this feels like a promising omen.

There is a lot to be said for both 'local' and 'partnership' in this context. It is a model that works. In Finland, which not only has the most forest (as a percentage of land area) in Europe, but is also increasing its forestry faster, there is a partnership between the government and very local owners. In 1947 Finland nationalised all its forests and the government then redistributed them to the adjacent farms: 35% of Finland's forests are owned by local farmers who work them together with their traditional agricultural land. This has not only made the forests better and more sustainably managed, it has kept rural farming viable and thus maintained the rural population.[7]

I begin to feel more hopeful, despite the bleak weather and the sense that winter still has a long time to go. I am cheered too by the knowledge that organisations like the CVCWT have followed the lead of the national Woodland Trust and are bringing our woods under more loving care. I know I am not alone in feeling a small measure of optimism. Rackham has commented that in the 1970s he felt that old British forests were doomed, but more recently there has been a true shift of consciousness:

> Those who expect me to predict the next 40 years should ask whether in 1966 anyone could have predicted the state of woodland by 2006. Forty years ago there seemed no future in natural woodland. Who would have predicted that a goodly number of ancient woods would still be there in the twenty-first century, that plantation forestry would lose [its] economic base ... that the Forestry Commission would be leading the way in recovering replanted woods and that the idea of new National Forests presented as imitating natural woodlands would attract huge popular support?[8]

Perhaps that will prove true for the fairy stories too.

At the top of the slope I come to a gate in the deer park wall; close to, the wall seems even more magnificent than from a distance; it is taller than me and both elegant and sturdy. Beyond the gate there is a wide slope of rough grass and bracken, but I follow a little track, grassy and clean, across it, toward the edge of the trees. Just before I walk into their embrace, I look round, down across the plain I have just climbed and then beyond to the bigger hills whose tops are sparkling with snow. I become aware then that the light is lifting and the sky clearing. And as soon as I slip between the first trees I am out of the wind; I can still hear it in the canopy, but on the ground it feels sheltered and hushed. These are old oaks and the ground is vivid with green moss. The path winds a little to avoid the trees. I may be searching for Sleeping Beauty's castle, but I am walking Red Riding Hood's path: I am not much tempted to wander from it; it feels just wintery enough to remind me to be glad that there are no longer any wolves and I am quite safe. There are no other people in the wood today, which adds to the sense of being in a magical place.

The path rises along the flank of a fairly steep hill – here and there I can see out to the fields and other woods, but mainly I am enclosed by the rough oak trunks and the ups and downs of the topography. There is a bright and busy burn which has cut its way down into a rocky gully, where in summer ferns and wild flowers scramble, along with briars and nettles and blackberries. The gully has almost vertical sides, and suddenly above me I feel a change of light and look up and there is a ridge with a line of huge silvery smooth trunks holding feathery twigs and horizontal branches right overhead; I cross the burn and scramble up the track, which is running with water itself, almost a stream, rocky and muddy. Because I need to watch my feet, I come very suddenly to the top. The ground levels off in front of me, creating a little artificial platform with the ground dropping away sharply. And here on this level space, the trees crowding around it, edging closer, hiding it protectively from view and disturbance, and at the same time, slowly and inexorably destroying it, is Sleeping Beauty's castle.

It is ruined now, but you can still see that it was once a tower house, the defensive square keep of medieval Scotland. One corner is still standing nearly as high as the trees around it, and it is possible to pick out the plan of two ground-floor rooms, the base of a turnpike stairway, window lintels and a keyhole gunloop, but even the most solid section of the wall is being broken up now by bright moss, dark ivy and small aggressive rowan trees. The stone frame of the grand fireplace remains; once it carried a mantel frieze carved in relief with swags of foliage springing out of the mouths of human heads. Outside the main block of the castle are the remains of a courtyard and ranges of buildings now reduced to heaps of stone, much of it buried in bright moss. It is very silent in the winter woods; although it is still early afternoon there is already a sense that the light is dimming and the cold waiting to pounce. It is beautiful and very sombre. It is hard to believe that the wood or its enchanted princess will ever wake up.

There is something haunting about ruins in woods. They often feel to me as though they came straight out of the fairy stories. Castles like this and little cottages with their gable-end walls still intact despite the trees pushing up against and into them are reasonably common and fit easily into the stories, but something takes root deeper in the imagination because often the buildings cannot have any association with the tales except the simple fact that they are in the woods.

I find myself thinking of the magical loveliness of the lime wood on Welshbury Hill in Gloucestershire. Limes were once the commonest tree in Britain (and one possible positive effect of global warming might be that we get more of them as they seem to need hotter summers to germinate than we now have). At Welshbury the prettiness of the ancient limes is transformed into something more weird and magical by the fact that they share the hilltop with an Iron Age hill fort, growing over and between the still-visible earthworks, huge ramparts and ditches hidden among the trees. No one knows which came first – the pretty trees or the massive earthworks; whether the trees moved in after the fort was abandoned, or whether this was one of the defensive hideouts in the 'impassable forests' to which Julius Caesar complained the Britons were escaping.[9] Whatever the origins of the fairy stories we now have, we can be pretty certain they did not come from Iron Age Britons, and were not told in the Welshbury hill fort, but still you would not be very surprised if birds spoke to you there, or a bold Little Tailor bustled up eager to trick you, or a merry third son came striding by in pursuit of his true love and fortune, or a witch enchanted you for no reason other than malice.

The ruined farm at Laggangairn, high on the Southern Upland Way, was abandoned and turning to ruin well before there were any trees there at all; it was desolate open moor before it was all converted into the least romantic, least 'natural' forestry plantation imaginable, but it still has an atmosphere of fairy story about it.

Perhaps such places remind me that there was once a far more intimate relationship between people and forests. The forests were busier and more inhabited – but at the same time, lonely and perilous lives were lived there. The atmosphere of so many of the stories seems to emerge out of lives lived deep in the woods – scary, optimistic, beautiful and cruel. Agreeable safe strangers came seldom, and people must have made merry when they did, sung songs and told tales, and both stories and forests flourished in such a relationship to each other. I want very much for this connection to continue somehow.

So I pause at Garlies Castle and I start to ask myself what I think should happen next to keep this alive. I remember Will Anderson saying to me years ago that you cannot get people to 'act well' in ecological matters out of high moral imperative alone. There has to be beauty and love. Beauty and love and, I would add, knowledge. They may even all be part of the same thing.

So, as I have argued in Chapter 4, I think we need to change the way we teach children about ecology. We have developed an approach which presents human beings as the 'baddies' and nature as a delicate, fragile little thing that our every action will damage and endanger. Additionally, nature is increasing located 'far away' in the rainforests and the deserts, rather than here and now, just round the corner. We need to give children a stronger sense that we are forest people. Our first ancestors followed the forest north as the ice cover retreated. The woods are our home. We need to give children confidence in their own roots, to remind them – and ourselves – that northern European deciduous woodland *likes* human beings; it flourishes best in relationship with human beings, and it rewards human beings who go into it and get to know it. This is what the fairy stories tell us and it happens to be true.

Stories and woodland are alike in a particular way – they are specific. Stories have lots of things in common with other stories, but they are different from every other story; woods are the same – of course they have things in common, but each wood is different too. Stories and woods are actual, not abstract: you cannot learn about stories or woods by reading books about stories or woods – or by watching films about them, or hearing lectures on them. To know about woods you have to go into woods. So if we want healthy children in healthy forests we need to get the children out into the forests, and to do that, we need to see the forests as friendly, generous places, but also as tough and determined. Germans and Austrians are typically better at this than we have been in Britain, partly because forests are frequently closer to towns and cities in those countries, but also because the tradition of family walks in the woods has remained stronger there. In 1975 Germany established a long-distance (600-kilometre/370-mile) walking route – the Fairytale Trail – from Hanau to Bremen to enable this sort of connection to be more readily made. On the whole, British long-distance routes are more about 'wilderness experience' and less child friendly.

This is an additional argument for keeping the management of amenity forest, and particularly the management of ancient forest and woods, local. There needs to be a real and continuing practical connection between woods and local primary schools – ideally, there needs to be some sense of ownership, which entails both gains and responsibilities. I believe this is more likely to happen when the wood is near to hand and 'belongs' to individuals a child might actually know.

After a little while I start to feel cold, and the moss has proved rather wet to sit on, so I continue with my walk. Rather than returning along the path I came by, I push further into the woods, north of the castle. Here there is no path at all and a real sense of being in a wild place; there are gaps between the trees in places – wide meadows with fine ancient maiden oaks standing free and on their own; there is a low-lying and faintly sinister-looking patch of bog, all long grass and willow scrub too wet to push through; and a shallow pond that in summer is packed full of yellow flag irises. But there are particular winter pleasures too: I come upon a vast sprawling willow whose branches have fallen and re-rooted and regenerated to form a tangled web partly growing in a small burn, and every branch and root bright green with moss: once it has leafed up it will be impossible to see how very ancient it is – it will look just like any sallow tangle; the fact that it is a single tree will disappear.

Eventually I come to the boundary wall again; here, in places, it is over ten feet high, and I notice something that I could not have noticed a few years ago, because I would not have known what I was seeing. In this wood there is very little evidence of coppicing – almost all the oaks grow on single straight trunks. But right along the wall there is a remarkable number of multi-stemmed trees. They must have been felled right to the ground in order to build the wall and then thrown out new growth as though they had been coppiced. Since this was presumably done only the once, they do not have wide boles.

Although my walk loops round, it is not in fact entirely random. Without haste but with purpose I am making my way to one of my favourite woodland places. The burn that charges down the scarp beside the castle and crashes through the oak trees to the bottom of the valley meets two other burns descending just as fast from different directions; all the descents are steep and the water leaps down carved gullies and miniature chasms, over cascades and falls foaming around rocks, but at the confluence itself the land flattens abruptly and all the water slows down. Over the years it has flattened out a green moss dancing floor. Although at this time of year it is far too waterlogged to do any dancing, I love the sudden coming together of all these waters into a calm and secret place. I think that it is like the fairy stories, collected from all sorts of places further up the hills, shaped by the slopes it tumbles down, but also shaping them, and coming together in a deep, serene pool.

I walk through this very particular bit of wood on this cold February day and I find myself thinking about all the woods I have walked in during the last year and how they have all been lovely and at the same time so very different. Not just the woods in this book, but all the other woods too.

I think about the fairylike birch woods that dance down the mountainside to Loch Hope on the tiny road between Tongue and Altnaharra in Caithness, perhaps the most northern forest in Britain, and totally unexpected as one leaves the wild, empty coast and drives south into the wild, empty hills.

And about the oaks growing right down on the seashore and trailing their branches in salt water in the Sunart Forest in Ardnamurchan; the sweet chestnut groves of the Blean in Kent where the last armed battle in Britain was fought in 1838; the soggy-bottomed alder and hazel woods around Weymouth; Grizedale in Cumbria with its sometimes bizarre sculptures, including Goldworthy's wonderful 'Taking a Wall for a Walk'; the magnificent distortions of the ancient pollards at Burnham Beeches; the deep sweet silence of the Hammer Wood at Chithurst Buddhist monastery where the monks and nuns practise in the tradition of the Thai Forest Masters; the stunted downy willow and juniper heath of the montane forest at Ben Eighe ...

... and about all the woods I did not walk in, the forests I do not know the names of, all beautiful, all different. Because you cannot learn the woods from a book – they call to a different kind of learning and knowing, an imaginative and creative engagement with the actual. From *this* sort of learning comes knowledge and love and an awareness of beauty.

The fairy stories are the same: I have been endeavouring to pick out common themes, but in fact in the Grimms' collections alone there are 210 stories – and they are only a tiny fragment of a much older and more extensive heritage (like our remaining forests).[10]

Each one is different, and I have picked and chosen according to my themes and my memory.

I realise why so many of the forests and woods I have been writing about have been either here in Galloway or other woods I knew and played in as a child.[11] It is because they are connected in my imagination to the fairy stories that informed my childhood or that I have absorbed into that inner world through regular and intimate connection. The same can be said of the fairy stories I love best, the ones that I have retold, rather than just discussed, here and elsewhere. Suddenly I do not feel I have 'proved' my thesis – that we have the stories we have *because* we are people whose roots are in the northern European forests – but this is because it is about a sort of knowledge that is not amenable to, not available to, the sort of 'proof' we have come to accept. It is an imaginative rather than a logical connection, and none the worse for that.

What seems worryingly possible is that we will diminish, degrade and even destroy these common roots, these shared stories, leaving us increasingly isolated and without any sense of collective identity; so I think that as well as getting the children (and the adults too) back into the woods, we also have to get the stories back into the social culture. I start to have a little fantasy: when a child's birth is registered, together with a birth certificate they should also be given a book of fairy stories – a gift from the whole community to a new member. Although it is impossible to create a 'bias-free' text, these stories should be from the earliest sensible version or as literal a translation as possible (they should not contain my, or anyone else's, attempts to make them more 'morally correct'). They should be as they were when they were first written down. There are plenty of places and opportunities for examining the presumptions and developing new versions: that is what education is for. What we need is a body of work that is shared,[12] that belongs to us all, that is part of our identity. The fairy stories have a number of claims to be this text: they are anonymous – we will not celebrate their author, but their tellers and audiences; they belong to everyone, not to any educated or wealthy elite; they are comprehensible to everyone, even children; they unite us with our fellow Europeans in a democratic and non-bureaucratic way – they are something we already have in common.

And for as long as we have the absurd 'Citizenship Test', everyone who passes it should also receive a copy of the same book – a simple symbolic way for the community to welcome new adult citizens on equal terms with newborn ones. There are not many books suited to all ages.[13]

At the same time, I decide, the new citizens, by birth or adoption, could be assigned to a tract of forest. This is not a 'plant-a-tree' scheme. They would not be given an individual tree: trees, especially saplings, die, which could very discouraging for the sensitive. I am trying to revive the tradition of 'common land', not encourage the individualism of personal ownership. Everyone would have a 'special relationship' with everyone else who had been assigned to that same hectare or so of the forestry estate of the nation. You might never go there, though you would have to know where it was or at least what its name was, but it would be nice to think that patterns and customs of visiting would develop and it would become part of people's identity: your own forest-piece location, like your date of birth or your Zodiac sign, would establish bonds and mutual interests.

Such thoughts engage me with amusement and hope as I drop down along the conjoined burn and cross it at an alarmingly deep ford. There has been more quad-bike traffic here. The CVCWT has been planting new trees – they are still inside their ugly but invaluable plastic sleeves which protect them from deer, squirrel and other depredations while they establish themselves and dig their roots in deep. We cannot go back to the beginning, but we can re-make woodland and create new woods where the old ones have been lost.

Just as I come down towards the gate I came into the wood through, a thin low sun breaks through the clouds, barely bright enough to cast decent shadows, but certainly enough to lighten and brighten the whole world. And suddenly I see a clump of crystal brain fungus (*Exidia nucleata*). Crystal brain fungus looks like what it is called: a brain-shaped, wrinkly convoluted jelly, almost transparent but with little white 'crystals' deep inside, which are actually accretions of calcium oxalate. It is not rare, but you can only see it in wet weather – it dehydrates quickly and shrivels into a hard, thin, barely visible membrane when it is dry. They are one payback for walking in wet woods. They are weird and unexpected, and the sun catches this one and makes it gleam. Before I identify it properly it looks like frogspawn. And then, woods being surprising, unexpected and magical, the very next pool, barely more than a puddle by the path, is full of real frogspawn. It is very like the crystal brain fungus actually, except that it is in the water as opposed to on a rotting branch, and the flecks in the middle of the jelly are black future tadpoles rather than white granules.

Frogspawn is bizarre: if you pick it up it has a strange texture, being both lumpy and slimy at the same time; each cell is quite distinct, but if you try and drip it through your fingers it moves as a single organism – the cells do not separate easily, and to a bare hand on a cold day, it seems curiously alive and eager. But today it is also a herald of the spring, an end to winter. A little way away from the puddle is a toad, squatting quietly and apparently looking at me. Frogspawn and toad spawn are supposed to be easily distinguishable: the books tell you that toads lay their eggs in lines and frogs in heaps, but I have never been certain I can tell the difference. I can, however, tell toads from frogs – toads are dry and warty, frogs are smooth and slimy; frogs hop and toads crawl, and this is a toad. It does not offer me any treasures, as toads so often do in fairy stories; it probably feels that I have had enough treasures today, and it is right.

Or perhaps it does offer a magic gift, because I suddenly start to notice other things. Hazel trees make their catkins in the autumn – all winter they hang small and tight under the branches, but now they are starting to stretch a little; looking closely, I see my very first neon-red female catkins, like tiny tufts of punk hair. There is a honeysuckle that has formed an unnaturally perfect spiral round a very straight hazel wand; and, halfway up and for no particular reason that I know of, is my first spring leaf, one, alone, just breaking green from its bud.

As I go back up the lane towards my car I see something that I should have seen on my way out, but did not. The lane that leads from the end of the tarmac road to the open plain where I started this chapter is itself rather wonderful and full of fairy-tale features. It starts beside an old mill and follows the mill race up to where it joins the river; it then runs, with a grassy ridge down its centre, through a little patch of wood and out between high hedges through fields. During the summer the ground under the hedges is a tangled mass of grass and wild flowers – in a week or so primroses will be flowering here. Tangling here and up into the hawthorn of the hedge are brambles and wild roses. And someone had, not more than a few days before, cut back the brambles. I went to look for springtime and for Sleeping Beauty's castle, and someone had pre-pared my way for me, cutting back the briars which guarded her for a hundred years.

The wood is not dead, just sleeping; it is turning now, waking up, beginning again. The stories are safe while toads deliver gifts and someone cuts briars back on the paths towards the fairy-tale castles.

I find I am laughing aloud as I go on my way back to my car, happy ever after.

The Dreams of the Sleeping Beauty

Once upon a time there was a princess, as lovely as the dawn.

Once upon a time when she was sixteen she ran up a spiral staircase and came to a little solar high in a tower of her parents' palace where she had never been before. And there in the warm sunshine there was a twirling, moving, dancing bobbin, and a little old woman with busy, busy fingers; the wheel hummed, and the flax danced and the light caught all the movements and spun them into diamonds, busy and playful and pretty. 'Oh,' cried the princess, enchanted and delighted, and she reached out to touch and she pricked her finger and fell down and down and down into the deep cold place where her dreams were waiting for her.

And for a hundred years she dreamed while the forest grew around her. Each dream took a whole year, and acorns became oaks trees while she dreamed.

1 She dreamed a great wall of ice that pushed across the first forest, scouring it down, killing all the trees. There was an unbroken silence for a long time.

2 She dreamed that it grew warmer and the ice melted slowly and there was the music of many waters.

3 She dreamed the witches' tresses and the gold coins of lichen crawling out across the erratic boulders that the ice had left behind.

4 She dreamed mosses and ferns and horsetails and liverworts; and sharp-faced weasels who had survived the cold.

5 She dreamed soft breezes that wafted in birch pollen and trees that began to sprout.

6   She dreamed the spring when there were first wind-flowers and primroses.

7   She dreamed the first brave insects, buzzing and skittering on the dark bog pools of the new forests.

8   She dreamed the first swoop and song of birds; swallows from the far-away deserts and kites spreading their forked tails on the thermals above the scrub woods that were growing, growing, growing.

9   She dreamed the huge dark eyes of deer and elk and hare.

10 And aurochs and lynx and bear and wolf; foxes and badgers and frogspawn and the dapple of fish in the clear streams.

11 She dreamed the small dark people, drifting northwards, following the deer.

12 She dreamed the fresh, bright red-gold of fire and of warmth and light in long chill nights.

13 She dreamed the stone-chipped arrowhead deep in the flank of the stag, and the dancing and laughter of the hunters.

14 She dreamed the sweet crunch of hazelnuts and the honouring of the trees that offered such treasure.

15 She dreamed the laborious wrestling and effort to raise the great stones and mark the rhythms of the years, and the singing of the songs for the gods.

16 She dreamed the sheep grazing under tall trees and the first sweet warm milk taken from an irritable cow.

17 She dreamed there were apples and blackberries and mushrooms from the generous forests, and later grain, carefully grown, gathered and ground.

18 She dreamed the piles of rocks to mark the homes of the dead, and the planting of trees for their comfort.

19 She dreamed a young woman stooping under a low doorway and raising her newborn child to see the dancing of sunlight under the canopy of leaves.

20   And, in the long northern night, the small dark people
     round the bright fire telling stories from the forests.

21   She dreamed the birch fingers, swaying, singing silently,
     holding the moonlight in their paper bark.

22   She dreamed the dark drift of the northern pines, scaled
     dragons with heavy limbs, tenacious in their grip on the
     rock face.

23   She dreamed the sallows and alders with their roots in the
     black bogs, their leaves whispering in harmony with the
     flow of the water.

24   She dreamed the dancing keys spiralling down, down from
     autumn ash trees.

25   She dreamed the deep cool shade under elm trees in
     wood pasture and the fat cattle that mourned their
     passing.

26   She dreamed the hazel coppices, bright with yellow
     catkins, and the detritus of red squirrels collecting winter
     stores.

27   She dreamed the cathedral ceilings and gothic columns of
     beech groves, gold green in springtime, and the bare red
     floors beneath them.

28   She dreamed the shining hollies, sharper than the spindle
     pin in the solar in the tower and their blood-red berries
     like the drop on her finger – the last thing she saw before
     she slept.

29   She dreamed the pollard oak, strangely contorted, abun-
     dantly welcoming, ancient, everlasting and magical.

30   And, greenest and brightest of all, the lovely lost limes,
     the woods that will never return.

31   She dreamed a king, like her father but French, coming
     with long ships and an army to subdue the people and
     claim the throne.

32   She dreamed that the king, like her father, loved hunting

and afforested the woodlands: the New Forest, and Dean, Rockingham, Sherwood, Epping, Hatfield, Braden, Exmoor, Windsor, Savernake, the Wirral and more.

33 She dreamed the elegant fallow deer, hind and hart, dappled flanks like sunshine in the woods in high summer.

34 She dreamed a king, not like her father. Not first among equals, but an absolute monarch – powerful, brutal and sexy.

35 She dreamed herself awake and beautiful, mounted on a black palfrey, hunting the pure white hart along the green rides.

36 She dreamed a great wild boar, bristled shoulders and blooded snout, and the dogs that bring him down.

37 She dreamed the sad limping mastiff, pathetic and declawed, so that it should not kill her father's deer.

38 She dreamed the handsome outlaw, hiding in the greenwood and laughing at the King, her father.

39 She dreamed the ancient forest rights – of pannage, perpresture, agisment, assart, estover and turbary – and the long, cold winters for the peasants without firewood.

40 And how, huddled in the dark, they sang the songs and told the tales of freedom.

41 She dreamed all the abused children lost or abandoned in the forest, crying from hunger or cold or fear, and all the dark and scary things they may encounter, and she was one of those children.

42 She dreamed cliffs and crags and caves and the sudden black bogs that will suck small children down.

43 She dreamed red-spotted fly algaric, pink mycena, slimy glaucous *Stroparia aeruginosa*, and the innocent-looking shining *Amanita phalloides* – the death cap toadstool.

44 She dreamed giants, smashing up the woods in their foolish wrath, and goblins and pixies and the Devil himself searching for his own.

45 She dreamed feral mink, cutting and slashing their way through the stream beds, killing without mercy.

46 She dreamed barons and landlords and government officers destroying the woodlands for profit.

47 She dreamed nettles, imported by the Roman legions, and briars and gorse and vicious barbed-wire fences.

48 She dreamed ruthless robbers in their dens and lairs, grinding bones for bread and swilling great cups of blood.

49 She dreamed witches and stepmothers, who are too often the same and who trick her with promises of sweetness and then eat her up, and gobble her down.

50 And wolves.

51 She dreamed the forests shrinking, retreating, enclosed by ditch and fence, the common land stolen from the trees and the plants and the animals and the insects and the people.

52 She dreamed the pain of trees grubbed out, the hacking of root and branch, of foxes hunted and badgers baited, and of the deep cut of metal plough destroying the woodruff and the bluebells.

53 She dreamed the brutal Black Act and the swinging gallows for the hanged poachers and the landowners who valued a human life less than a pheasant.

54 She dreamed the huge machines that demanded huge fields and tore up the hedgerows and cut down the wood pasture and killed the song birds and the fritillaries and the field mushrooms.

55 She dreamed the sulphur smoke from finger-pointed factory chimneys leaching out calcium, raising acidity and killing the forests.

56 She dreamed roads and railways and airports cutting through the forest, breaking up the ancient patterns, and of pylons and cables and deer fences killing the bats and the birds.

57 She dreamed a war-weary people who clear-felled ancient forests, destroying the trees, leaving acres that looked like the battlefields of France, and to no useful purpose.

58 She dreamed *Scolytus scolytus*, the large elm bark beetle that carries the fungi that attack the great elm trees and leave them skeletal, then dead and gone.

59 She dreamed the years of the locusts, the vast march of foreign conifers invading the country, supported by the fifth column of tax concessions and destroying the natives.

60 And poor John Clare, lost and crazed in a landscape he could not recognise because the woods he loved had been stolen.

61 She dreamed the wind flowers, *Anemone nemorosa*, fairy white and gold, and all the sweet and lovely things that are only found in the forests.

62 She dreamed cow wheat, food for the heath fritillary butterfly, and herb paris, sanicle, wood sorrel, dog's mercury, woodruff and yellow archangel.

63 She dreamed the sun-bright thick-ridged girolle mushrooms and the white clusters of angel's wings and the mysterious rays of the earthstars in beech-leaf litter.

64 She dreamed the tiny red spoons of the carnivorous sundew along the drainage ditches and the wet places of the woods.

65 She dreamed toothwort and the ghost orchid that grow in the darkest shade and have no chlorophyll, no green, but are cream coloured and waxy and rare.

66 She dreamed pure mornings when the low sun caught the dew in spiders' webs on dark gorse bushes and they danced like diamonds.

67 She dreamed the wet blue smoke of bluebells drifting away from sight and the sharp acrid scent of the ransom carpet.

68   She dreamed the climbing-twining, twining-climbing rich-smelling strangulation of honeysuckle and dog rose, tangling in her hair and between her breasts.

69   She dreamed the frothed extravagance of meadow sweet and the dark pink sweetness of wild strawberries, juice dripping from fingers and lips.

70   And of sweet violet and primroses and the stories of springtime they modestly whisper.

71   She dreamed two little children, Hansel and Gretel, lost in the forest, and cold and frightened and tired, nibbling at the sugary little house until the wicked witch came out to punish them

72   She dreamed the dark tanglewood where the wolf lurked waiting for Little Red Riding Hood to come trotting down the path on the way to her grandmother's house.

73   She dreamed the Goosegirl-princess, duped on a road through the forest, whose horse was slaughtered and whose joy and love were stolen.

74   She dreamed the dark stories and then she dreamed Snow White running terrified through the forest but finding comfort and love in the home of the seven dwarves.

75   She dreamed the twelve naughty princesses who vanished at night through forests of gold and silver and jewels and danced their shoes to rags and laughed at all their suitors.

76   She dreamed a girl imprisoned in a high tower deep in the forest, who let down a strong rope of her own golden hair and hauled up a life of love and hope.

77   She dreamed an abused child who fell down a well into a lower forest where, through hard work and good manners, she earned an unending stream of gold.

78   She dreamed the faithful silent sister, sitting in a tree in the forest, sewing shirts for her swan brothers – pure and courageous and strong.

79   She dreamed all the young women who, frightened and

abused, found safety in the forest and learned the language of the birds and the language of their own hearts.

80 And of a princess, who was herself, asleep in a green forest, waiting for springtime to wake up, preparing for love and joy.

81 She dreamed her mother's breast, sweet and round, her nipple like a wild strawberry, juicy, sun-warmed.

82 She dreamed her father, the King, at the castle gate, holding up his lovely newborn daughter to the cheers of the populace.

83 She dreamed he planned a party, with dinner and dancing, with fireworks and feasting to celebrate her birth.

84 She dreamed that kings and commoners, princes and peasants came to the party, and twelve old women, gossips and friends, welcome for their wisdom.

85 She dreamed they gave her eleven gifts: intelligence, beauty, grace, laughter, kindness, health, green fingers, serenity, courage, courtesy, a voice like a singing bird ...

86 She dreamed a dark presence; a thirteenth old women, bitter and jealous, whom her father, the King, had neglected or rejected, who had not been invited to the party and who was cold and mean.

87 She dreamed a shriek and a curse – before she became a woman she would prick her finger on a spindle and die, die, die.

88 She dreamed the twelfth old woman weeping; and then, swift as thought, changing her gift from wealth to redemption: she would not die but sleep and sleep and sleep until her beloved came.

89 She dreamed her long, golden, sheltered childhood and her father the King pushing her on a swing, higher and higher, his arms strong, his love embracing her.

90 But still she ran away, up a spiral staircase to a little solar high in a tower. There was a twirling, moving, dancing

bobbin, and a little old woman with busy, busy fingers; the wheel hummed, and the flax danced and the light caught all the movements and spun them into diamonds, all busy and playful and pretty. 'Oh,' she cried, and reached out to touch and she pricked her finger and fell down and down and down into the deep cold place where her dreams were waiting for her.

91   She dreamed the dog roses twining over her, sweet smelling, sharp thorned, red and pink and white.

92   She dreamed the hazel catkins, which had passed the winter tucked under their twigs, began to swell and stretch, stiff and thick with pollen.

93   She dreamed a Swedish scientist with a wig and a Viennese doctor with a beard and glasses who both said it was all about sex and the hazel catkins giggled nervously.

94   She dreamed dark curling moss growing between her legs, soft and damp and luxuriant.

95   She dreamed the forest was stirring now, the days longer and the wind gentler, and the larches flushing rose pink.

96   She dreamed the swallows in the hot, dry desert gathering themselves, flickering the hot air, yearning for small flies over dancing little rivers and turning northwards for the long journey home.

97   She dreamed a hibernating hedgehog turning and grunting deep in the leaf litter under the hawthorn hedge, uncurling and rolling before sleeping again.

98   She dreamed her belly swelling with new life.

99   She dreams that the dream time is coming to an end.

100   And that when she is ready, when the spring comes sweetly and the primroses flower, a prince will cut his way through the protective undergrowth and kiss her awake.

And this will not be a dream; she will wake up and love him and they will live happily ever after in her beloved and lovely forest.

ACKNOWLEDGEMENTS

Some of the walks in this book I did on my own, but for several I had companions and I would like to thank them all:

I walked in the Saltridge beech wood with Peter Daly and Ed Brammel (and Solly, their dachshund); in the Great North Wood with Will Anderson; in Epping Forest with Rob Macfarlane; in the forest at Mar Lodge with Liz Holden; in Staverton Thicks with Maggie and Lottie Lawrence; in Kielder Forest with Max McLaughlin; down the Hopewell Mine in the Forest of Dean with Dan Morgan and John Daniels, Free Miners; in the Glenlee Ravine with Cathy Agnew.

I also walked in Glenknapp Forest with Janet Batsleer and Margaret Beetham; in the Blean with Ruth Matthews; in Wightham Wood with Jo Garcia.

And in some of these and many others with Adam Lee, a great walking companion, a great photographer and a great son.

I thank them all.

I have also shared many of my walks in the last few years with Zoe, my enthusiastic border terrier, and I thank Hugh Poward for giving her to me, at, I fear, some cost to himself.

I could not have written the book without the work of Oliver Rackham, historian of British woodland, and Jack Zipes, Grimm expert and translator, nor without the help and knowledge and kindness of Rob Soutar, Forestry Commission Scotland's regional manager for South West Scotland. I was generously supported by the Wingate Foundation (a fairy-story funder in the best sense of the word) and by the Scottish Arts Council.

I thank Jenny Brown, the sort of agent other writers complain does not exist any more; Sara Holloway, my editor; and everyone at Granta.

Finally, I thank my father Adam Maitland, who, over half a century ago, introduced me to both forests and fairy stories. I like to hope I may finally have written a book he might have enjoyed.

NOTES

1 Airyolland Wood

1 The old proverb says of tree leafing: 'If the oak before the ash, we will only have a splash; if the ash before the oak, we will surely have a soak.' Each spring I try to notice if this is true, but have not come to any definite conclusions.
2 Jack Zipes, The Brothers Grimm: From Enchanted Forests to the Modern World (Palgrave, 2002).
3 Julius Caesar, *De Bello Gallico*, verse 21.
4 Zipes, Brothers Grimm.
5 I note with considerable joy that *Our Island's Story* by H. E. Marshall (Galore Park Publishing, 2005), first published in 1905, is back in print. That is what I mean by 'history stories'.
6 Not much more suitable really, because Rapunzel still manages to have twins without ever getting married – but hopefully the mid-nineteenth-century child would not put two and two together here.
7 The first collection was published in 1812, and added to with a second volume in 1815. These contained 87 tales. The brothers (but increasingly Wilhelm) continued both to edit and to add to their collection. The final edition was published in 1857, and contained 210 stories (which include 10 that were called 'legends' and are more explicitly pious than the 200 tales). Zipes (and others) have expanded this to 268 stories, by including some that were so heavily edited as to constitute new or different tales and others that for one reason or another were not included in any of the editions that the Grimm brothers edited (although some were published elsewhere). In his 2002 edition, Zipes also includes 11 tales which were found in letters in the Grimm archive but that were never edited by them.

8   Padraic Colum, *The Complete Grimm's Fairy Tales* (RKP, 1975), Introduction.

9   *Cod: A Biography of the Fish That Changed the World*, by Mark Kurlansky (Vintage, 1999), always seems to me to be a perfect example of this latter phenomenon.

10 Oliver Rackham, *Woodlands* (Collins, New Naturalist Library No. 100, 2006), p. 34.

2 Saltridge Wood

1   Tree species vary in their gregariousness. Obviously trees that propagate clonally appear in clumps near each other, but hornbeam, lime and beech, for example, are gregarious; ash and maple are random in their preference in this respect. Crab apple is anti-gregarious (it is highly unlikely that the tree next to a crab apple will be another crab apple) – a habit it shares, perhaps surprisingly, with many tropical rain forest trees.

2   The spring of 2011 came exceptionally early (probably because the extreme cold of the previous winter also occurred early, with the spectacularly low temperatures and heavy snow falls all over before Christmas). The wood was probably more May- than April-like when I was there.

3   J. B. Priestley.

4   It looks gentle, in fact the area is ferociously rich – one of only two areas outside London and the South East that makes it onto the list of the 20 richest locations in the UK, with a median household income of over £60,000 a year. This certainly helps the aesthetics.

5   Oliver Rackham, *Trees and Woodland in the British Landscape* (Dent, 1990), Preface to the revised edition, p. xviii.

6   Trees seldom behave as they should. Rackham cites a pre-plantation beech as far north as Durham, and they flourished in more of East Anglia, and also in Lancashire, in prehistoric times.

7   Before these dates, planting woodland was very unusual, so woods growing by that time were very likely to have developed naturally. However, in the eighteenth and nineteenth centuries it became common practice to replant new trees within ancient woodland. Such woods are called 'planted on ancient woodland sites'. (There are a few sites, especially from the 1920s, where ancient woods were clear felled, but then never replanted: here you have relatively young trees growing

on ancient rootstock – but since the land will have been exposed to more light after the felling, they do not have the sort of flora that a genuine ancient wood has.)

8 Paul Nash, *Outline: An Autobiograph (The Lively Arts)* (3rd ed., Columbus Books, 1988), p. 73.

9 'To a birch tree cut down and set up for a Maypole' (Gruffydd ap Dafydd, *c.*1340-70).

10 S. T. Coleridge, 'The Picture or the Lover's Resolution', 1802.

11 R. Mabey, *Flora Britannica* (Chatto, 1996), p. 85.

12 J. C. Loudon, The Encyclopedia of Trees and Shrubs, 1842.

13 Unnamed correspondent in Mabey, *Flora Britannica*, p. 86.

14 This may be a little rhetorical. Just as it is difficult to ascertain what is genuinely ancient woodland, so it is difficult to address this kind of particular in fairy stories. When the stories move from place to place, as such stories do, translators have a problem: not only may the species in the original not be known to the new listeners, they may have rather different associations. A classic example of this is the name Rapunzel. She was called this because it was the plant her mother craved in pregnancy, and it was stealing it for her that led to Rapunzel's father promising the baby to the witch. Unfortunately, the plant which is 'rapunzel' in German is, in fact, 'rape' in English; obviously you cannot have a fairy-story heroine called 'Rape'. A more casual example can be found in hagiography (a rather similar form to fairy stories, both in genre and in distribution, and widely disseminated through oral retelling); even in modern printed texts I have read that St Anthony, to fight off (sexual) temptation, threw himself into a bed of 'nettles'. This makes the hagiographer's point very effectively, but in fact there are no nettles in the Sinai desert; a literal translation of Athanasius' original would probably be 'thorn scrub'.

15 Gilbert White, in 1789, in *The Natural History and Antiquities of Selborne*, described the beech as 'the most lovely of all the forest trees'.

16 Deuteronomy 32:8; Job 31:33. Clearly, though, the story was known – the name occurs five times in the New Testament – four of them show Paul trying to contrast Jesus with the 'old' sinful (fallen) humanity (Romans 5:14; 1 Corinthians 15:22, 45; 1 Timothy 2:13, 14; and Jude 1:14). The Eve references in the New Testament are both Pauline – 2 Corinthians 11:3, and 1 Timothy 2:13.

17 Corinne Saunders, *The Forest of Mediaeval Romance* (D. S. Brewer, 1993).

18 In *A Midsummer Night's Dream* and *As you Like It* (and you could make a good case for a number of other plays too) Shakespeare does seem to be playing the two off against each other – not just in the contrast between the 'hero class' and the rustics, but in more complex narrative ways as well.

19 Laurie Lee (1914-1997) wrote *Cider with Rosie* (published in 1959, and entitled *Edge of Day* in the USA) as an autobiographical account of his rural childhood in the Cotswolds. It is one of the most popular English books of the twentieth century. He lived in Slad, a small village nearby and purchased the field in 1972 to protect it from developers – and then gave it to the cricket club.

3 The New Forest

1 Robert Frost, 'Nothing Gold Can Stay', *New Hampshire* (1923).

2 It is frequently claimed that 'bluebells' in Scotland are a different plant, the high summer harebell – a very different and very lovely delicate little thing; but Robert Burns used 'bluebell' to describe the spring flowers, just as his English contemporaries did. (In fact, it was the Romantic poets who made the name popular; prior to that, what we now call bluebells seem mainly to have been called hyacinths.) If it's Scots enough for Burns, it's Scots enough for me. Indeed, Richard Mabey claims that it is almost always the English who make the distinction and tell the Scots what we mean by 'blue bell'.

3 Don't.

4 I say 'almost' because I was also influenced by having spent a very happy weekend here many years before in a little cottage deep in the woods, with my friends Sabine Butzlaff and Alan Green.

5 In the very earliest version of Robin Hood, he was not in fact a nobleman at all, but a 'yeoman'. His steady elevation through the ranks of British culture for 600 years rather emphasises my point.

6 William Shakespeare, *Macbeth*, III. iv.

7 Indeed, in Sweden, for example, this remains the case, even today. All forest products remain 'free' regardless of who owns the forest. (Hazel nuts are the one exception; they belong to the owner of the tree.)

8 Thomas Hughes, *Tom Brown's School Days* (1857).

9 As a nation we are becoming increasingly anti-bloodsports of all kinds, and undoubtedly this will end up affecting the way we see

poachers, but it has not done so yet. Poachers (and curiously also pirates) have a romantic image that robbers most certainly do not. It is not imaginable that cabinet ministers robbing banks, breaking and entering, or pickpocketing, even in fiction, would be seen as amusing and courageous. This is similar to defining who is a 'freedom fighter' and who is a 'terrorist'.

10 John Buchan, *John McNab* (Polygon, 2007[1925]).

11 Zipes, *Brothers Grimm*, p. 80 (there are also 27 stories in which animals are the central characters).

12 Zipes, *Brothers Grimm*, p. 81.

13 Chartists supported the People's Charter of 1838. It was one of the first organised workers' reform movements in Europe. Comparing the demands of this Charter with those of the Magna Carta clarifies the difference between 'conservative' and 'radical' demands. While the demands in Magna Carta were to restore older privileges, the People's Charter demanded brand new rights – among them: (1) universal male suffrage; (2) a secret ballot; (3) no property qualification for members of Parliament; (4) pay for members of Parliament (so poor men could serve); (5) constituencies of equal size; (6) annual elections for Parliament. Chartism 'began among skilled artisans, such as shoe-makers, printers, *and tailors*' (my emphasis) – precisely the heroes of eighteenth-century fairy stories.

14 And, of course, Americans, Australasians and Canadians. The enter-prising poor made up a very large proportion of the emigrants of the nineteenth century.

4 Epping Forest

1 Particularly later on by Henry VIII and Elizabeth 1, for hunting in. Down at the southern end of the forest, nearest to London, there is still a handsome Tudor building called Queen Elizabeth's Hunting Lodge – although in fact it was built by Henry VIII in 1543, and was originally called The Great Standing. The two upper storeys of this timber-framed construction were originally open-sided, creating a sort of raised pavilion with a panoramic view from which to observe the hunt on the open Chingford Plain below.

2 Arthur Young, *General View of the Agriculture of the County of Essex*, vol. 2 (Board of Agriculture, 1813).

3 So successful, indeed, that the corporation bought up other woods

around London, such as Burnham Beeches, for the same purpose. But because of its accessibility from the East End, Epping was particularly associated with impoverished Cockney communities.

4 Gerard Manley Hopkins, 'God's Grandeur', in *Poems*, 1918.

5 Robert Macfarlane, personal communication.

6 'Swarming' trees (that is, climbing straight up a relatively slender trunk that is narrow enough to get your arms round) is apparently one of the lost arts. In fact, I only know about it from classic children's fiction, but in (for example) *Tom Brown's School Days* there is a detailed and practical description of how to go about it. Tom and his friends (with convincing difficulty) climb a tall fir tree by this method. Interestingly, they go out with 'spikes' – obviously something like mountaineers' crampons – well prepared for this activity. I do not know of any teenager who swarms trees now.

7 Richard Louv, *Last Child in the Woods* (UK edition: Atlantic Books, 2010). This book is very American – Louv's concept of 'nature' and 'wilderness' are rather different from a European one – so it needs to be read carefully (especially in his leap to psychological pathology). Nonetheless, it should be read.

8 A possible exception might be feral American mink, but they have no particular connection with the 'dark depths' of 'dreary' forestry plantations; being semi-aquatic, they prefer waterside habitats.

9 Of course I believe that children should learn about the larger world – and ecology is part of this – but I believe such learning should be more grounded in real, concrete contact and observation – in experience. This is, in other fields, an educational truism.

10 I developed my ideas (and indeed adopted the word 'resilience' to describe them) through a conversation with Peter Powell, a consultant pediatrician now at the West Suffolk Hospital. I thank him.

11 This is one of the few stories that actually spells out its moral: 'The grandmother ate the cake and drank the wine which Red-Cap had brought, and revived, *but* Red-Cap thought to herself; "as long as I live I will never by myself leave the path, to run into the woods, when my mother has forbidden me to do so".' The Grimms' version of this story also has, uniquely, an epilogue in which the readers see Red-Cap, after she has profited from the lesson, repeating her mission obediently and thereby outwitting the wolf and drowning him in a water trough. Then 'Red-Cap went joyously home, and no one ever did anything to harm her again.'

12 This last one is a very weird story; one of its peculiarities is that the children are *not* brother and sister. Marlinchen is the daughter of the wicked stepmother, but nonetheless she is entirely on her stepbrother's side against the evil machinations of her own mother.

13 Thumbling stories follow a slightly different pattern. He is well loved and not abused, and he leaves home because of an assortment of accidents related to his small stature. However, he has a 'physical disability' instead, inflicted upon him by his parents' foolish wishing.

14 'A little brother took his little sister by the hand and said, "Since our mother died we've not had one moment of happiness. Our stepmother beats us every day and when we come near her, she kicks us away with her foot. We get nothing but hard crusts of bread, just leftovers for food, and the dog under the table is better off ... come let us go off together into the wide world"' (Opening paragraph of 'Brother and Sister').

15 I have heard it proposed that this a pre-historical memory, hardwired into us during the aeons on the savannah, but, like the terror of snakes that I discussed in the previous chapter, it seems a rather bizarrely selective process. Why would consumption by other animals be a more useful 'memory' than 'don't eat fungi or unidentified berries', something that children will regularly do?

16 *Brendan Chase* is in fact set in the woods of Kent and BB is a careful observer, especially in his detailed descriptions of English wildlife.

17 'A Counter-Desecration Phrasebook', in *Towards Re-Enchantment: Place and its Meanings*, ed. Di Robson and Gareth Evans, 2010, p. 116.

5 Great North Wood

1 Quoted in J. Corbet Anderson, The Great North Wood with a Geological, Topographical & Historical Description of Upper West and South Norwood in the County of Surrey (printed for subscribers, 1898), p. 66.

2 'Fairings' are things bought at fairs – modern fairings would be candyfloss and goldfish in little plastic bags, but more traditionally they were ribbons, laces and scarves. (The word 'tawdry' to describe tacky goods of this kind derives from St Audrey's Fair in Ely, where the laces were considered particularly shoddy and garish.)

3 Thomas Frost, Reminiscences of a Country Journalist, 1886, p. 4.

4 Anderson, The Great North Wood.

5   Until the middle of the nineteenth century, 'collier' applied equally to charcoal burners and mineral coal miners.

6   In the first half of the twentieth century the Forestry Commission was convinced that you could grow trees anywhere – and the disastrous attempts to plant forests in peat bogs (as in Ranoch Moor, for example) demonstrate the obverse of what is happening in South London.

7   Actually, you tend not to see as much death in the woods as you might expect – nature is very efficient: there might be a puddle of feathers where a fox has killed a pigeon or pheasant, but the body is gone; carrion is taken and bones are swiftly cleaned and dispersed. Road kill, unless humans remove the corpse, lingers longer.

8   This is an interesting story because it is one of the few where the heroine actually does start out as a real princess and ends up marrying a real prince. As I've pointed out, this is not as common as we tend to think: like other actual princesses, she 'loses' this status and has to re-establish it.

9   The Grimms have two stories involving brothers who are turned into birds and subsequently rescued by their little sister. In many subsequent collections of fairy stories, these two have been combined into a single story using elements from each. Many people have the two confused in their minds, although originally they are very different (even the number of brothers varies between 6 and 7). In one story the enchantment is brought on by the wicked stepmother (whom the King only marries because he is so scared at being lost in the forest); in the other, it is caused by the King's careless stupidity rather than by any malice.

10 All these years later I cannot remember the name of the writer – if she recognises herself, she should get in touch; I would love to thank her for this tale which has lived with me for over fifteen years, and give her the acknowledgement she richly deserves.

11 'Beauty and the Beast', which is a more grown-up version of this story, is not in fact in the Grimms' collections –but it makes this point very clearly. Here, Beauty becomes entangled with the Beast, not because of a promise of her own, but because of one of her father's. When she kisses the Beast she has no reason to know his true identity – she does not seek to liberate him from an enchantment or gain herself a handsome husband; she kisses him out of kindness alone, and for that she is rewarded.

6 Staverton Thicks

1 Rackham, *Trees and Woodland*, p. 12.

2 Rackham, *Trees and Woodland*, p. 547.

3 George Peterken has surveyed Staverton – see 'Development of Vegetation in Staverton Park, Suffolk', *Field Studies*, 3(1) (1969). Rackham comments that if Staverton were in Czechoslovakia, it might be categorised as 'virgin forest'. Countries in Europe designate their own 'virgin forests', and there is no formal standardisation or regulation. Britain, Ireland, the Low Countries and Denmark claim no virgin forest – all the woodland in these countries has been worked, used, affected by human culture in one way or another; Sweden, second in the list, enters 38 woodlands in this category – whereas Czechoslovakia has named 123 sites. The general professional view is that Czechoslovakia uses a looser definition (which might include places similar to Staverton, although in the UK the evidence of pollarding would exclude it); the alternative possibility is that Czechoslovakia does in fact have a different forest history from the rest of Europe.

4 In some parts of the country pollards were also used as marker trees – for example, on a boundary, or as 'signposts'. Oak trees in Scotland were more likely to be coppiced than pollarded, partly because the native sessile oak does not pollard as successfully as its southern relative. Most ancient oak pollards in Scotland are single examples in areas of coppice or timber trees, and are now believed to have been designed to give some sort of information, like boundaries or way-markers.

5 I say 'almost' because trees that develop through 'cloning' cannot really be dated the way other trees can. Cloning species put up new trunks from the underground root – so a ten-year-old tree trunk may be growing on centuries-old roots and be part of a centuries-old organism.

6 I have no idea why this is the case – and neither, apparently, does anyone else. Rackham speculates that newer trees tended to be planted closer together and this may affect their root formation (particularly because he records that trees on the edges of plantations do better in relation to windblow than those in the centre of large groups).

7 T. R. E. Southwood, 'The Numbers of Species of Insect Associated

with Various Trees', *Journal of Animal Ecology*, 30 (1961), pp. 1–8. But it is important to understand that 'no one individual tree of a particular species will harbour all the species of insects/mites/lichens known to be associated with that tree species. Indeed, no single woodland is likely to contain all of the species associated with its constituent tree species.' Nonetheless, the numbers are actually even higher because Southwood was specifically counting tree-foliage eaters. However, trees obviously provide a range of resources for species other than those simply eating their foliage. Southwood further concentrated on species specifically linked to particular tree species and deliberately omitted those insects feeding more generally on a range of trees.

8 A 'maiden' tree is one that has never been coppiced or pollarded, but that has been grown for its tall, straight trunk. These are also called 'timber' trees.

9 Now perhaps 60, because in his (magical) book *The Butterfly Isles* (Granta, 2011), Patrick Barkham records seeing a pair of Queen of Spain fritillaries mating in West Sussex.

10 Christopher Marlowe, *The Tragical History of Doctor Faustus*, Act 1, scene i.

11 The magi or 'wise men' of the Greek original did not become kings for several centuries. The word 'magic' may be derived from these magi, although this is not certain.

12 There are two versions of this story in the Grimms' collections – one puts the blame on the stepmother, and the other on the father.

13 It is well-nigh impossible to see how anybody could sew anything at all out of starwort (*Callitriche stagnalis*) – a tiny fleshy flower growing in water in wet mud. Its flowers are minute and its stalks are not fibrous. Perhaps her success is truly magical – and certainly skilful.

14 Zipes uses 'spit', but it is fairly clear from the narrative that something more vulgar was intended; the RKP complete edition of the Grimms' stories uses 'spews from back and front'.

15 There are also a few stories in which the Devil – or his grandmother, or an angel or saint, or, occasionally Jesus – appears and rescues the deserving. These are more ethical stories, but they are not 'magical' in any usual sense of the word.

16 This was Wilhelm Grimm's belief by the end of his life: the stories were 'fragments of belief dating back to most ancient times ... the mythic element resembles small pieces of a shattered jewel which are

lying strewn on the ground all overgrown with grass and flowers ...
Their signification has long been lost, but it is still felt.'

17 Rackham, *Trees and Woodland*, p. 547.

7 Forest of Dean

1 It is from this story that Cinderella's 'magical coach' was drawn – the
son's third task is to find 'the most beautiful woman in world'. The
toad humorously comments that she doesn't 'happen to have her right
to hand', but then offers him a hollowed-out turnip, six little mice and
one of the baby toads. Immediately the toad is transformed into a
'remarkably beautiful maiden', and the turnip and mice into a coach
and horses.

2 Aeneas' descent to Hades in Virgil's epic is a well-known instance of
such a visit.

3 There is archaeological evidence that coal was used on Bronze Age
funeral pyres, but it would seem that this was 'outcrop coal' – coal
lying on or very near the surface.

4 In 1848 a railway tunnel under the Severn was opened, and there was
also a railway bridge between Sharpness and Lydney (which collapsed
in 1960).

5 Fashions change – now the tall, straight oaks with tidy bushy heads are
less admired than the more romantic, multi-trunked irregular old oaks
with their infinite variations of leaf size and epicormics – the little
tufty shoots of twigs found on their trunks. Now we like epiphyte
ferns, mosses and lichens which all prefer irregular spreading trunks
and branches. We prefer sessile to pedunculate oak trees.

6 The global danger of illegal logging is not that forests are being used,
but that they are being exploited by non-local industries which have
no local base and therefore no particular interest in managing the
forest sustainably. This was simply not the case in Europe through the
early modern period.

7 I have found no discussion on this, but given how soon this is after the
serious social protest that led to the army being called out in force following the enclosure legislation, I cannot help wondering if the
miners got these rights so clearly legalised because the government did
not want to face another similarly difficult situation.

8 http://www.legislation.gov.uk/ukpga/Vict/1-2/43/contents

9 Sea coal, which we would now simply call coal, was so named to

distinguish it from char-coal (coal produced by charring or burning). It seems to have been called sea coal because it was first gathered not from mining but from pieces thrown up on beaches. The word 'collier' originally referred to both charcoal burners and miners.

10 Ochre is a clay used in dyeing – and it is often mixed with oak bark to make a preservative paint for buildings and ships' sails.

11 This is a very complex and confusing (and unusually long) story, which appears to be an amalgamation of a remarkable range of themes and tropes. I have picked out only one of them.

12 The dignity and independence of spinning has left an odd, hidden mark on the English language. A spinster was a woman who could spin; it was as a compliment that the word was extended to all unmarried women, because it implied that they did not need a husband, but chose freely to love or live singly. 'A spinster of this parish' comes to have her banns called not from dire necessity, but from a position of equality and independence.

8 Ballochbuie and the Forest of Mar

1 In the nineteenth century the term 'forester' referred to someone who worked not in the woods but in the deer 'forests', where there were unlikely to be any trees at all. In the twentieth century these employees became known as 'stalkers' – a word whose meaning has changed in a rather sinister way – or as 'game-keepers'.

2 As the fashionable enthusiasm for all things Scottish grew in the UK in the second half of the nineteenth century, a great many Scots pines were planted as ornamentals in other places – just as beech had been transported northwards earlier.

3 In Russia the startsy, hermits of the Russian Orthodox tradition, dwelt in the coniferous forests there, and there is Buddhist eremitical 'forest tradition' too – the Theravada forest tradition of north-east Thailand. The Theravada monks have a monastery in Sussex. The Irish tradition hermits seemed to have preferred islands, but there are numerous place names and chapels that inform us that the forests of the Middle Ages provided isolation for hermits throughout the UK. However, the hermits of the northern pine forests seem to generate a great deal of legend and lore.

4 Bible: 1 Peter, 5:9.

5 Shakespeare, *Macbeth*, IV. i, l.92.

6 I have not been able to confirm or source this, and in Ballochbuie and other woods the same feature occurs; however, I do hope that it is true.

7 Red deer stags collect does in the autumn and defend them energetically from other challengers (to the point of engaging in serious fighting). During this time they make the most extraordinary and indescribable noise somewhere between a cough and a roar, but with enormous carrying power and volume. It is always uncanny, and can be scary when you first hear it.

8 Kenneth Grahame, *The Wind in the Willows* (1908). Although Grahame is wonderfully precise about the feeling and the fear, he is rather more vague about the botany of his Wild Wood. It cannot, of course, truly be Caledonian forest, because the countryside around it is clearly the rich shire counties of Middle England. Nonetheless, it feels like it.

9 *OED*, 1971(1933). 'Uncanny' is one of those fascinating and unusual words which is negative in form and either has no positive version or, as in this instance, did not develop one for several centuries.

10 Eighth Amendment to the United States Constitution (1787), derived there from the English Bill of Rights (1689).

11 G. K. Chesterton, *Orthodoxy* (Bodley Head, 1908), p. 73.

12 These punishments are meted out, respectively, in 'Snow White', 'Cinderella', 'The Little Goosegirl', and 'Hansel and Gretel'.

13 It is not clear exactly why the red deer population has been growing since the mid-nineteenth century – even the loss of territory to, for example, fenced plantation forestry, roads and expanding villages has not halted their increase.

14 Other reintroductions have been happier. There seem to be no problems with the return of the osprey or the sea eagles off the west coast of Scotland, and the wide forked tail of a red kite riding the evening thermals on easy wing cannot but cause the heart to lift with joy. The capercailzie in the Cairngorms, which are now causing concern, are themselves a nineteenth-century reintroduction. We do not yet know the outcome of bringing beaver back home to Glenknap in Argyle.

15 It is difficult, to put it mildly, to describe this weird life form, which is bright red or salmon pink and looks like one of those Chinese ivory filigree balls – like a cage – with a sort of fetid green slime lining (called gleba) that smells of rotten meat.

16 This is not just me: even experts need a microscope to be certain of what they are seeing.

17 This is an immensely complex field, as there is a range of classification systems presently in use. In the classical period the philosophers recognised two different sorts of 'life' – animals and plants. These came to be called 'kingdoms'. Subsequently, and especially after the invention of microscopes, this simple binary system proved inadequate, and was gradually made more complex. Some classifications no longer use the idea of 'kingdoms' at all, and (to make our lives more difficult) the USA and Europe, including the UK, are presently using different systems as standard. In the UK the most commonly used organisation is into five kingdoms: prokaryota, protozoa, plantae, animalia and fungi.

18 There is a fungus called *Coprinus atramentarius* (the common inkcap) which makes excellent eating, unless you drink alcohol with it – in which case it becomes deadly. I cannot help but wonder how many unwanted husbands have been permanently dispensed with via a Coprinus casserole: the couple eat it together and then he goes off to the pub for a pint or two – and how would anyone ever know?

19 Richard Mabey, in *Flora Britannica*, records that Geoffrey Grigson (1905-1985) collected 70 local/idiomatic names for bird's-foot-trefoil (the little bright yellow, scrambled-egg-shaped flower).

20 Liz Holden, *Recommended English Names for Fungi* (desk study for British Mycological Society, English Nature, Plantlife and Scottish Natural Heritage, 2003).

9 Kielder Forest

1 I had wimped out on this occasion, declining the tent and insisting on a proper Bed and Breakfast establishment. Rough camping in England is a more dubious enterprise than in Scotland – and trying to do it somewhere we did not know and would not reach until dark seemed too much.

2 This creates a slightly odd situation – the establishment of the Scottish Parliament in 1989 meant that various issues were 'devolved' to that assembly while others (defence, for example) remained in the hands of Westminster. One area that was devolved was forestry. Already there have been some divergences of practice – most recently, the present government's consultation document which outlined possibilities for selling off (or long leasing) much of the Forestry Commission's estate only applied to England and Wales. The Scottish Parliament has made it clear that it has no plans to

reduce the Commission's role. In Kielder, uniquely, this could lead to obvious management problems.

3 These small rectilinear blocks in the middle of moors and hill country are often called 'pepper pots'. The very worst version of this is
sometimes called 'pyjama planting', where larch and spruce are
planted in separate but adjoining straight strips, and from even fairly
short distances the difference in the colours of the two trees creates a
very weird striped effect.

4 For example, far more than most private landlords, in Scotland the
Commission has embraced not just the letter but the spirit of the
access laws of 2004, opening up access to enormous swathes of rural
countryside, and positively welcoming visitors, especially walkers.

5 For good measure, the Commission was also given research and training functions.

6 Not quite all, actually – because, as I have already explained in the
case of Epping, a few of these had already been hived off into various
different sorts of arrangements.

7 *De Re Rustica* is a massive 12-volume work, fortunately preserved in its
entirety, and one of our principal sources for agricultural practice in
the Roman Empire. Very little is known about Columella: he was
probably born in Cadiz, served in the army, and on retirement took
up farming.

8 Although not highly valued now, poplar wood was extensively used in
earlier periods – for example, for making shields, because it was as
sturdy as oak but considerably lighter.

9 John Reid, *The Scots Gard'ner* (Edinburgh, 1683).

10 This figure has been contested. C. Smout argues that a good deal of
scrub and small woodland was not counted properly, and that the
actual date is sometime in the 1880s.

11 This is a management-level job. McLaughlin has a degree in forestry
from New Rigg College in Cumbria. Although there are still senior
managers who began 'axe in hand' as part of the workforce, the
Forestry Commission increasingly recruits at graduate level.

12 Mason, Kerr and Simpson, *What is Continuous Cover?* (Forestry
Commission internal note, October 1999).

13 Ninety per cent of forestry wood for sale is still clear felled.

14 See Chapter 2.

15 Rackham, *Woodlands*, p. 466. He goes on: 'Do similar considerations
apply to wind farms, now being objected to on similar grounds?' It is

heroic of me to even raise this question, since a highly likely place for 'blanket' wind-farm construction would be precisely where I live – an upland region with very good winds and a very small population. Nonetheless, it is worth thinking about: would it be better to have six hundred wind turbines on these hills as closely grouped as possible, and leave all the other hills and moors free? The Forestry Commission Scotland has just granted wind-farm development and exploration licences to a number of energy companies, so now is a good time to raise this possibility.

10 The Purgatory Wood

1 They argue (truly) that it is non-biblical, and sometimes that it is explicitly forbidden in Jeremiah 10:1-5.
2 Mabey, *Flora Britannica*, p. 125.
3 There is, in fact, considerable doubt as to whether Sawney Bean ever existed at all – and if so, when. The reports are confused and inconsistent. Nonetheless, he is well established in local folk legend; his story was rehearsed, along with a large number of similar cases, in broadsheets and scandal/horror literature, especially in the eighteenth century, and he is still cited extensively in discussions about cannibalism.
4 Quoted in O. Rackham, *The History of the Countryside* (Dent, 1986), p. 258.

11 Glenlee

1 Howard Colvin, A Biographical Dictionary of British Architects, 1600–1840 (Yale University Press, 1995).
2 Robert Lugar, *Villa Architecture* (1828).
3 The Ramsar Convention (the Convention on Wetlands of International Importance, especially as Waterfowl Habitat) (1971) is an international treaty for the conservation and sustainable utilisation of wetlands. Globally, there are nearly 2,000 designated sites, 168 of them in the UK.
4 There is no evidence that Young Lochinvar ever really existed, but he appears in local ballads and songs before Scott.
5 Walter Scott, *Marmion* (1808).
6 John Syme, letter to Alexander Cunningham, 1794.

7 J. Buchan, *The Thirty-Nine Steps* (Blackwood, 1915).

8 Compact edition of *Oxford English Dictionary* (OUP, 1971[1933]).

9 This is pure speculation on my part – I can cite no source or evidence beyond the coincidence itself.

10 The Southern Upland Way follows Garroch Burn down from the Galloway Hills to cross the Ken Valley– one of its loveliest sections.

11 Deer were hunted with hounds on Exmoor until the practice was outlawed in 2004. In the New Forest, deer were hunted more traditionally until 1997, when the last pack was disbanded. In Scandinavia deer are still hunted with hounds, but the dogs are used to drive the deer onto a strategically placed line of guns, rather than to bring the deer down. Deer are, as I have mentioned elsewhere, still hunted in forests throughout Britain (as well as stalked on open ground in Scotland), but the 'kill' is now done by rifles, not by hounds. Unlike in the USA, throughout Europe shooting deer with a bow and arrow is illegal.

12 H. Repton, *Observations on the Theory and Practice of Landscape Gardening* (1803).

13 There are still about 30 traditional deer parks with deer in them in the UK – the most famous is probably Richmond Park, near London.

14 Although *Northanger Abbey* was not published until 1818 (posthumously), it was written about 20 years earlier, and finally revised (to what extent is unclear) in 1803.

15 Some, indeed, did too well: a great deal of woodland across the country has been wrecked (or at least seriously degraded) by rhododendrons, discovered in the Himalayas and introduced into Britain by Joseph Hooker in 1849. They proved immensely successful, partly because many would flower under trees, in woodland; however, one version, *R. ponticum*, has turned out to be destructively invasive, destroying the underfloor of woods by suppressing other species.

16 One hundred and fifty feet high when it was last officially measured (not an easy undertaking), in 1979. As it is still in full health, it will certainly have put on more height in the last thirty years.

17 Alan Mitchell, in *Scottish Forestry* (1979).

18 This is one of the reasons why I wanted pictures in this book.

19 *Complete Grimm's Fairy Tales* (Constable, 1900 and 1909).

20 There is *no* suggestion that he did. There were many ornamental forests like Glenlee at the time, though, curiously, Barrie drew his inspiration for *Peter Pan* in Galloway.

21 To make this work, the film invents a bucolic male chauvinist for her to reject – a new sort of 'villain' for fairy stories. The only sadness for me was the way the Beast was finally turned back into the most regressive and old-fashioned style of handsome prince it is possible to imagine (and, in the process, he also lost his wonderfully sexy growly voice).

22 A blackhouse is the traditional highland dwelling house (found especially in the Western Isles); they were built with double dry stone walls, lined with earth, and thatched. They had flagged or packed-earth floors, single open space inside and no chimneys.

23 My mother gave each of her nineteen grandchildren a traditional 'firestool' with their initials carved on them, so for me they are still very particularly associated with childhood.

24 Thomas Hobbes, *Leviathan, or the matter, forme, and power of a commonwealth, ecclesiasticall and civill* (1651). The full phrase is 'solitary, poor, nasty, brutish, and short'.

25 Terri Windling, 'White as Snow: Fairy Tales and Fantasy', in *Snow White, Blood Red* (Avonova Books, 1993).

26 See Chapter 8.

27 When Prince Philip was taken into hospital just before Christmas 2011, I was surprised by how much the media made of the fact that he would not be able to organise the 'Boxing Day Shoot': we do not know who carves the turkey at the royal Christmas dinner; we do not know where or when members of the royal family open their presents; but we do know (because it happens outside) that they go 'hunting' on Boxing Day – and apparently this is something we are still interested in knowing.

28 See Chapter 7.

12 Knockman Wood

1 It is not clear in the story whether the compulsion is in his human identity – proving him to be royal by nature – or in his deer identity – nourishing the happy (and surprisingly common among pro-hunting people) conviction that deer and foxes enjoy being hunted.

2 Nothing in the story says he was a white deer, but I have always imagined that he was (perhaps because the girl gives him a golden collar), and was quite surprised when I went back to the text to check, and found no mention of his colour. He is a white fawn in my personal version.

3 The present management strategy is to try and weed out new beech seedlings (and also sycamore, another introduction), but the old trees are so handsome and have become so much a part of the 'flavour' of this wood that they are being left.

4 Wood of Cree, for example, where fast burns and high waterfalls crash down the escarpment, was clear-felled in the 1920s, its ancient oak trees cut to the ground, but then no one did anything with the ground. The oak trees regenerated spontaneously on the ancient root stock, so there is now a wood of young, apparently identically aged, oaks with the ground flora of an ancient wood.

5 Taken from the CVCWT website, www.creevalley.com

6 The Buchan Wood's survival is partly down to its real isolation, high up in the sparsely inhabited hill country, and on the way to nowhere. Additionally, however, it was the site of Robert the Bruce's first major 'come-back' victory in 1307 against the English army – a bold, guerrilla-style ambush from the heights above Loch Trool. The woodland here has probably been protected as a result of its iconic status.

7 My enthusiasm for local partnership is not meant to derogate other organisations, like the Woodland Trust, the UK's largest woodland conservancy charity, which has been a fairy godmother to little, threatened Cinderella woods all over the country since it was founded in 1972. It has probably also been the major force in publicising the perils facing the woods and teaching us to value our forests and woodlands more and understand them better. The Woodland Trust now owns over 1,000 woods, a total of more than 20,000 hectares (50,000 acres) of deciduous woodland. However, it is clear that some of the Trust's woods are very small, and for full habitat conservation you need some big forests as well, but it would be expensive for the Woodland Trust to acquire these. One particular benefit of a partnership model is that you can link woods together to form corridors or chains of related land, overriding ownership.

8 Rackham, *Woodlands*, p. 525.

9 Julius Caesar, *De Bello Gallico*, verse 21.

10 For example, *Jack and the Beanstalk*, a very well-known fairy story, is *not* in the Grimms' collections and appears to be purely British in origin. We have no idea how many stories have been entirely lost.

11 Three of the twelve woods I have written about – Saltridge, the Great North Wood and Staverton Thicks – were entirely new to me; I went to explore them because of writing the book.

12 In Britain, the Authorised Version of the Bible used to provide this 'common text', but obviously this is no longer appropriate. We need a replacement.

13 I am making this an endnote because I do not want to suggest improvements to a test that I believe should be abolished, but in the Citizenship Test at present there are no ecology or physical geography questions, and the only cultural ones are either about Christianity (e.g. 'What and when are the Patron Saints' Days of the four countries of the UK?' 'What are bank holidays?' 'What and when are the main Christian festivals?' 'What other traditional days are celebrated?') or about sporting events and cinema classifications (plus a very peculiar reference to the National Trust). Access law and questions like 'How many dwarves did Snow White meet?' or 'What was Cinderella's slipper made of?' seem to offer a more cohesive and generous view of citizenship and shared cultural identity.